The Smear

Also by Sharyl Attkisson

Stonewalled

The Smear

||||||||||||||||||||||||||||||||||||||||||||||||||||||||||||||||||||||||||||||||

**How Shady Political Operatives
and Fake News
Control What You See,
What You Think, and How You Vote**

||||||||||||||||||||||||||||||||||||||||||||||||||||||||||||||||||||||||||||||||

Sharyl Attkisson

HARPER

NEW YORK · LONDON · TORONTO · SYDNEY

HARPER

A hardcover edition of this book was published in 2017 by HarperCollins Publishers.

THE SMEAR. Copyright © 2017 by Sharyl Attkisson. All rights reserved. Printed in the United States of America. No part of this book may be used or reproduced in any manner whatsoever without written permission except in the case of brief quotations embodied in critical articles and reviews. For information, address HarperCollins Publishers, 195 Broadway, New York, NY 10007.

HarperCollins books may be purchased for educational, business, or sales promotional use. For information, please email the Special Markets Department at SPsales@harpercollins.com.

FIRST HARPER PAPERBACKS EDITION PUBLISHED 2018.

Designed by Joy O'Meara

Library of Congress Cataloging-in-Publication Data has been applied for.

ISBN 978-0-06-246817-8 (pbk.)

18 19 20 21 22   DIX/LSC   10 9 8 7 6 5 4 3 2 1

Contents

⅃⅃⅃⅃⅃⅃⅃⅃⅃⅃⅃⅃⅃⅃⅃⅃⅃⅃

Acknowledgments vi

Author's Note vii

Introduction 1

Chapter One
Birth of the Modern Smear: Spies, Bork, and the Clintons 9

Chapter Two
David Brock's Smear Frontier 35

Chapter Three
The Smear Industrial Complex:
Smear Merchants and Scandalmongers 67

Chapter Four
Media Matters (but Money Matters More) 94

Chapter Five
Plausible Deniability: Conjuring an Astroturf Reality 119

Chapter Six
Transactional Journalism:
The Black Market Information Trade 140

Chapter Seven
The Anti-Smear Candidate (and the Disloyal Opposition) 166

Chapter Eight
The Road to the Conventions 195

Chapter Nine
General Election 214

Chapter Ten
Brave New World of #FakeNews
(and Chilling Efforts to Censor It) 249

Epilogue: The Smear Gone Global 275

Index 287

ACKNOWLEDGMENTS

||||||||||||||||||||||||||||||||||||||||||||||||||||||||||

With much appreciation to those who shared their experiences; to Tab Turner, who continues to be a devoted warrior for truth and transparency; to Keith and Matt at Javelin; to Matt and the entire Harper team; and to Jim and Sarah and my whole supportive family.

AUTHOR'S NOTE

||||||||||||||||||||||||||||||||||||||||||||

The content of this book is drawn from extensive reporting and research as well as my own opinions, experiences, observations.

Some proceeds from this book are being donated to the Brechner Center for Freedom of Information at the University of Florida. A donation was also made to Project Censored.

*A lie gets halfway around the world
before the truth has a chance to get its pants on.*

Introduction

IIIIIIIIIIIIIIIIIIIIIIIIIIIIIIIIII

Nearly every day, my overloaded email in-box is peppered with pleas from viewers asking—no, *begging*—me to investigate tales of the implausible and unbelievable. They're w that the truth is being hidden from them on a massive scale. That someone is manipulating what they see on the news and online. Conspiring to hide select facts and advance particular narratives. Colluding on plots to smear certain people.

Their suspicions are correct, even if their notion of truth is often confused. In fact, the confusion is often by grand design.

At the end of campaign 2016, one story they urge me to investigate is #Pizzagate. It's a twisted conglomeration of unthinkable accusations about Democratic presidential nominee Hillary Clinton and her inner circle. "News" of this shocking scandal has been circulating on the Internet, and conspiracy theorists believe the mainstream press is covering it up. The allegations are whispered about and forwarded through social media, quasi-news sites, blogs, and videos posted by nameless sources. The stories are filled with names of real people and places, blended with fabricated tales of child rape, a porn ring, and a pizza parlor supposedly trafficking in underage sex through a basement tunnel. A mysterious video posted under the moniker "Anonymous" promises that the final week of the campaign will reveal irrefutable evidence of indictable crimes. The sources of this as-yet unrevealed information, according to the video, have been contacted by the FBI, which is getting ready to sweep in and make arrests.

I'm busy working on pressing stories for my weekly news program, *Full Measure.* But I poke around in case there's anything to any of it. I look at the websites. I check out the videos. I consult sources who might know if there are real law enforcement investigations under way. I quickly detect telltale signs of misinformation.

Meanwhile, Donald Trump faces his own parade of false accusations, and I'm getting emails about those as well. Viewers want to know why I'm not reporting on the story about him having raped a child. I look into that one, too. There's a lawsuit pending, and the players involved are at least as dubious as the ones promulgating #Pizzagate. Still, the Trump story gets picked up by the likes of the New York *Daily News, Politico, BuzzFeed, New York* magazine, the *Independent,* and the *Atlantic.* As cameras gather for a news conference to hear the sordid tale from the supposed rape victim, she evaporates. There are more concocted stories—that Trump's New York City modeling agency was "caught trafficking young girls and hiding them in basements"; that Trump is a secret "plant" who entered the presidential campaign as a pettifogger, surreptitiously working to get Clinton elected; and that he's a stooge of Russian president Vladimir Putin in a "Manchurian candidate" scenario—a reference to the 1962 film about an American soldier who was brainwashed into carrying out communist plots.

Not a day goes by without the voting public getting pummeled by countless narratives—some based on grains of truth; others wholly invented for the audience. Racist, Wall Street lackey, crooked, liar, cheat, white nationalist, socialist, womanizer, misogynist, corrupt, xenophobic, homophobic, Islamophobic, anti-immigrant, basket of deplorables, fraudster, loser, alt-right, delusional, dangerous, mentally ill, pay-for-player, and tax cheat. Assisted by ideologues, shady political operatives, and dark Internet outfits seeking moneymaking clicks, Campaign 2016 shatters all records in the smear department.

In this environment, the ability to execute a character assassination becomes more pivotal than any other singular campaign strategy. Operatives spring into action, exploiting the latest technology and tactics.

Once relegated to grocery store tabloids, smears now figure prominently in most every mainstream news publication. Reporters pursue sordid narratives with the fervor of Jimmy Olsen chasing an exclusive for the *Daily Planet*. Smears become embedded in the fabric of our everyday existence. So common, we barely flinch at the most audacious claims. With distrust of the news media at an all-time high, a skeptical public looks to alternative information sources and becomes easier to bamboozle. It's in this space, devoid of principles, where smears and fake news thrive. It's no longer a stretch for news consumers to believe that the press is covering up important stories or is in the tank for corporate and political interests.

We didn't get here overnight. The past two decades have served as an ideal incubator for an industry of smears and fake news. The tools and tactics have evolved from old-school to high-tech. Incredible amounts of money change hands, yet some of the most damaging smears can be accomplished with little more than an idea and an Internet connection. By 2016, a Pew Research Center report found more than 44 percent of the American adult population got its news on Facebook, which had 1.09 billion active daily users. Some of that news is true. Some of it's not. Today, an entire movement can be started with a few bogus Twitter accounts and 140 characters or less.

"You don't have to spend millions on political ad buys anymore," observes one operative in the business. "You can spark wildfires with just a tiny little stick now, which is a new thing."

What, exactly, is a smear?

That depends on who you ask. One man's smear is another man's truth. In simple terms, it's an effort to manipulate opinion by promulgating an overblown, scandalous, and damaging narrative. The goal is often to destroy ideas by ruining the people who are most effective at communicating them. What you may not know is that a lot of this manipulation is done through methods that are utterly invisible to the average consumer. Paid forces devise clever, covert ways to shape the total information landscape in ways you can't imagine. Their goal is to fool you. Public ideas are meticulously orchestrated to appear random. Op-eds printed in major news publications are ghostwritten by paid agents in the name of shills who rent the use of their signature. Private eyes dig up dirt on enemies by dumpster-diving for embarrassing information and compromising material.

Fox News host Tucker Carlson cites his own dicta for a successful modern-day smear. First, it must be inherently interesting and, preferably, salacious. That means anything of a tabloid nature—sex, greed, or venal sin. Second, the smear has to be explainable in a sentence or two. Even better if it can be encapsulated in a catchy phrase. "War against women." "Crooked Hillary." "Gun show loophole." And finally, the smear must confirm what a lot of people want to believe. If it's too disconnected from the realm of the desirable or credible, it won't work. For example, Carlson says, smearing the pope by claiming there's video of him worshipping Satan probably wouldn't work. It's too far from the realm of what most people would consider credible. But link a Catholic figure to a male prostitute and that may be enough in the minds of the audience to make them think it might be true. It confirms their preexisting suspicions. Repeat it often enough and it becomes undeniable—something "everybody knows."

Professor Mark Feldstein of Philip Merrill College of Journalism at the University of Maryland is author of *Poisoning the Press: Richard Nixon, Jack Anderson, and the Rise of Washington's Scandal Culture*. Before becoming a professor, Feldstein was an award-winning investigative reporter and producer at ABC, NBC, and CNN. As a journalist who stepped on toes of the influential and political, he says he found himself the target of many smear campaigns by powerful interests—"beaten up, subpoenaed, sued, and detained." In 1998, as an NBC producer investigating alleged misconduct by United Nations troops in Haiti, his correspondent and crew were forced off the road by armed guards who stole their notes, belongings, and camera equipment. The U.S. embassy notified them that the Haitian police had opened some sort of criminal investigation into them and that they were about to be arrested. They were being set up. They left.

Feldstein has a view similar to that of Carlson on the ingredients for a successful smear.

"A lot of what resonates has to do with whether it seems consistent with the persona or whether it resonates with some issue that's radioactive in society," he notes. "The rumor about Hillary throwing the lamp at Bill

[Clinton]. . . if someone said that about Laura Bush it wouldn't gain currency because it's so at variance with who she seems to be."

As corporations and political operatives jockey for control, they've found uncanny success in exploiting news organizations, quasi-news outlets, and brokers of so-called fake news to lend legitimacy to their efforts. We in the news media have allowed ourselves to become co-opted by political, corporate, and other special interests. We permit them to dictate the story *du jour*. We let them dominate the opinions we consult and quote. We plaster our news reports with political pundits not offering independent opinions but serving their masters. We've invited political operatives into our fold as consultants, pundits; and even made them reporters, anchors, and managers in our newsrooms. We've become a willing receptacle for, and distributor of, daily political propaganda. And because we invite both sides to feed us, we call it fair. In many ways, some media outlets have become little more than thinly veiled political operations.

Adding to distrust of the media are stark changes in how the news has come to operate. Policies that once firewalled news from opinion, that resisted interference from political and advertising interests—*voop!* Evaporated. Relationships and practices regarded as the most egregious breaches of ethics a few years back are now commonly accepted. Now, intermingling is not only tolerated, it's encouraged.

They've figured out how to marginalize those who are still seeking the facts. Not long ago, if a journalist reported a true but damaging story about a key political figure, the politician might try to deny the report and discredit the reporter—but the effort wouldn't gain much traction.

It's different today.

Now, the news story, reporter, and outlet are hit with highly organized, offensive smears. Strategic communications firms spring into action. False information, rumors, and innuendo are circulated against the reporters on blogs and social media. Negative "press releases" are dispatched to long email lists of reporters and pundits. Pretty soon, these astroturf efforts drown out the real story and overtake the news narrative. *Politico, Infowars, The Huffington Post, Breitbart, Salon, Vox, The Right Scoop, Mother Jones, Rolling Stone, Wired, DailyKos,* the *Washington Post,* the *New York Times,* CNN, MSNBC, the *Hill, BuzzFeed,* and *Mediaite* are some of the media entities known to peddle clickable concoctions of legitimate news and sometimes-good journalism alongside partisan opinions, vicious agendas, misinformation, mischaracterizations, and smears against other journalists. It blurs together until there's virtually no meaningful distinction between credible reporting and propaganda.

One of the biggest casualties is nonpartisan investigative journalism. The PR spinmeisters, corporate collusion, and political flacks have made it increasingly difficult for good reporters to do independent reporting on important topics. Good reporters hate what's happened to the news.

The disturbing dominance of this "transactional journalism" has further opened the floodgate to clandestine collusion between reporters and special interests. As a result, it can be impossible to separate fact from fiction. Even self-proclaimed truth-tellers and fact-checkers have been co-opted.

"Everybody's in fucking battle mode all the time," a notable player in this murky universe tells me.

The smear is a malleable creature, without loyalties or compunction. It's equally happy to be the tool of government, corporations, special interests, Democrats, or Republicans. All aim to be its master. But some prove far better at it than others.

That's where the smear artist comes in: a character assassin driven by passion, ideology, and money. The smear business is interminable and eminently profitable. It's silently turned into one of the largest white-collar industries in Washington, D.C. It's making thousands of people rich. It's becoming one of our biggest global exports.

Within these pages are smear secrets exposed. Some are buried in emails and government documents never meant for outside eyes. More come from current operators who agreed to reveal tricks of the trade as long as they could remain anonymous. Together, we'll trace the incredible money that pours into major smear efforts, and we'll review the fatalities. And you'll see how, once in a great while, a smear backfires. The operator may find herself in the crosshairs, as did Democratic National Committee chairwoman Debbie Wasserman-Schultz in 2016 when WikiLeaks exposed some of the duplicitous shenanigans Wasserman-Schultz's DNC conducted against the party's own presidential candidate Bernie Sanders.

In my thirty-five years as a journalist, I've encountered countless operatives who are pros at peddling smears. They don't *say* that's who they are or what they do. They pose as advocates, watchdogs, tipsters, and public relations agents. They work at global law firms, PR companies, crisis management groups, nonprofits, think tanks, blogs, and strategic communications firms. They send me research, ask to have coffee, press a business card into my palm, whisper into my ear, invite me into their fold, and point me to "sources." They use tried-and-true propaganda techniques to attempt to persuade reporters like me to further their narratives. In fact, if they're really good, they convince us it's all *our* idea: *we're expert journalists whose connections and skills have gotten us an exclusive story!*

And if we aren't useful to the effort? We might find ourselves the target of a smear. It happened to me.

In my two decades as a national television investigative reporter, I make it a practice to follow the facts wherever they lead. My exposés on giant corporations like Enron and the pharmaceutical companies, on charities such as the Red Cross, and on problematic initiatives under Democrats and Republicans alike have been recognized with top journalism awards. As a result, I've made enemies of some of the most powerful interests on the planet. The subjects of my stories deploy their apparatus to controversialize and silence my reporting. Yes, independent-minded reporters like me have plenty of public defenders, but they aren't among the powerful. We don't have important friends in high places or retainers with expensive PR firms. Our supporters lack the kind of influence that money can buy. They don't control a bevy of fake news sites to do their bidding.

As a target, I've learned to sniff out smears a mile away. They're inescapable. Turn on the TV. Fire up the computer. Flip on the radio. News, entertainment, philanthropy, advertising, social media, book reviews, rumors, memes, nonprofits, even comedy acts—they're all used in smear campaigns. We're living amid an artificial reality, persuaded to believe it's real by astroturf engineered to look like grassroots. Success of the paid forces hinges on their ability to remain virtually invisible. To disguise what they do and make it seem as if their work is neither calculated nor scripted. It must appear to be precisely what it is not.

Nothing is more exemplary of these efforts than the sudden frenzy over fake news. I find an Internet search returns no common mentions of "fake news" among news stories until precisely the moment an orchestrated effort was launched in September of 2016. It's quickly followed by an October announcement from President Barack Obama, in which he claims there's a burning need to "curate" news on behalf of the public. From that point forward, the topic of fake news dominates headlines on a daily basis. It's as if the media has its assigned narrative and is marching forward. Headlines read, "The Real Danger of Fake News," "How Fake News Helped Donald Trump Win," "Why Facebook and Google Are Struggling to Purge Fake News," "How to Fix the Fake News Problem." But it isn't the public that's clamoring for content to be filtered, censored, or otherwise "curated." The push is coming from corporate, political, news, and special interests who want to dominate the narrative and crush information that's contrary. Can *they* be trusted to separate fact from fiction?

Many will not survive the smear.

How can somebody with no power, no megaphone, and no media cooperation begin to counter the propaganda muscle of a government-corporate-media attack? Victims frequently express hopelessness and desperation. Pushing through the day as the target of a character assassination can take every ounce of mental strength. Imagine trying to focus on your job or family while professional smear artists engage in a 24/7 operation to discredit and controversialize you. To them, it's second nature. They've perfected their techniques. They maintain a constant pressure. Their slander alienates your bosses, clients, colleagues, and the general public. They isolate you from your support system. Eventually, your own family and friends start to wonder about you. You feel the icy chill of distancing from those you consider closest.

So, what do you get out of this journey? The truth. You'll see how public consensus is shaped and how opinion strings are pulled. Not by ordinary citizens, but by people whose names you've never heard. By the time you finish this book, you'll have become adept at recognizing smear campaigns—and maybe seeing through them.

Today you're viewing the world through foggy glasses. I'll help you take them off, wipe them clean, and see things more clearly.

Chapter One

||||||||||||||||||||||

Birth of the Modern Smear:
Spies, Bork, and the Clintons

As vicious as our modern politics are, they aren't the beginning of the smear. To understand the tricks of the trade and how they figure into attempts to manipulate your opinion, it helps to examine how we got here. It turns out smears are a tradition in American politics dating back to our earliest days. In fact, our founding fathers knew very well the power of a sharp character assassination.

"Hamilton and Jefferson were planting stuff on each other's sex lives and writing anonymously for their partisan newspapers," says Professor Mark Feldstein, of Philip Merrill College of Journalism at the University of Maryland. He's an avid student of historical scandal. Back in the 1790s, the efforts were relatively unsophisticated, he tells me.

"In those days it was kind of obvious who was behind the smears, because the first Treasury secretary, Alexander Hamilton, had this sexual affair with a woman named Maria Reynolds and Thomas Jefferson published it. And Jefferson was banging Sally Hemings, and it was the Hamilton paper that surfaced it," says Feldstein.

While rumor and innuendo have long been the bedrock of political assaults, I think you could say the modern smear came into its own during

World War II. And it's only natural that the U.S. intel agency responsible for perfecting psychological warfare and propaganda techniques became accomplished in the art of the smear. Back then, they called it "Morale Operations."

In 1943, the U.S. Morale Operations Branch opened under the Office of Strategic Services, the precursor to the CIA. The mission: misinformation and deception. The tools: white, black, and gray propaganda, all still widely used by today's players in the smear game. White propaganda openly reveals its source and relies on "gentle persuasion and public relation techniques." Black propaganda is misinformation that claims to be coming from one side but is actually produced by the opposing side. Then there's gray propaganda, which the CIA considers the most mysterious of all "because the source of the propaganda is never identified." (Relate that idea to today's political dark-money groups, which don't have to disclose who their donors are.)

The CIA also knows that when demoralization and demonization are the order of the day, nothing does the trick like a good old-fashioned rumor. To paraphrase an historic figure: A lie can travel halfway around the world before the truth gets its pants on. During World War II, the Morale Operations Branch initiated about twenty rumors per week. They were typically "short, memorable stories concerning famous people and events . . . meant to cause fear, confusion, and distrust." Success was measured by "comebacks"—the number of times the rumors surfaced in the press.

In addition to using word of mouth and the press to deploy rumors and other forms of propaganda against the Nazis, the government's secret operators had another first-rate device at their disposal: radio. The Morale Operations Branch used "black" propaganda radio stations to broadcast disinformation on behalf of the United States and its allies. In 1944, the "gray" propaganda radio station Soldatensender (Soldier's Radio) went live in England, denouncing the Nazis amid news, music, and entertainment. American movie stars took part in musical black ops on Soldatensender. According to the CIA, Bing Crosby, Dinah Shore, and Marlene Dietrich performed black propaganda lyrics written for German and American songs. One instance involved a tune called "Lili Marleen." It's a nostalgic, pessimistic melody. Adolf Hitler's chief propagandist, Joseph Goebbels, considered it demoralizing and banned it in Germany.

Outside the barracks, by the corner light
I'll always stand and wait for you at night

Despite the ban, Dietrich recorded the song in German and English and it was played on Soldatensender, which German troops could hear. The idea was to make them homesick. It worked.

Meantime, Goebbels was busy perfecting textbook propaganda techniques of his own that also stand the test of time today. As head of Hitler's Reich Ministry of Public Enlightenment and Propaganda from 1933 to 1945, Goebbels was obsessed with controlling virtually every form of message in German society whether from government, churches, films, reporters, or mass media. Obsessive control was necessary to lead the German people down the path of fanatical support for a dictator. It was the only way the masses could be convinced to stand by—even take part—as their government was transformed into a fascist state.

"It would not be impossible to prove with sufficient repetition and a psychological understanding of the people concerned that a square is in fact a circle," Goebbels observed. "Repeat it until even the densest has got it." We're afforded a window into Goebbels's thinking by virtue of his diaries, which he wrote nearly every day beginning in 1923 at age twenty-six, and continuing until less than a month before his suicide in April of 1945. Prior to his death, Goebbels took steps to make sure his diaries were preserved, correctly predicting that they could be of great interest to future generations. Contained in the Goebbels diaries are the tactical secrets he deployed over a decade, and his observations about which proved to be the most successful. "Propaganda works best when those who are being manipulated are confident they are acting on their own free will," he noted.

Other applicable remarks found within the pages of the Goebbels diaries include:

- "A lie told once remains a lie but a lie told a thousand times becomes the truth."

- "Not every item of news should be published. Rather must those who control news policies endeavor to make every item of news serve a certain purpose."
- "The truth is the greatest enemy of the State."
- "It is the absolute right of the State to supervise the formation of public opinion."
- "Propaganda must facilitate the displacement of aggression by specifying the targets for hatred."

From Goebbels's propaganda playbook I think we can glean three discrete smear techniques:

1. The bigger the lie, the more people will believe it.
2. If you repeat a lie often enough, it becomes the truth.
3. An attempt to convince must confine itself to a few points and repeat them over and over. Persistence is the first and most important requirement for success.

In short: Tell a big lie. Focus and repeat—until the audience recites it in their sleep. Pretty soon, they'll have no choice but to believe it.

Postwar, the CIA remained in the forefront of the propaganda game. The spy agency was apparently responsible for promoting the phrase *conspiracy theory* for use as a powerful device in the lexicon of the smear artist. Before the covert CIA effort, which we can pinpoint to a secret memo in 1967, there was nothing controversial about discussing or exposing "conspiracies." After all, a conspiracy is simply an agreement by two or more people to commit a bad act. Bonnie and Clyde were conspirators. Jesse James, Butch Cassidy, the Ku Klux Klan, the Weather Underground, mobsters, the Mafia, criminal gangs, and drug cartels all involve conspiracies. Whether it's Iran-Contra, Watergate, the Enron scandal, bank fraud rackets, illegal sports betting, identity theft rings, financial crimes, kidnappings, robberies, or political corruption, millions of schemes each year are conspiracies.

"Americans had always been quite receptive to the idea of elite conspiracies against their rights and property," says Mark Crispin Miller, professor of media studies at New York University. "The Declaration of Independence is a conspiracy theory from beginning to end. Americans never felt they had to apologize for suspecting that the elites may be up to no good."

Yet *after* the CIA secret memo, the public and media were brainwashed into dismissing out of hand those labeled as "conspiracy theorists," as if only the mentally unbalanced would believe in the existence of conspiracies. *How was this propaganda feat accomplished, and for what purpose?*

The CIA memo was written in 1967 because the agency was concerned about "a new wave of books and articles" questioning whether Lee Harvey Oswald really acted as a "lone nut" in assassinating President John F. Kennedy. The spy agency worried that the "publicity problem" could reflect negatively on President Lyndon Johnson and on America as a nation. So the CIA issued its secret dispatch.

"Conspiracy theories have frequently thrown suspicion on our organization," reads the internal CIA memo dated April 1, 1967. "The aim of this dispatch is to provide material for countering and discrediting the claims of the conspiracy theorists."

The memo proves to be instructive in showing some of the early efforts by government players to manipulate politicians and the media, and by proxy, use government power and influence to control the narrative. CIA station chiefs were instructed to reach out to "friendly elite contacts (especially politicians and editors)" and "urge them to use their influence to discourage unfounded and irresponsible speculation."

The CIA memo foreshadows what would become a cornerstone of future generations of smears: cultivating and exploiting close ties with the media. Today, reaching out to "elite contacts" is one of the most basic and effective ways to discredit a target: using a seemingly impartial voice— typically a reporter or journalist—to sell the smear to their viewers, readers, or followers.

The CIA memo goes on to advise station chiefs to "employ propaganda assets." They were told that "book reviews and feature articles are particularly appropriate for this purpose." And you'll likely recognize some of the suggested talking points included in the memo's recommendations:

- Argue there's nothing new.
- Insist that a large-scale conspiracy would be impossible to conceal in the United States.
- Smear critics as politically or financially motivated, hasty and inaccurate, or infatuated with their own theories.

Largely as a result of that CIA memo, Professor Miller argues, the "conspiracy theorist" meme became a propaganda tool routinely used to assassinate the characters of those who threaten the powers that be, particularly in the news media. Once labeled as conspiracy theorists, the targets are to be doubted, viewed with suspicion, and disregarded, even though proven conspiracies, as a matter of fact, are exceedingly common.

"Labeling something as a 'conspiracy theory' is a far more efficient way to tame the press [into disregarding a source or viewpoint] than actually whacking journalists the way they do in other countries," Professor Miller tells me. "It's a subtle form of intimidation and a much more effective way to keep people in line. Once journalists have internalized the notion that there's something crazy about someone who suspects a conspiracy, they're useless as guardians of our freedom. Just call something a conspiracy theory and journalists snap into attack mode, roll their eyes, and jeer."

The CIA's legacy can further be found in a maxim often used by today's spooks. When confronted:

- Admit nothing
- Deny everything
- Demand proof
- Make counterallegations
- Discredit the opposition

Those eleven simple words encapsulate basic smear tactics and the reason they're exercised, usually as a counteroffensive.

The Verb *Bork*

There were plenty of smears in the 1960s and 1970s, but the organized political smear entered the contemporary marketplace circa 1987 with President Ronald Reagan's nomination of Robert Bork, a conservative judge, to the Supreme Court.

The blueprint for fighting Bork's nomination had actually been drawn a year before when Reagan nominated Republican U.S. attorney Jeff Sessions to a federal judgeship. Sessions had suffered a vicious defeat in the Senate amid accusations that he'd made racist comments in the past. The difference with Bork, besides being a Supreme Court nominee, was that his highly orchestrated character assassination was hatched and played out in real time, on live television, before a national audience. It was all-out war, and liberal forces mobilized as never before in a Supreme Court contest. In a nationally televised speech, Senator Ted Kennedy, a Democrat, claimed:

> *Robert Bork's America is a land in which women would be forced into back-alley abortions, blacks would sit at segregated lunch counters, rogue police could break down citizens' doors in midnight raids, schoolchildren could not be taught about evolution, writers and artists could be censored at the whim of the government, and the doors of the federal courts would be shut on the fingers of millions of citizens.*

Bork's confirmation fell to a crushing defeat in the Democrat-led Senate, with a number of Republicans joining Democrats in voting nay. "Too often, character assassination has replaced debate in principle here in Washington," complained President Reagan at the time.

Eventually Anthony Kennedy filled the Supreme Court vacancy. And a new verb was coined. Getting *borked* came to mean becoming the unfortunate target of an unfair, relentless, organized character assassination. The term would later be added to the *Oxford English Dictionary,* defined as: "To defame or vilify (a person) systematically, esp. in the mass media, usually with the aim of preventing his or her appointment to public office; to obstruct or thwart (a person) in this way."

Both sides learned new lessons from the fight over Bork. A few years later, in 1991, Democrats revived and repeated the tactics when conservative Clarence Thomas was nominated to the Supreme Court. A feminist addressing a National Organization for Women conference told the audience, "We're going to *bork* him," referring to Thomas. "We're going to kill him politically. . . . This little creep, where did he come from?"

But this time, Republicans were ready. While Thomas was getting borked by the left, the right was plotting to destroy one of his chief critics: former law professor Anita Hill, a former assistant to Thomas, who had been trotted out by liberals to testify at his Senate confirmation hearings. She accused Thomas of lurid sexual harassment, claiming he initiated inappropriate discussions about films showing group sex or rape scenes. In one infamous anecdote, Hill testified that, one day at work, Thomas looked at the soft drink can on his desk and asked, "Who has put pubic hair on my Coke?"

Republican senator Orrin Hatch defended Thomas, and accused Hill of working with special interests and "slick lawyers." For his part, Thomas insisted he'd been subjected to a "high-tech lynching for uppity blacks" by white liberals. In the end, he survived his borking and achieved a spot on the high court—by a narrow vote.

Hill would spend the better part of the next several years as the target of a hatchet job led by a writer for the conservative *American Spectator* magazine: David Brock. In 1992, Brock dug for dirt on Hill, publishing articles that negatively exaggerated what he'd learned. He topped it all off with his 1993 book, *The Real Anita Hill: The Untold Story,* which discredited Hill along with her claims against Thomas.

The Clarence Thomas Supreme Court nomination showed both sides that the best way to fight a smear might not be to take a defensive posture—but to mount an offensive countersmear. Going after the accuser, whistleblower, fact-finder, or truth-teller would prove to be a critical strategy for smears in the coming decades.

It was about this time that the *American Spectator* set its sights even higher, on the most prominent U.S. political couple of the next three decades, a couple that would be at the nexus of innumerable smear efforts, both as victims and masterminds: Bill and Hillary Clinton.

The Clinton Era

If you ask people to identify a coming of age for the modern-day smear, it's amazing how many political insiders—both Democrats and Republicans—consider it to be the Clinton era. It's impossible for any outsiders to know exactly how the Clintons became adept at engineering smears to deflect from their controversies. But a hint may be found in the thesis Hillary wrote at Wellesley College in 1969. It was about Saul Alinsky's work and philosophies.

In case you're not familiar with him, Alinsky was a self-proclaimed radical. A liberal Chicago "community organizer" who authored a book that was required reading in one of my college classes: *Rules for Radicals*. At the time, I wondered, *Were we supposed to be inspired or repulsed by his ideas?*

I think, in retrospect, the professor hoped we would question, be inspired by, or even admire Alinsky. Certainly, Hillary Clinton fell into the latter category. She and Alinsky exchanged friendly letters, and Hillary's thesis paper was seen as generally sympathetic to the controversial radical—she called him "a man of exceptional charm." She says he even offered her a job but that she chose law school instead. (Interestingly, at the request of the White House, Wellesley kept Hillary's Alinsky-themed thesis under lock and key until 2001, until long after Bill was finished with the presidency.)

Alinsky's *Rules* and his ends-justify-the-means approach were intended to right perceived societal wrongs. An ardent supporter of wealth redistribution, Alinsky pitted the so-called haves against the poor have-nots and endorsed use of guerrilla tactics to organize and accomplish the mission: to make things right and fair in the eyes of the self-appointed equalizers.

From Alinsky's *Rules*:

- Ridicule is man's most potent weapon.
- Keep the pressure on, with different tactics and actions.
- [Develop] operations that will maintain a constant pressure upon the opposition.
- The threat is usually more terrifying than the thing itself.

- If you push a negative hard and deep enough it will break through into its counterside. In other words: Turn a negative around to your benefit.
- Pick the target, freeze it, personalize it, and polarize it.

As you might expect, some of Alinsky's tactics are equally as effective in the context of executing a wicked smear. The Clinton smear machine, whether by subliminal accident or intentional design, is lubricated with the oil of Alinsky's *Rules*. Perhaps Hillary innately recognized how to apply them in a new context. Not to accomplish social goals, but to marginalize, controversialize, and defeat a political enemy. (And then convince yourself you're accomplishing social goals.) These strategies, from ridiculing enemies to pushing a negative and keeping the pressure on, are easily recognized in the Clintons' subsequent handiwork.

One of the earliest smear campaigns perpetrated by the Clintons began even before Bill announced he was running for president, when Hillary was busy devising a preemptive strike against women rumored to be involved with her husband. According to journalist Carl Bernstein in his biography *A Woman in Charge,* Hillary reportedly sought to get sworn statements from women Bill was rumored to have slept with. It was said that she wanted to convince the women to swear they had no relationship with him. She was correct to anticipate trouble.

In 1992, Bill was steeped in his election campaign when salacious claims began to surface from more than a half dozen women who said they'd been victims of his sleazy advances or improper sexual behavior, or that they'd carried on illicit affairs with him. Myra Belle "Sally" Miller, Miss Arkansas 1958, claimed she had an affair with Clinton in 1983 and was later threatened by a Democratic official not to go public.

"They knew that I went jogging by myself and he couldn't guarantee what would happen to my pretty little legs," Miller alleges the official told her. Clinton vigorously denied even having met her. The media largely ignored her claim as unreliable.

They weren't so quick to brush off the allegations from another accuser, Gennifer Flowers. Flowers alleged she met Clinton while she was a TV reporter in Little Rock in the 1970s and carried on a twelve-year affair with him. In a palpably awkward appearance on the CBS News program *60 Minutes*, Bill and Hillary denied the accusation, with Hillary proclaiming, "I'm not sitting here some little woman standing by my man like Tammy Wynette."

Flowers would later allege in a sexual harassment suit against Bill that Hillary had devised a "war room" during the 1992 campaign dedicated to smearing, defaming, and harming her and other Clinton enemies. In subsequent years, critics would come to call Hillary—who portrays herself as a committed feminist and women's rights defender—the architect of the first real "war on women." Though Hillary has repeatedly denied any effort to disparage or harm her husband's accusers, former Bill Clinton adviser Dick Morris has another view. He says he still finds Hillary's actions repulsive all these years later.

"What really turned me off was what I call secret police, when [Hillary] hired this fleet of detectives to go around examining all of the women who had been identified with [Bill] Clinton," Morris told *Breitbart News* in 2014. "Not for the purpose of divorcing Clinton. Not for the purpose of getting him to stop. But for the purpose of developing blackmail material on these women to cow them into silence . . . that had a Nixonian quality that I hold against her."

The deputy chair of Clinton's 1992 campaign, Betsey Wright, labeled allegations against Clinton as "bimbo eruptions." As more women emerged, the campaign against them was nicknamed the "nuts and sluts" defense, borrowing a term apparently coined years before by attorney and feminist Susan Estrich. Taking a page from the Clarence Thomas fight, the Clinton application of Nuts and Sluts meant Bill's accusers were portrayed—much like Anita Hill—as being crazy or of questionable moral character. This was done partly in the hope that they wouldn't be considered credible, partly so others would be discouraged from stepping forward and opening their mouths.

For Gennifer Flowers, Nuts and Sluts meant she got stamped as "trailer trash" and a "saloon singer." Clinton surrogate James Carville coined his now-infamous slur about her: *If you drag a hundred-dollar bill through a trailer park, you never know what you'll find.* But it turned out, Flowers had the goods: audio recordings proving her relationship with Clinton, and she called a news conference to make them public. Later, under oath in 1998, Clinton finally acknowledged he'd had sexual relations with her.

Women weren't Bill's only problem. Besides the accusations swirling about his affairs, there were questionable business dealings, which came to be known simply as "Whitewater." They threatened to undermine his candidacy. Perhaps no one had a better understanding of Whitewater and its significance, then or now, than Pulitzer Prize–winning reporter Jeff Gerth. In fact, if there's one journalist who most knows what it's like to be in the crosshairs of the Clinton smear operation for the long haul, it has to be Gerth. From the moment he wrote his first *New York Times* investigative article about the Clintons' shady Whitewater dealings on March 8, 1992, he was a marked man.

Branded. Like Chuck Connors in the 1960s TV series.

Gerth would remain a favorite whipping boy of the propagandist left for the next two decades, and then some. The Clinton smear machine has a long memory, and an even longer reach. Besides, the credibility of the smear target is directly proportional to the imperative to discredit him.

Gerth's entrée into the dark side of the Clinton universe was his original 1992 *New York Times* article headlined "Clintons Joined S&L Operator in an Ozark Real-Estate Venture." It was widely acclaimed in journalism circles as an important break in the Whitewater scandal. Today it remains in many ways a definitive dissection of the Clintons' complicated entanglements with an insolvent savings and loan, a money-losing real estate deal, and a business partner later convicted of fraud.

That's in the real world.

In the distorted world of the smear artist, things are very different. Up becomes down and down is up. It's Alice in Wonderland and somewhere down the rabbit hole there's a tea-sipping Mad Hatter stirring the pot.

"There was certainly a coordinated effort against me back in the 1992 campaign," Gerth tells me, with the benefit of hindsight. "There was a whole department aimed at me and other reporters who were looking at the Clintons, the women, the Rose Law Firm." Rose Law Firm is the Arkansas company where Hillary Clinton was a partner.

"I always knew at the *New York Times* it was difficult writing about Democrats," says Gerth. Yet, he says, his two editors were supportive of his

Whitewater piece. "They certainly didn't kill it or downplay it." In fact, they helped write the top of the story on a Friday night. It ran two days later on the front page of the Sunday paper.

"The Clinton campaign went after me the day the story was published," recalls Gerth. The attacks were ultimately successful in keeping him from being able to publish the many follow-ups the story begged for. It even prevented Gerth from reporting on how the smear machine was targeting him personally. Gerth's editor told him, "I don't want you writing about [them coming after you]. Since they're criticizing you, you have a conflict of interest."

Gerth says that's just what his attackers wanted. "If the target of a story need only attack the reporter to get him knocked out, because he's then deemed controversial, then it's easy to pick off all the journalists doing proper coverage," he tells me.

"I don't know all the things that went on between the Clinton world and my [*New York Times*] bosses," Gerth says today. He says he knows only one thing for sure: the *Times* didn't want him to do any more Whitewater articles.

"I do remember being told 'we don't want any Whitewater stories.' They said, it's like 'piling on.' Obviously I was not happy. But you just go onto the next thing. I never went and asked my two editors, 'Did the Clintons weigh in on you? Did friends of the Clintons complain?' I'm not sure they'd tell me anyways."

Only a full twenty-four years after Gerth's article did the full level of hysteria it triggered in the Clinton camp become clear. That revelation was provided by documents made public in January 2016 after they were obtained by the conservative watchdog Judicial Watch, in a Freedom of Information Act lawsuit. The documents include an internal case memo from the now-defunct Office of the Independent Counsel (OIC), which investigated the Clintons' Whitewater dealings back in the 1990s.

The memo, dated April 22, 1998, indicates the independent counsel considered filing a case against Hillary Clinton and even went so far as to outline the legal terms. Ultimately, any idea of prosecuting the first lady was discarded as unwinnable. But the thirty-two-page memo, titled "HRC Order of Proof," serves as a testament to how important—and damaging—Gerth's journalism was assessed to have been. His White-water article was repeatedly mentioned as the spark setting off frenetic responses from Clinton interests.

For example, there was a flurry of suspicious "activities" in Little Rock, Arkansas, triggered by the first whispers of Gerth's impending *Times* article. On Saturday night, March 7, 1992, "when the Gerth story hit the wire," Clintonites allegedly arranged a hasty nighttime rendezvous in the parking lot of the Rose Law Firm to accomplish a mysterious transfer of documents. The independent counsel's memo states that Clinton White-water lawyer Loretta Lynch (no relation to Obama attorney general Lo-retta Lynch) "received documents from Webb Hubbell in the [Rose Law Firm] parking lot that night." Hubbell was Hillary's onetime law partner. *What was it about Gerth's article that prompted Hubbell to transfer documents to Lynch in the dark of night? What did the documents show?*

Clinton interests would seek to smear Gerth in hopes of diminishing the impact of his powerful work and—more importantly—discouraging him from staying on the trail.

That smear was accomplished by the 1996 publication of *The Great Whitewater Hoax*. In it, liberal author Gene Lyons blamed Gerth for stir-ring up unfounded public hysterics over Whitewater. Using the language of astroturfers, Lyons called Gerth's work "debunked" and "discredited," and said the Whitewater controversy itself was a "hoax." (Lyons was still on the scene twenty years later, defending Hillary amid her wayward email practices and secretive Wall Street speeches.)

"Nobody [in the general public] read the [Lyons] book, but they dis-tributed it to every Democratic member of Congress," Gerth tells me. Ex-cerpts were published in *Harper's Magazine* and circulated by PBS and other news media.

Even then, Gerth wouldn't have predicted that the cyclone he'd con-jured would follow him like a menace for many years.

"I don't think I recognized [the organized smear] the first time around," Gerth tells me. "I didn't think that much of it until a year or two later when the Whitewater story came back again and there was an independent counsel investigation." About that time, Gerth says, the pro-Clinton response "grew more robust, and eventually the 'back to business' committee was set up." "Back to business," he says, referred to the Clinton allies' plan to "move on" the public from the Clinton controversies and a push to impeach the president for alleged perjury and obstruction of justice. It was the genesis of MoveOn.org.

MoveOn.org started up in 1998, the year the Whitewater independent counsel's Order of Proof memo against Hillary was drafted. At its inception, MoveOn was an email group that passed around a petition to censure (rather than impeach) Bill Clinton. MoveOn undertook aggressive smears of those who stood to hurt the Clintons (or, depending on your viewpoint, they undertook the task of setting the record straight for the Clintons).

In the end, at least some of the tactics used against Gerth and others worked. As serious as the accusations surrounding Bill Clinton appeared to be, they didn't derail his candidacy. Both sides took copious notes; the same sort of counterattacks Republicans had made against Anita Hill had now worked for Democrats. Ultimately, Democrats were able to insulate Bill from political death by smearing his accusers.

Once Clinton became president, scandal continued to hound him. This was no accident. Conservative billionaire Richard Mellon Scaife had launched a vendetta against President Clinton, focusing on the salacious womanizing angle.

A supporter of the presidential campaign of noted conservative Barry Goldwater, Scaife inherited his family's oil, shipbuilding, and banking fortune. After becoming convinced that Democrats were outdoing Republicans in the "war on ideas," he set about to change the balance. He became an early supporter of the conservative Heritage Foundation and a crucial funder of the rise of the right from the Reagan era forward. According to an account in the *Washington Post,* Scaife donated $200 million to conservative causes over the eighteen years leading up to Clinton's election.

Following the 1992 election of Clinton, Scaife decided to spend millions more pursuing an anti-Clinton crusade. A friend later quoted Scaife from a 1994 luncheon as saying, "We're going to get Clinton." Clinton ally James Carville referred to Scaife as "the archconservative godfather in [a] heavily funded war against the president." By the end of Clinton's presidency, the *Washington Post* reported Scaife was officially "the most

generous donor to conservative causes in American history." To date, he's
said to have given at least $340 million to fund a "war of ideas against
American liberalism."

There were many beneficiaries of Scaife's generosity along the way.
But one in particular, the *American Spectator,* drew blood at the start of
the Clinton administration. In 1993, Scaife supported a new venture at the
Spectator known as the Arkansas Project. There were reportedly strings
attached: the money had to be used to dig for dirt on President Clinton.
Scaife later told the *Washington Post* that he had doubts that the *Post* and
"other major newspapers would fully investigate the disturbing scandals
of the Clinton White House . . . I am not alone in feeling that the press
has a bias in favor of Democratic administrations."

It didn't take long for Scaife's money to hit gold. The Arkansas Project produced a high-profile exposé, "Troopergate," written by none other
than Anita Hill smear merchant David Brock. The first article in the 1993
series was titled "His Cheatin' Heart."

"His Cheatin' Heart" had every element of a delicious smear. Sex,
scandal, cover-up, and the president of the United States. Four Arkansas troopers told lurid stories of Clinton's supposed womanizing, claiming
they'd acted as de facto pimps for Clinton when he was governor of Arkansas. The troopers said they scouted for women, got their contact information, secured motels, and kept watch. There were dozens of affairs,
Brock wrote, ranging from one-night stands to long-term relationships.
He reported that the troopers viewed the Clinton marriage as "an effective political partnership, more a business relationship than a marriage."
It was later reported that the troopers had each been paid $6,700 after the
Troopergate articles were published.

Fox News Is Born

In the mid-1990s, as Scaife and other conservatives complained that the
left-tilted press was failing to give due coverage to Clinton's scandals and
shortfalls, the entire media landscape was about to change in a fundamen-
tal way.

It was 1996 and President Clinton was running for reelection. His opponents were Republican Bob Dole and Independent Ross Perot. Clinton's interests were fighting on two different fronts: playing defense on his scandals and pressing an offense to smear his attackers. In four short years, he'd already managed to weather a panoply of scandals. Besides Gennifer Flowers and Troopergate, there were the feds' disastrous handling of a cult holed up in Waco, Texas, in 1993, which resulted in seventy-six deaths, including four federal agents; and the mysterious death in July 1993 of White House counsel and Hillary confidant Vincent Foster. President Clinton had managed to rise above the ghost of Whitewater and survive the abysmal failure of Hillary's health-care initiative. He'd ridden out Filegate, Travelgate, and a Commerce Department bribery scandal punctuated by the strange demise of commerce secretary Ron Brown in a plane crash—while Brown was the subject of a grand jury investigation.

Although the press had widely reported on all of these Clinton controversies and more, conservatives perceived that the first couple had received kid-glove treatment relative to the seriousness and frequency of their alleged offenses. Enter Fox News.

The Fox News Channel first went live on October 7, 1996, one month before the election. The cable news network was founded by Australian-born tycoon Rupert Murdoch and GOP strategist Roger Ailes. A hefty national audience quickly embraced Fox as the alternative to a lineup of longtime, left-leaning mainstream news. With Fox's entrée as a bold, unafraid actor in the media game, the mainstream would become less likely to filter out or ignore some of the more salacious and lurid claims surrounding the Clintons. Before Fox, the mainstream press could act as an effective filter. If they didn't pick up a story, or didn't advance a particular take on one, it might as well never have happened. Now if the traditional media turned their nose up at a story or scandal, viewers could find it on Fox. It was in this news environment that President Clinton's sex scandals grew larger, threatening his presidency.

A loyal Democrat volunteer named Kathleen Willey unwittingly entered the fray in January 1997. She was called to testify in a sexual harassment lawsuit filed against President Clinton by one of his former associates, Paula Jones. According to Willey, her nightmare began back in

1993, when she was a White House volunteer aide. She was with President Clinton in a room off the Oval Office when he began consoling her over her husband's apparent suicide that day. The president's hugs of consolation, Willey claims, morphed into a groping session where he fondled her breast and pressed her hand against his genitals. There's no way to sugarcoat it. She makes the president sound like a panting, out-of-control adolescent who could cross the line into being dangerous. (Clinton denied any inappropriate conduct.)

Once her allegations became known, Willey says, she was chewed up and spit out by the Clinton smear machine. She recently talked with me about the experience, which still leaves her shaken all these years later.

"It's like being physically attacked. Where do you go? What do you do? Who do you tell?" she says. "These people really mean business."

Smears can manifest as physical threats, at least in the minds of weary targets like Willey, who became paranoid and despondent. She recounts what happened to her on January 8, 1997, two days before she was scheduled to give her deposition in the Jones case: Willey is walking her three dogs early in the morning near her house. Her cat has recently—mysteriously—disappeared. A stranger in dark sweat clothes and a baseball hat approaches and calls Willey by name. First, he asks about her missing pet.

"Hey, Kathleen, did you ever find your cat?"

"No," she replies.

"He was a nice cat," says the stranger.

A chill runs up Willey's spine. In recounting the story to me, she says, "The hair stood up and I thought, *This is trouble.*"

"Who are you, what do you want?" she asks.

"He just looked," Willey tells me. "I'll never forget the look. And he asked me how my children were doing, by name, and referred to where they live."

"What do you want?" she asks the man again.

"You're just not getting the message, are you?" says the stranger.

Willey tells me, "Frankly, I thought, *I'm gonna die right here.*"

She turns and runs as fast as she can, her dogs in tow.

"I got home, and I'll never forget as long as I live," says Willey, now seventy-one years old. "I remember thinking, *This is way out of your league. These people really mean business.*"

Two days after the scare, Willey detailed the harrowing encounter to the judge in the Jones lawsuit. The judge demanded confidentiality from both sides. But within seventy-two hours, someone leaked the story out onto the street. Willey says the next thing she knew, one of Bill Clinton's advocates was smearing her. Telling people she's a "fucking floozy female flake."

When smears do their job, the victims are eschewed by their friends and associates. They're separated from their support structure. Their resolve is weakened. They're broken. Willey notes she'd been a lifelong Democrat but, once smeared, found herself desperately alone.

"I had done much work for the party for years," she says. "I was a loyal Democrat. And not one person came to my defense." Today Willey insists she was subjected to more than a smear. She calls it a "terror campaign" orchestrated by Hillary Clinton that still affects her twenty years later.

For her part, Paula Jones's lawsuit alleged Clinton propositioned her and exposed himself years earlier as governor of Arkansas. Clinton eventually paid her an $850,000 settlement, but he admitted no guilt. Settlement or not, the damage to the reputations of both Clinton and Jones had been done. The case seemed to trigger an endless parade of additional women accusers. Dolly Kyle Browning claimed in a sworn statement for the Jones lawsuit that she had a sporadic twenty-two-year sexual relationship with Clinton (which he denies). She said Clinton described himself as a "sex addict." In 1998, Elizabeth Ward Gracen, Miss America 1982, claimed a one-night stand with Clinton when he was Arkansas governor. The story broke on the *Drudge Report*. Juanita Broaddrick alleged in 1999 that Clinton raped her twenty-one years earlier. Clinton denied it and was never charged. President Clinton ended up in the absurd position of spending his public life as Leader of the Free World while seeing his private time consumed by strategy sessions anticipating the next sexual accusation.

"Sid" Vicious

To help in his defense, Clinton hired journalist Sidney Blumenthal in August 1997 as a special adviser. At the time, *Newsweek* had just published its first story about the president's alleged groping session with Willey, the Jones lawsuit was moving forward, and Clinton was trying to break off his secret sexual relationship with White House intern Monica Lewinsky. He was in deep trouble. Blumenthal came to the rescue, managing intimate details of the Clinton quagmire.

Before landing the White House job, Blumenthal wrote for a series of liberal publications, including the *Washington Post, Vanity Fair,* and the *New Yorker.* In the 1984 presidential race, he'd gotten caught helping Democrat Gary Hart with speeches at the same time he was writing positive news stories on the Hart campaign. Next he penned positive stories about then–Arkansas governor Bill Clinton for the *Washington Post.* In 1992, Blumenthal praised presidential candidate Clinton in articles for the *New Republic* while attacking Clinton's opponents, President George H. W. Bush and Ross Perot. Once Clinton set up residence in the White House, Blumenthal became Washington correspondent for the *New Yorker.* His ardent support for the Clintons continued as the first couple slogged through their self-inflicted controversies, from Travelgate to Hillary's failed health-care proposal. As *Vanity Fair* later observed, for years Blumenthal "played both sides of the street as a journalist and a committed partisan."

Five months into Blumenthal's newest job as Clinton's adviser, the tawdry Monica Lewinsky affair exploded onto national front pages. The *Drudge Report* published rumors that *Newsweek* had the lurid story—but was delaying publication. Two days later, January 21, 1998, the news made headlines on the *Washington Post, Los Angeles Times,* and ABC News. Clinton was forty-nine years old when the affair began. Lewinsky was fresh out of college at age twenty-two. Rumors of the relationship had first surfaced as part of the Paula Jones lawsuit, for which Lewinsky had filed a false affidavit denying she ever had sex with the president.

As the news broke, the White House launched into panic mode behind the scenes. That afternoon, Blumenthal met privately with Hillary, then Bill. Five months later, in grand jury testimony, Blumenthal would imply that Bill deceived him in those early conversations, falsely assuring him that absolutely nothing untoward had taken place between Lewinsky and Bill. And being a trusting, naïve sort of fellow, Blumenthal claims, he believed Bill.

Here's what Blumenthal would later tell independent prosecutor Ken Starr's grand jury about his discussion of Lewinsky with the president:

> *I said to the President, "What have you done wrong?" And he said, "Nothing. I haven't done anything wrong.".... He said, "Monica Lewinsky came at me and made a sexual demand on me." He rebuffed her. He said, "I've gone down that road before, I've caused pain for a lot of people and I'm not going to do that again." She threatened him. She said that she would tell people they'd had an affair....*

A grand juror wanted to know if President Clinton admitted to any sexual activity with Lewinsky. Blumenthal replied that "the opposite" was true:

> *[Clinton] told me that she came on to him and that he had told her he couldn't have sexual relations with her and that she threatened him. That is what he told me.... [I] certainly believed his story. It was a very heartfelt story, he was pouring out his heart, and I believed him.... My understanding was that the accusations against him which appeared in the press that day were false, that he had not done anything wrong.*

Blumenthal not only allegedly helped sully Lewinsky; he also took on Starr and the grand jury. How does one go about smearing a grand jury? By publicly claiming they'd asked inappropriate questions about his dealings with the news media. After his first grand jury appearance, Blumenthal put on his most sincere offended face, telling reporters, "I never imagined that in America I would be hauled before a federal grand jury to answer questions about my conversations with members of the media."

Blumenthal continued: "Today, I was forced to answer questions about conversations, as part of my job, with the *New York Times*, CNN,

CBS, *Time* magazine, *U.S. News,* the New York *Daily News,* the *Chicago Tribune,* the *New York Observer,* and there may have been a few others." Members of the media began sweating it out. *What did Blumenthal tell the grand jury about our private conversations?*

Some in the media joined Blumenthal in his outrage at the grand jury's supposed line of questioning. Reporters secretly worried that if their candid and sometimes clubby private dealings with the Clinton operative were exposed, they wouldn't come out looking clean.

It turns out Blumenthal wasn't telling the truth. The grand jury hadn't asked him to detail his dealings with specific news organizations at all—at least, not according to the grand jury. In fact, the jurors were so outraged by Blumenthal's public accusations, they took the unusual step of calling him on it. After Blumenthal made another appearance before the panel, the forewoman admonished him: "We are very concerned about the fact that during your last visit that an inaccurate representation of the events that happened were [*sic*] retold on the steps of the courthouse," she said. She asked Blumenthal to *this* time "really represent us the way that events happened in this room."

Of course, it was Blumenthal who had the last word. In his 2003 book, *The Clinton Wars,* he wrote that the grand jury forewoman's comments were "distorted and highly inappropriate." In his book he also criticized legions of reporters and other perceived Clinton enemies. One of them was fellow journalist Michael Isikoff, who remarked about the book, "Time and again, in the book as in life, [Blumenthal] rearranges facts, spins conspiracy theories, impugns motives, and besmirches the character of his political and journalistic foes—all for the greater cause of defending the Clintons (and himself)."

Blumenthal proves himself a quintessential smear artist and model for others to follow. He defends his liege from any grievance, real or imagined, and works with a friendly press to advance his agenda. He attacks any accusers with a take-no-prisoners ferocity that some believe to be unrivaled—whether his targets are political enemies, members of the press who are off the narrative, or anonymous grand jurors doing their job as civil servants. One other key tactic Blumenthal would pioneer and perfect: the art of getting his story or view—even when incorrect—widely circulated in the media. He knows that if his version of events is later disputed or proven false (as was the case with the grand jury), the intended harm would have already been done. Many people would hear the original narrative; few would learn of the retraction.

Mission accomplished.

"It Was Only a Kiss"

Not many people know this, but in 1998, while President Clinton was busy lying about his relationship with White House intern Monica Lewinsky, his surrogates were floating the idea of telling a little, teeny, selective bit of the truth. They wanted to see how it played in the press and would develop their future strategy accordingly. So they privately leaked the following to the CBS News White House team: the president might admit to having a physical relationship of sorts with Lewinsky, but he will insist it was "only kissing." The idea was to see if the public could be convinced that Lewinsky was exaggerating their relationship.

Thus in late February 1998, CBS News reported its exclusive on the *Evening News*: Clinton might admit to kissing Lewinsky! It was a bombshell since the president had to date denied any relationship.

After the CBS story aired, the White House apparently wasn't pleased with the public reaction to the trial balloon it had just floated. It decided Clinton *wouldn't* go public with the "kissing relationship" narrative, after all. In fact, after CBS had reported its exclusive, White House adviser Rahm Emanuel appeared on another CBS program, *Face the Nation,* and denied such a strategy was ever considered.

Instead, Operation Nuts and Sluts moved full speed ahead, with Clinton allies expanding on the playbook that had successfully undermined Anita Hill and Kathleen Willey. Hillary attempted to portray Lewinsky as crazy, telling a friend that the young intern was a "narcissistic loony tune." (The name-calling was revealed much later, in notes taken by a close Hillary friend, upon the friend's death.) For his part, Bill called Lewinsky a liar. Clinton surrogates fanned out on-message. Blumenthal reportedly told his pal, journalist Christopher Hitchens, that it was Bill who was the victim in all this; Lewinsky was a "stalker." Both of the Clintons and Blumenthal were spreading the word.

"I have never had sexual relations with Monica Lewinsky," Bill would insist under oath in a deposition in January 1998. "I've never had an affair with her." He would later repeat that false claim to the American public in a now-infamous news conference. "I want you to listen to me, I'm gonna say this again. I did not . . . have . . . sexual relations with that woman." As the president spoke in a serious, angry tone, he wagged his finger at the press corps and television cameras for emphasis. He wagged it so hard, it hit the podium.

Hillary called the attacks on her husband a "feeding frenzy." In an appearance on NBC's *Today* show, she denied Bill had a relationship with Lewinsky and announced, "The great story here for anybody willing to find it and write about it and explain it is this vast right-wing conspiracy that has been conspiring against my husband since the day he announced for president." Whether it was "vast" or not, Hillary had a point, considering efforts like Richard Mellon Scaife's at *American Spectator*. However, this particular smear wasn't based on a fabrication. Bill had, indeed, secretly engaged in sexual relations with the young White House intern, then lied about it under oath.

Blumenthal and the White House firmly denied any effort to smear Lewinsky or other women. Blumenthal has consistently denied telling lies or using dishonest tactics. In his world, *he's* the victim of unfair smears.

Porno Smear

Ultimately, on December 19, 1998, the president was impeached by the House of Representatives on two charges stemming from the Lewinsky affair: perjury and obstruction of justice. But it's the Senate that decides whether to convict or acquit on impeachments. As the Senate deliberated, the Clintons got a big assist in their PR war from an unlikely ally: porn king Larry Flynt. Flynt, publisher of the hard-core pornographic magazine *Hustler,* decided to apply his naked creativity to the penetrating world of politics. Like other character assassins, his idea was to smear Clinton's enemies. To redirect focus toward Clinton's political accusers. Turn the tables. Change the conversation. It's not about the president's misconduct; it's about political hypocrisy.

Flynt bought a full-page ad in the *Washington Post* brazenly soliciting ammunition for the smear. He offered a toll-free number and promised up to a million dollars in cash to anyone who could prove they'd had adulterous sex with a current member of Congress or high-ranking government official.

Two thousand calls flooded in. *Hustler* editor Allan MacDonell told the *Post* in an article published January 11, 1999, "every voicemail that the calls were routed to was full, and every time we took down the numbers and deleted the messages, the system would immediately fill up again."

Flynt solicited photos, home video, "taped phone conversations and answering machine messages, dinner and drink receipts, phone bills, witnesses, divorce papers, angry spouses." Nothing was off-limits. He even hired an established investigative firm to knock on doors and check out leads. His private eyes were said to be ex-FBI and -CIA. Word got around. A nervous chill fell over the U.S. capital.

The mere threat of a smear proved enough to take down one major figure calling for Clinton's impeachment: House Speaker–designate Bob Livingston, a Republican from Louisiana. Flynt claimed he'd identified four women who'd been involved with Livingston. The day of Clinton's House impeachment vote, Livingston abruptly resigned.

Government officials who remain in the political mix today still shudder at the thought of that *Hustler* smear campaign. All these years later, one confides in me. He says that Flynt's sleazy investigators had approached one of his (the official's) ex-girlfriends, offering her $250,000 to sign a paper claiming she'd had an abortion from their relationship. Fortunately for this official, the woman didn't sign the paper or take the money.

In another incident, a source tells me, one member of Congress became so convinced his infidelities would be exposed by Flynt's scheme that the congressman went home and confessed a multitude of sins to his wife. The joke was on him: in the end, Flynt never mentioned him.

Flynt's targets at the time weren't just sitting politicians. *Hustler* editor MacDonell told reporters the hit list included pundits "who go on TV and keep attacking Clinton." It was a warning shot across the bow. Speak out against the president and you'll pay the price. Guilty-minded commentators began self-censoring. Suddenly some of the television analysts weren't so hard on Clinton. In fact, some of them switched to defending him. In February 1999, the Republican-majority Senate voted to acquit Clinton.

It's no wonder that today when political figures make decisions that seem to defy logic, their colleagues and staffers openly joke, *I wonder what they've got on him?*

Lewinsky forever wears the stain of her encounter with the president. And today she probably suffers more from her media assassination than the ex-president suffers as a result of his own actions and lies. I'll bet a dozen black berets that if you invoke Lewinsky's name to most anyone born after 1990, he'll chuckle and identify her as the intern with the sullied blue dress who gave the president a blow job. The young person probably won't be able to tell you that Clinton's misbehavior with Lewinsky was why, in 1998, he became only the second U.S. president in all of history to be impeached. Yes, critics note that Bill is oft remembered fondly, his transgressions forgiven and largely forgotten. In fact, it's one of the Clintons' greatest, yet most unheralded accomplishments: that history and the media widely regard his scandals while president to be little more than conspiracy talk, disproven myths and witch hunts. It's largely thanks to the smear. In this way, the Clintons elevated the smear to an art form and pioneered new methods: using the media to target enemies and to undermine uncooperative journalists. Together with their aides and friends, they wielded the tools of the trade with remarkable precision and paved the way for political smears over the next twenty years.

In January 2001, when the Clintons exited the White House, they took with them a clear playbook outlining how they'd managed to survive the previous eight years. It was a playbook they would build upon and revise, as needed. One they believed would help return them to the White House. In moving forward, they would strengthen their relationships with both Blumenthal and Brock: like-minded character assassins who possess a very particular set of skills. These two men would populate the Clinton orbit for two decades. Together they would build an indomitable smear network that evokes fear and awe and has come to set the standard for operations like it, both liberal and conservative.

Chapter Two

||||||||||||||||||||

David Brock's Smear Frontier

"David Brock is a fascinating person to watch because he's so entirely full of shit and so creepy," says a notable cog in the Washington, D.C., smear machine, with equal parts admiration and disgust. "But people throw money at him."

Of all the creations that the smears of the 1990s produced, perhaps the most provocative and perplexing is Brock. He had worked on the inside of the right-leaning media to build mountainous scandals out of molehills. And so it came as a shock to much of Washington's political class when he abruptly switched sides during the final years of the Clinton presidency. Brock crossed over from far right to hard left, bringing with him his conservative tricks and institutional knowledge.

That was just the beginning of Brock 2.0. In the years since his about-face, Brock has placed himself at the center of a remarkable smear movement. His name isn't evoked with the recognition or regularity of liberal billionaire donor George Soros, yet his influence on the left, especially in the media, is now legendary. His political reach stretches down a deep rabbit hole, placing him in close proximity to nearly every modern scandal developed against his paid and personal enemies.

Brock has cultivated an impressive body of liberal megadonors and assembled an eclectic collection of no fewer than thirty smear-related projects, most notably his flagship "media watchdog," Media Matters. This collection of groups was cited to me by nearly every Democrat and Republican operative I interviewed as the most ubiquitous and successful operation of its kind in its first decade.

Brock is the front man; a face for those who would rather remain faceless. And over the years, he's rewarded himself handsomely. He's collected salaries from at least seven of his organizations. It could be more, but he keeps those details secret. Brock repeatedly declined to be interviewed for this book, and would not disclose his compensation or provide a list of the organizations he's involved in. Over the course of many months, I pieced together information available from a myriad of tax documents and public reports. One thing is clear: Brock has made millions from his tax-exempt groups.

Perhaps more significant, he's had a dramatic impact on how the media functions, the kinds of stories it tells, and journalists' unwillingness to critique the left with the same zeal they attack the right.

You can think of Brock's empire as an anthill from which many tunnels radiate, surfacing elsewhere as other anthills. To those observing aboveground, each anthill may appear deceptively distinct, unrelated to the others. But an underground cross-section view reveals the intricate connections. They're single-minded in terms of their far-left agenda and no-holds-barred approach:

- **9 Nonprofits and Tax-Exempts**: American Bridge 21st Century Foundation, American Democracy Legal Fund, American Independent Institute, Citizens for Responsibility and Ethics in Washington (CREW), Common Purpose Project, Franklin Education Forum, Franklin Forum, Media Matters, Media Matters Action Network.
- **6 PACs, Super PACs, and Party Committees**: American Bridge 21st Century, Correct The Record, Franklin Forum, Priorities USA Action, American Priorities, and American Priorities 16 Joint Fundraising Committee.

- **15 Miscellaneous (training, websites, LLCs)**: Barrier Breakers project, *Blue Nation Review,* Bridge Project, Conservative Transparency, DropFox.com, Equality Matters, Franklin Strategies, Message Matters, Political Correction Project, Unnamed "polling and predictive" modeling destination, Progressive Talent Initiative, Progressive Media USA, ProgressiveAccountability.org, Shareblue, True Blue Media.

Brock's smear machine has proven potent and effective. It whirs, clanks, and chugs away, creating the false impression of overwhelming support for or against an idea, candidate, or person. It has successfully led campaigns to saturate the Web, social media, and news landscape in a way that directs and dominates the narrative. The goal for all these related groups: to mainstream and legitimize the controversial positions Brock's interests support. To sway thought among members of the public, politicians, and unquestioning reporters.

The Brock-affiliated groups coordinate in a way that has led critics to accuse them of violating IRS rules, but no authority has alleged wrongdoing. Together the entities spend millions upon millions advancing the interests of a relatively small group of donors. They spread money under different monikers to give the impression of great breadth and diversity. They dig up dirt to use against their targets. If they can't find any, sources indicate, they're not beyond repeating unproven or discredited information. They amplify their message with simultaneous, relentless attacks that exaggerate the impression of their numbers. They train armies of messengers in the art of how to use propaganda to shape the news media and political agenda. They conduct secret polls. When the results show a negative view of an interest they support, they set about changing the narrative. Unpopular concepts are reinvented, renamed by left-leaning interests, and then pushed by Brock entities to the public. Americans aren't buying "global warming"? Call it "climate change." The term *liberal* scores negatively? Change it to *progressive.* Need to alter the way people think about "illegal immigrants"? Smear those who use the phrase as "racist" or "white nationalists."

Brock's groups pay to have one-sided "reporting" conducted and pub-

DAVID BROCK'S EMPIRE

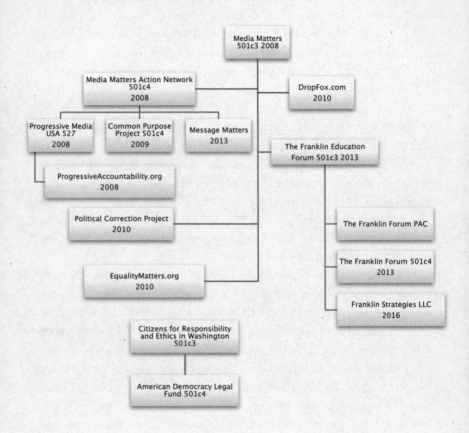

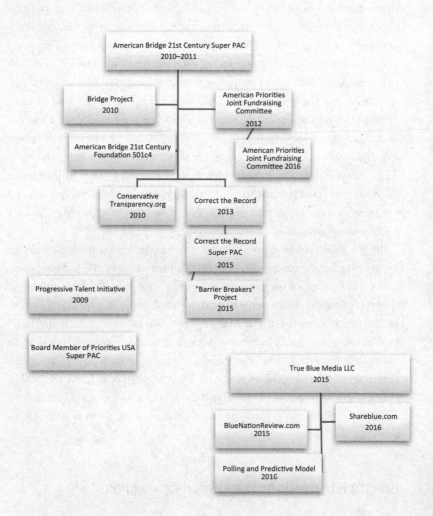

lished in the popular press. They controversialize opinions that threaten their agenda. They give speeches, hold press conferences, issue position papers, write blogs, pen letters to the editor, exploit social media, and serve as experts at think tanks. Their disciples are booked on the evening news and cable channels, and quoted in national publications. The idea for each new campaign is hatched by paid operatives, disseminated at meetings, spread among the groups, taught to the messengers, distributed as talking points, and ratified by politicians. They can masterfully steer the national agenda by launching a meme, coining a new phrase, or advancing a charged term. *Microaggression. Body shaming. White privilege. Alt-right.* They can use their vast network to implant propagandist terminology in the daily lexicon of Americans. The malleable press adopts the jargon and pretty soon even opponents are using it, unwittingly codifying the very ideas they oppose.

Brock didn't develop his game plan overnight. He built his knowledge by working inside the news media on both extremes of the political spectrum. He learned of the hopes and fears of each side and how to exploit them. He studied their strengths and vulnerabilities. But most important, he learned how to use the media as a tool. Brock experienced firsthand how conservative and liberal newsrooms operated. He understood what motivated reporters, what their thinking process was, and what influenced their editors. Building on the Clinton playbook from the 1990s, Brock's second volume in the 2000s centers on the rising popularity of cable news, the Internet, and eventually social media as new weapons in an established war.

Brock's Liberal Birth: The Clinton Connection

The backstory to Brock's entrée into liberal circles has to qualify as one of the most curious tales in politics. To understand why, it helps to look at his modus operandi as a conservative entering the prominent political reporting scene around 1992. He was on assignment for the conservative *American Spectator,* defending Supreme Court justice Clarence Thomas and attacking Anita Hill. By his own admission, Brock employed ruthless and dishonest tactics. Some of them had echoes of blackmail. In one instance, Brock approached a Hill friend named Kaye Savage to try to convince her to renege on her public support for Hill. He pressured Savage by obtaining, and then threatening to publicize, nasty accusations about her from a sealed child custody dispute.

"He knew all this personal stuff," Savage later told reporters about Brock. "He wanted me to take back what I had said [in support of Hill]. I couldn't. It was true. But I was intimidated, and so I faxed him something innocuous. I was scared."

Later, in his tell-all book *Blinded by the Right,* Brock would admit to using underhanded methods, and to misleading readers. In discussing how he'd switched political loyalties, he confessed that—as a conservative—he wrote "virtually every derogatory and often contradictory allegation" he could find to make Hill seem "a little bit nutty and a little bit slutty." He also wrote that he "demonized Democratic senators, their staffs, and Hill's feminist supporters without ever interviewing any of them." In a private memo unearthed in 2016, Brock also wrote specifically about the deception he used against Hill's friend Kaye Savage: "Though I confronted Savage with the [negative information from her divorce proceedings] in an effort to get her to recant, she never did, although I made it appear otherwise by journalistic sleight-of-hand."

Brock compiled his reporting against Hill into the 1993 book *The Real Anita Hill: The Untold Story.* The *New Yorker* said "Brock's book was filled with things that weren't true." Supreme Court reporter Lyle Denniston summed it up this way in the *Baltimore Sun:*

> *Mr. Brock scoured the gutters. The result is an almost astonishing display of political meanness, masquerading as objective investigation. . . . The two main characteristics of Mr. Brock's work are its breathtaking leap to conclusions, and its clumsy—sometimes even brutish—use of innuendo . . . beneath its tissue-thin veneer of respectable writing, this book speaks—in the main—in filthy whispers.*

It was after Brock's successful smear of Anita Hill that he took on an even bigger assignment: a hit job on President Clinton's wife. Brock reportedly pocketed a one-million-dollar advance to write *The Seduction of Hillary Rodham.* But when the book was published in 1996, it was far from the blockbuster the right had hoped for. Some reviewers said it was more apology for Hillary than critical examination of her transgressions. With no "scoops," Brock's book netted poor reviews and disappointing sales.

It was around this time that Brock made his peculiar political transfiguration. It's hard to know exactly what triggered it. He claimed it was a sudden attack of conscience. Others noted that he knew his flop of a book about Hillary would finish him off in right-wing circles, so he was in need of reinvention. Either way, in 1997, Brock officially switched political teams by writing an article for *Esquire,* "Confessions of a Right-Wing Hit Man." In it he attacked his own reporting methods and the conservative right for funding them. In a follow-up article the following year, Brock apologized to the Clintons for his earlier, salacious attacks against them. He continued the theme with his 2002 book, *Blinded by the Right.*

Coincident with Brock's transformation, it just so happened that Fox News was achieving unexpected dominance by appealing to the underserved conservative audience. By the early 2000s the cable news network had become a ratings leader, often outperforming its two best-known cable competitors—CNN and MSNBC—combined. Liberal interests were scared to death of Fox's success. Fear is a great motivator. It's against this backdrop that the converted Brock was formally recruited into the Clinton fold.

In January 2003, former president Bill Clinton personally placed a call to Brock. According to Brock's book *Killing the Messenger: The Right-Wing Plot to Derail Hillary and Hijack Your Government,* Bill wanted to build upon what Brock had begun with the rejection of his conservative roots and apparent newfound admiration for Hillary. *If Fox News is the conservative answer to the Clinton smear machine, then what's the liberal answer to Fox News?* At that moment, the idea was born for the crown jewel of Brock's groups: Media Matters. Hillary invited Brock to the couple's home in Chappaqua, New York, to present the concept to donors and the seeds for Media Matters were officially sown. Brock officially founded the group as an educational nonprofit in 2003, according to IRS records.

Years later, Hillary would take credit for "helping to start" Media Matters. At a 2007 convention in Chicago organized by the liberal blog the *Daily Kos,* then-senator Clinton spoke of the effort to develop a vast propaganda web to challenge conservative views:

We are certainly better prepared and more focused on, you know, taking our arguments, and making them effective, and disseminating them widely, and really putting together a network, uh, in the blogosphere, in a lot of the new progressive infrastructure, institutions that I helped to start and support like Media Matters and Center for American Progress.

Media Matters was started under the same IRS tax-exempt category as charities and religious organizations. It's called a 501(c)(3). There's no limit to how much money these groups can accept from individuals, corporations, and unions. In return for this wide latitude afforded by the IRS, and to theoretically keep the corrupting influence of big money separate from political campaigns, 501(c)(3)s are barred from engaging in political campaign activity. The IRS says such groups can't favor or oppose any candidate. (This was precisely the explanation the Obama IRS would later offer for launching its slow-grinding inquiries into the activities of dozens of Tea Party groups, many of which were ultimately denied tax-exempt status.)

Upon its founding, Brock presented Media Matters as a media watchdog to help balance conservative-tilted reporting in the mainstream media. In tax filings, the group provided this rationale for its educational mission:

Media Matters for America (MMA) believes that news reporting and analysis by the American media, with its eye on profit margin and preservation of the status quo, has become biased. It is common for news and commentary by the press to present viewpoints that tend to overly promote corporate interests, the rights of the wealthy, and a conservative, Christian-influenced ideology.

But it quickly became clear that the actual agenda of Media Matters was far less high-minded. To critics, Media Matters engaged in political activity day in and day out right from the start, in blatant violation of IRS rules. Years later, it seemed like Brock himself admitted as much. In a June 2015 blog, he wrote that he and Media Matters played a "role in specifically defending Hillary Clinton from the Republicans' unfair attacks" after the 2012 terrorist assaults on Americans in Benghazi, Libya. However, to date the IRS hasn't accused Media Matters of doing anything improper.

Although Media Matters initially described itself, inauspiciously, as a progressive research and information center, it quickly earned its stripes as a pro-Democrat smear group. It exists to obliterate conservative thought and eradicate any person, place, or thing that's perceived to be a threat— particularly to Hillary Clinton throughout her two presidential campaign attempts. It declared damning facts to be "bonkers," "phony," "anti-science," "witch hunts" that have been "discredited" and "debunked" as "myths" and "conspiracy theories." It assassinated the characters of Clinton's enemies and controversialized anyone who stood in the way.

But Brock had still bigger plans. They involved starting an arcane array of splinter groups. Some fell under the Media Matters umbrella, with various levels of oversight, accountability, and tax structures. Along with Media Matters, Brock also founded in 2003 the Media Matters Action Network, a tax-exempt 501(c)(4). "Social welfare" groups with this tax designation are allowed to engage in unlimited lobbying and can even work to help political campaigns, as long as that's not their primary activity. In other words, Media Matters Action Network can engage in political activities that Media Matters is forbidden from doing under the law.

Media Matters: Money Magnet

Almost from its inception, Media Matters became a magnet for elite left-wing patrons. When I added up the income from its beginning through 2014, it came to a whopping $94 million.

Who are the big-money players funding the cause? It's not an easy question to answer. Media Matters isn't required to name its donors. In 2010 Brock praised his own supposed openness in disclosing a $1 million contribution from the billionaire hedge fund manager George Soros. Besides that, there's not much in the way of transparency. But it's possible through reverse engineering to identify some contributors because the IRS requires certain entities to report their donations. That's how we know various progressive foundations have provided Media Matters at least $30 million over the years.

Two foundations figure prominently in Media Matters' early financial development: Tides Foundation and the Stephen M. Silberstein Foundation. Stephen Silberstein is a member of Patriotic Millionaires, an exclusive group of more than two hundred millionaires who "believe that the country's current level of economic inequality is both dangerous and immoral." Silberstein also belongs to Democracy Alliance, another network of liberal funders. In 2003—in Media Matters' infancy—the Silberstein Foundation made out a $100,000 check to "Tides Foundation—Media Matters for America," as if the two entities were one and the same. Silberstein would go on to become a top donor to the Hillary Clinton for President effort in 2016, contributing to three of her major super PACs.

As for Tides, it's the brainchild of wealthy liberal activist Drummond Pike. It functions as a donor pass-through for many left-wing causes. For example, those who prefer that their names not be publicly linked to radical causes can contribute to Tides, which then directs the funds to intended recipients like Media Matters. Critics liken it to a legal form of money laundering. Tides describes its mission as "building a world of shared prosperity and social justice, founded on equality and human rights, a sustainable environment, healthy individuals and communities, and quality education." Tides gave well over $4 million to Media Matters and its companion organization, Media Matters Action Network, in their first eight years. Other major supporters of Media Matters include the National Education Association teachers' union, which reported giving over $400,000 from 2009 to 2012; and labor unions, which gave $185,000 over several years.

But a lot of Media Matters cash is collected through a purely untraceable fashion—legally laundered, if you will—through Brock's favorite fundraiser, Mary Pat Bonner of the Bonner Group. Bonner earns millions by persuading Democrat megadonors to lighten their wallets to benefit

Brock's groups. Over the years she's collected commissions from at least *ten* of Brock's outfits. In 2013 and 2014 alone, she raised more than $21.9 million for Media Matters and got paid nearly $2.55 million in commissions, according to tax records. Bonner didn't respond to my repeated requests for information. I dissected what was publicly available by combing through hundreds of pages of documents from official filings submitted to the IRS and the Federal Election Commission. A partial tally of the Bonner Group's earnings from Brock's conglomerate comes to more than $15 million.

Brock and Bonner make up their own mutual enrichment society. Donor money is shuttled around among the groups in a dizzying dance that can make the original source of funds impossible for an outsider to trace. In 2014, the *Nation* declared Bonner to be Brock's "secret weapon." An insider calls the pair "probably the most effective major-individual-donor fundraising team ever assembled in the independent-expenditure progressive world." In fact, Brock and Bonner are so close, her offices are located in his Washington, D.C., headquarters, and the two are said to share a rental house in the Hamptons.

Bonner herself is a focus of controversy. She was at the center of a turf battle in early 2015 between Media Matters and a competing pro-Hillary smear group—all clawing for the same liberal donor dollars. The *New York Times* wrote about the spat, implying that Bonner reserves her richest donor connections for Brock because he offers a higher commission. The *Times* left the impression that there was something unseemly about their arrangement.

The Early Smears

The early years of Media Matters were spent establishing its reputation and getting to know the players in the news media. At the time, it functioned as the liberal version of the conservative media watchdog Accuracy in Media. Media Matters attacked a broad array of news targets. It even went after outlets generally seen as friendly to liberal causes, if they strayed from the preferred narrative. This included, believe it or not, select criticisms of CNN, PBS, and even MSNBC's Chris Matthews. Clearly, Media

Matters' strategy was not just to attack conservative targets, but also to spank liberal media actors when they got out of line.

Because the targets of Media Matters' early criticism included such a broad array of print and television outlets, the public and news media didn't widely recognize it as the fiercely partisan venture that it was. Further obfuscation of its motives was accomplished by the fact that the press often failed to do its homework on Media Matters' origins and financial backing, often treating the group as if it were a neutral media watchdog. In fact, if I were to isolate Brock's single most important achievement, it would be his uncanny ability to integrate Media Matters into the mainstream news culture as a news source. No other partisan group has been as successful at influencing the media and passing off its partisan work as news, or a newsworthy product.

Brock lorded over Media Matters as it built an impressive Listserv of Washington, D.C.– and New York–based reporter emails. Because many journalists personally agreed with Media Matters' criticism of news that defied the liberal agenda, they opened their minds to Media Matters' influence and took calls from Media Matters' staffers when the phone rang.

My own early experiences with Media Matters were friendly. Like other journalists, I didn't know much about them. As a reporter at CBS News, I didn't cover a lot of political topics. But occasionally my assignments would veer into that sort of territory and I'd get a call from a Media Matters staffer. I didn't know how the group got my contact information. My memory is that the staffers were knowledgeable and polite, and made their appeals in an affable manner. I recall one strategy a Media Matters operative used. He was trying to discredit a particular storyline in the news. He casually remarked that I, of course, as a reporter, was too smart to fall for *that* narrative. The tone was, *Everybody knows that story has been debunked. That source is discredited.* The implication was that anyone who reported the story was a patsy. *They want to fool you. But you're too smart for that.* Looking back, it was a clever psychological tactic. Nobody—least of all a reporter—wants to think of himself as a patsy, or be called one. As simple as such a strategy sounds, it can have the desired effect. The reporter subconsciously thinks to himself, *Yes, you're right, I'm too smart for that!*

Another reason Media Matters gained early prominence was that it was the first major effort to critique news from a liberal viewpoint. Most national reporters had never been called out in public by a group that so many other reporters and editors agreed with ideologically. Journalists began to cringe at the thought of being publicly shamed, their names and stories being highlighted on the Media Matters blog, where news colleagues and bosses might read it and wonder about them, with no opportunity to provide a counterpoint. In hindsight, news outlets should have recognized Media Matters as the partisan-motivated operation that it was and treated it accordingly. Forward-thinking news executives might have foreseen that Media Matters was on the leading edge of a potentially compromising trend of propaganda groups working to shape the news. Proactive news organizations could have developed policies and strategies to avoid compromise. But they didn't. The truth is, nobody was paying much attention on a macro level, and Media Matters was using that to its advantage.

As Media Matters worked to develop its voice, social media and the Internet were transforming the smear industry at the speed of light. Nobody could predict how dramatic the effects would be. In 2004, the social networking service Facebook was launched. In 2006, the microblogging platform Twitter fired off its first tweet. These free services, and others like them, were quickly identified as hypereffective tools for starting rumors and ruining reputations on a wide scale. They're game changers. No longer do propaganda campaigns require a large budget, strategy, and connections. Operatives can accomplish a smear faster than ever with the speed of the Internet and the power of social media. Rumor, innuendo, and lies in 140 characters or less. Media Matters used the reach of the Web to touch reporters via email on a daily basis and bring eyeballs to its website for its "media watchdog" blogs.

Conservatives were also making inroads, though no single group had the same "in" with journalists that Media Matters was busy developing. A 2007 article in the left-leaning *Nation* examined "the new right wing smear machine" and claimed it was conservatives who were taking full advantage of the new technological opportunities. It noted the expanding role that email and the Internet were beginning to play in advancing smears so that they became conventional wisdom widely accepted as fact. The article was subtitled "A web-savvy form of conservative propaganda, written anonymously and forwarded via e-mail, is altering the political landscape."

During this time, Brock developed bigger ideas and loftier goals. Media Matters' early years were spent nibbling at the edges of uncooperative media targets. It would soon formulate schemes to take down the targets. Discredit. Ruin. Destroy. Make an example of them. Chill other journalists from traveling the same territory. Once Media Matters found a successful formula, the casualties began to pile up. The first one worthy of note: radio shock jock Don Imus.

A Media Matters Smear in Six Steps: Imus

A "shock jock" is, by definition, a radio personality who entertains by expressing opinions in a deliberately offensive or provocative way. That's the whole point of the shtick. Don Imus invited guests from many ilks to appear on his program and became infamous for his politically incorrect humor and parodies. And he went on that way for decades, until April 2007.

Imus in the Morning was being simulcast on CBS Radio and on MSNBC television. Imus had already shown up on the Media Matters radar for his derogatory remarks about Hillary Clinton. In 2006 he'd referred to her as "that buck-toothed witch, Satan." Media Matters assigned a young "researcher" named Ryan Chiachiere to scrutinize every syllable that emerged from Imus's mouth in hopes of identifying a misstep to escalate into an all-out propaganda campaign. On April 4, 2007, with Hillary in the midst of her first failed run for the presidency, Imus delivered that misstep. In an on-air discussion with his producer, Bernard McGuirk, Imus referred to the predominately black Rutgers University women's basketball team in racially charged terms.

> **Imus:** So, I watched the basketball game last night between—a little bit of Rutgers and Tennessee, the women's final. . . . That's some rough girls from Rutgers. Man, they got tattoos and—
> **McGuirk:** Some hard-core hos.
> **Imus:** That's some nappy-headed hos there.

Initially the comments didn't generate much response. Imus's listeners are accustomed to provocative banter. But Media Matters was about to initiate a smear campaign that would serve as a prototype for many more to come.

Before we dissect those techniques, you may be wondering: What, exactly, distinguishes a smear from the truth? It's a fair question. After all, Imus uttered the slur. There's no denying it. The answer to what defines a smear often lies in the motivation behind, and scale of, the response. Expert smear artists take a sprinkle of truth—in this case Imus's objectionable comments—and pervert it into a weapon of mass destruction to advance a larger goal, often political or financial. That's what truly defines today's smear: its purpose is rooted in annihilation. It uses propaganda tools to amplify a misdeed out of proportion. It aims to obliterate any obstacle blocking a particular agenda. It gets personal. It goes for the jugular.

Here's how Media Matters systematically demolished Imus in about a week.

Step One: Launch

Within hours of Imus's comments, Media Matters posts a video clip and transcript, along with its first blog posting attacking him. A remark that relatively few saw or heard is now amplified with help from the Internet. "They publish a video and come up with a headline that will best activate supporters," an insider would later observe, speaking to the attention-grabbing technique. Another describes Media Matters' strength as in being "so fast, it's unbelievable. Its strength boils down to speed, volume and breadth."

Step Two: Distribution

Media Matters circulates its "news story" via email to hundreds of reporters on its email list. To build public pressure against Imus, word of his misdeed must spread like fire and soar beyond the level of a celebrity faux pas. The group counts on reporters' ignorance or complacency. Some of them use Media Matters as a source, as if it's a neutral media watchdog, and don't know better. Others are simply grateful to have a salacious story fall into their lap without having to do the legwork. And still more are sympathetic to the Media Matters agenda. "The right doesn't have a receptive audience in mainstream news," an observer tells me. "If you're sending a [conservative] Media Research Center email to an executive producer at any news channel except Fox, it's just going to get ignored, whereas Media Matters is taken seriously."

Step Three: Outreach

Media Matters identifies like-minded organizations to whip up outrage and further the smear. Since this instance involved a racial remark, Media Matters partners with black journalists, the NAACP, and other civil rights groups. Media Matters's Brock gets on the phone and personally calls "the heads of various liberal activist groups to coordinate a message."

Step Four: Escalation

Media Matters achieves success: the media begins to report the Imus incident as "news." The story has crossed over from gossip or a one-line news note into the mainstream. Media Matters knows it's hit paydirt and assigns fifty operatives to fan the flames. Their duties include publicizing previous Imus blunders to prompt second- and third-day news stories. CNN takes the bait and writes an article titled "Imus Has a History of Offending." Slate.com uses research provided by Media Matters to publish a comprehensive list of Imus's offensive comments through the years. The *New York Times* publishes stories three days in a row. In many publications, the shock jock's remarks garner coverage beyond that devoted to the Somali civil war, fighting by U.S. troops in Iraq, and the Duke lacrosse players who were exonerated on charges of rape, kidnapping, and sexual assault.

Step Five: Demands

Media Matters and its advocates demand and receive an apology from Imus. He publicly calls his remarks "thoughtless and stupid." CBS and MSNBC announce he'll be suspended for two weeks. However, the smear artist doesn't seek an apology for the purpose of putting a controversy to rest; he exploits it as an admission of guilt to exert pressure to further squash the target. The groups attacking Imus now demand that he be fired.

Step Six: Pressure

Media Matters' minions turn up the pressure with rapid-fire "stories," and convince advertisers to threaten to pull commercials from MSNBC. Imus ally and former New York City police detective Bo Dietl attempts to defend his friend, telling CBS chairman Sumner Redstone: "Two words ['nappy-headed hos'] should not ruin a person's career." But in eight days, it's all over: Imus is fired from both CBS Radio and MSNBC. A personality who once reportedly generated $25 million a year for CBS and $8 million for MSNBC is summarily dispensed with—over two words. Media Matters has managed to place a barely noticed remark on the dashboard of millions of Americans and escalate it into national outrage. As the *Wall Street Journal* later reports, "it soon became clear that events were moving at a speed [Imus] couldn't control."

Imus concedes that what he said was wrong. He recently told me, "I gave them the ammunition." That's the dastardly beauty of a smear: the agent need only lie in wait. Everybody slips up sometime. Add a little seasoning and spice to that grain of truth and one can cook up a career train wreck.

Double Standards

One mark of a smear outfit is that it zeroes in on its enemies but gladly overlooks the same behavior in its friends. It's worth mentioning some notables who made similarly distasteful remarks as Imus's, yet were not targeted by Media Matters or other hit groups. *Their* transgressions were ignored, justified, or quickly forgiven. Play along using the Substitution Game. What if the other side had made the gaffes recounted below?

- During a 2006 fundraiser, then–Senator Hillary Clinton, a Democrat, evokes a stereotype about Indians working at gas stations, joking that India civil rights leader Mahatma Gandhi "ran a gas station down in St. Louis for a couple of years." She later apologizes for her "lame attempt at humor."
- Also in 2006, then–Senator Joe Biden, a Democrat, makes a similar

joke. "You cannot go to a 7-Eleven or a Dunkin' Donuts unless you have a slight Indian accent. I'm not joking!" he says.

- In 2007, Biden comments on Barack Obama's candidacy for president, stereotyping and insulting the black race. He states, "I mean you've got the first sort of mainstream African-American who is articulate and bright and clean and nice-looking guy." Obama not only forgives the perceived racial slur; he also chooses Biden as his running mate.

- In 2008, it's then–Senate majority leader Harry Reid, a Democrat, who makes racial comments about Obama. Reid is quoted as saying that Obama could be a successful presidential candidate due in part to his "light-skinned" appearance and the fact that he speaks "with no Negro dialect, unless he wanted to have one." When the comments are publicized, Reid apologizes. Obama accepts the apology "without question."

- At a question-and-answer session in June 2013, Obama defense secretary Chuck Hagel facetiously asks an Indian man in the audience if he's a member of the Taliban, an Islamic extremist terrorist group that has no connection to India or Indians.

- In February 2015, Biden is at it again. He stereotypes Somali immigrants as taxi drivers, stating, "If you ever come to the train station with me, you'll notice that I have great relationships with [Somalis] because there's an awful lot of them driving cabs and are friends of mine. For real. I'm not being solicitous. I'm being serious."

- In a 2010 video eulogy, Hillary Clinton called Senator Robert Byrd, who had been a former member of and recruiter for the white supremacist Ku Klux Klan, a "friend and mentor."

None of these politicians was subjected to a trademark Media Matters smear campaign. The smear artist reveals himself by his disparate treatment of people and situations. He drapes himself in a superhero cape, claiming to defend the aggrieved. He pretends to right societal wrongs. In fact, though, he's motivated primarily by paid interests and his own selfish agendas. By definition, the job requires that morality and conscience be cast aside.

After its success in taking down Imus, Media Matters was emboldened, its taste for blood whetted. As soon as it learned of Imus's career demise, it published a blog putting other popular conservative personalities in the crosshairs.

"As Media Matters for America has extensively documented, bigotry and hate speech targeting, among other characteristics, race, gender, sexual orientation, religion, and ethnicity continue to permeate the airwaves through personalities such as Glenn Beck, Neal Boortz, Rush Limbaugh, Bill O'Reilly, Michael Savage, Michael Smerconish, and John Gibson," stated the website.

With its first high-profile takedown, Media Matters had accomplished something even more significant. It had proven to liberal donors, conservative foes, and the news media that it was more than a media watchdog. It was a force to be reckoned with. And it now had a diabolical recipe for success.

The Return of Jeff Gerth

While Brock's Media Matters waged war against Imus, it was fighting simultaneous campaigns against other adversaries, including Pulitzer Prize–winning journalist Jeff Gerth. Gerth had broken an important Whitewater story in the *New York Times* back in 1992. He remained in Brock's crosshairs for years.

At one point, while Bill Clinton was still president, Brock was said to have talked with Clinton White House lawyer Mark Fabiani about plans to "debunk" the Whitewater story. Fabiani was apparently so disturbed by Brock's stated intent to discredit Gerth that he took the unusual step of writing Gerth a personal memo about it. In the January 23, 1998, memo, Fabiani wrote that he had defended Gerth's Whitewater reporting and informed Brock that he believed "the heart of [Gerth's] original *Times* story remained intact to this day."

Fabiani further explained in his memo to Gerth, "I also said [to Brock] that the basic question raised by the *Times* story was still the basic question of Whitewater: Is it appropriate for a public official to enter into a private business arrangement with an individual who is seeking regulatory approval from the elected official or the official's appointees?"

Even though Fabiani, a Clinton insider, supported the facts and merits of Gerth's reporting, Brock didn't let that interfere with his agenda: Gerth remained a marked man. Fifteen years after Gerth's first Whitewater article, the familiar personalities were about to intersect and clash again.

It was 2007. Hillary had initiated her first White House run; Brock was building his pro-Hillary Media Matters empire; and Gerth was about to publish a new book about the "real" Hillary Clinton, *Her Way: The Hopes and Ambitions of Hillary Rodham Clinton.* (The book was cowritten with Gerth's fellow Pulitzer-winning colleague Don Van Natta Jr.) One month before the book's release, Media Matters stepped up its fictitious narrative about Gerth. One fanciful account was authored by Eric Boehlert, formerly of left-leaning *Salon* and *Rolling Stone,* who calls himself a Media Matters "senior fellow." In his blog, Boehlert hurled so many insults at Gerth, it reads almost like a parody. First, Boehlert wrote, Gerth is better known for the facts he got wrong than the stories he got right. In Boehlert's alternate reality, Gerth was "a Zelig-like figure during the 1990s. . . ."

Zelig is a Woody Allen film about a character with a gift for mimicry.

Boehlert rambles on for ages. He says Gerth appeared "at every crossroads where *The New York Times* lost its newsroom composure, and uncorked dark, convoluted tales featuring the conniving Clintons at the heart of a would-be criminal enterprise." He claims Gerth took a "shoddy approach to journalism," engaged in "corner-cutting," and wrote "accusatory stories that couldn't withstand close scrutiny and often didn't even make sense." He adds, "among mainstream reporters, perhaps nobody during the 1990s got more things wrong about Hillary and Bill Clinton than Jeff Gerth," and "Gerth's misfires became as predictable as his reporting style." A few more aspersions: "Gerth seemed to take bad writing, and camouflaging, to new heights during his discredited Whitewater adventures," "Gerth appears to be almost delusional about his flawed Whitewater reporting," and, for good measure, "Gerth is also a famously bad writer."

Why the overkill? Because Clinton supporters had a daunting task at hand: to discredit a prize-winning journalist before his newest book release. If nothing else, Boehlert's diatribe was intended to figure prominently in Internet search results and hopefully sway readers who didn't know better.

2008 Presidential Race

In the 2008 race, Media Matters was obviously pulling for Hillary. According to the *Daily Caller,* from February 2007 through January 2008, Media Matters ran 1,199 favorable posts for Clinton compared to 700 for Obama (and zero for Republican John McCain). But on June 7, 2008, Clinton conceded defeat to Barack Obama in the Democratic primary. Media Matters swiftly shifted its operation to defending Obama and attacking his enemies.

A large part of the strategy involved monitoring Fox News and taking on commentators and journalists who challenged Obama's campaign rhetoric. Media Matters targeted conservative analyst Ben Stein, NPR's Mara Liasson, and Fox News anchors Gretchen Carlson and Gregg Jarrett—all for their Fox News appearances and reports about Obama's tax plan. Liberal groups like Citizens for Tax Justice amplified the message by republishing excerpts of Media Matters' blogs.

Sean Hannity and the Fox News program he cohosted, *Hannity & Colmes,* constituted another major threat to the Media Matters agenda. Media Matters blogs regularly cataloged and exposed supposed "falsehoods" and "lies" presented on the show. While such blunt terminology is common in today's unvarnished Internet and social media environment, extensive use of such charged language at that time was a novelty. It drew the desired attention and shocked the sensibilities of those accused. It provided a chilling effect for those who didn't want to likewise end up in a negative light.

Media Matters was also an early adapter of other attention-grabbing techniques that got its messages widely circulated and quoted: its writers crafted headlines that tempted people to click on the articles and videos. They built lists and awarded dubious distinctions. "Top 10 Awful Displays

of Sexism on Fox News." "Sean Hannity: Media Matters' 2008 Misin-
former of the Year." "Top 6 Reasons Women Should Be Thankful Conservative Media Aren't Their Doctor."

Brock launched a joint project with MoveOn.org leader Tom Matzzie
and the left-wing Center for American Progress, which was founded by
John Podesta, a former Bill Clinton adviser and Obama official. Together
in 2008 they created an anticonservative war room called **Progressive
Media USA**, with Brock as its chair.

Unlike his other two Media Matters groups, Progressive Media was
formed as a different sort of tax-exempt nonprofit that worked to support or defeat political candidates. It was specifically dedicated to smearing Republican senator and presidential candidate John McCain. Initially
Progressive Media was conceived to serve as a major vehicle to collect
unregulated donations for negative TV ads against McCain. Organizers
boasted they planned to spend no less than $40 million: a huge sum. But
it turned out to be a pipe dream. During the election, Obama called on
so-called "outside" groups like Progressive Media to rein in their spending. The $40 million McCain smear would have to be dialed back before
it even began.

So Brock reinvented Progressive Media as a 501(c)(4) pro–Obama
White House operation called **ProgressiveAccountability.org**. Rather
than spending millions on attack ads, the new iteration dedicated itself to
"researching" McCain. Trackers were dispatched to videotape McCain at
campaign events, hoping to capture a misstep to build into a smear. (Today
both Progressive Media USA and ProgressiveAccountability.org appear to
be defunct.)

With the election of Obama as president in 2008, Brock continued
to spin the machinery of Media Matters into a growing and increasingly
complex tapestry. The resulting network would have a goal much grander
than any single takedown, issue, or election. It would serve as a conduit for
billionaire ideologues and select corporate interests, a way for their money
to be used to transform opinions, ideas, and even society at large.

The **Common Purpose Project** was another Media Matters–related
attempt to coax the news narrative to the left, this time in coordination
with the Obama White House. Started in 2009, it was a politically ori-

ented tax-exempt 501(c)(4). Organizers held weekly meetings on Tuesdays at the Capitol Hilton with officials from a variety of familiar left-wing organizations, such as MoveOn.org. According to *Politico*, the gatherings included "involvement" from an Obama White House communications official. The ultimate goal? To advance the Obama agenda. A primary mission reflected on Common Purpose Project's 2012 tax form was to defend Obamacare against its critics. The group also reportedly took part in a daily morning call run by Media Matters' interests and related groups, including an alliance promoting the president's budget. Common Purpose promised to disclose donors biannually; its last such report was made in 2013 and it now appears to be defunct.

The **Progressive Talent Initiative** was also established in 2009 as another subpart under Media Matters engaged in media training to "incubate a new generation of liberal pundits" for appearances on TV news to advance and defend liberal positions. It was an ingenious Brock creation, recognizing the great value that could be gained by going beyond attempts to influence the news media on the outside. This would work the news from the inside, coaching liberal ambassadors on how to effectively present their message and argue their points in a telegenic way before mass audiences. The twenty-four-hour cable television universe had an endless appetite for content and Brock rightly postulated that if his groups could train and offer up pundits, they'd get lots of exposure. By 2011, the Progressive Talent Initiative declared that it had already trained more than 100 pundits who had appeared a combined 800 times on television and radio. A partner organization described Progressive Talent Initiative as a female-centric group with a bold goal: to prompt a "true values shift among the public . . . In particular . . . identifying and training promising women in order to increase the presence of female progressive voices throughout the mainstream media."

Despite the money and effort pouring into the growing Brock network, it was still having difficulty chipping away at the biggest advantage conservatives were building: Fox News. An entire television news channel whose reporting was often out of step with the more controllable mainstream media. A forum for outspoken, conservative personalities who were able to reach and influence a mass TV audience like never before.

Media Matters would decide it wasn't enough to attack the messages on Fox. It would have to go after Fox itself.

Wrecking Beck

Just as President Obama took office in 2009, conservative radio personality Glenn Beck was getting inaugurated at Fox News. He'd left CNN Headline News for Fox's larger audience, and his viewership quickly surpassed that of his combined cable news competition.

Though new to Fox News, Beck had been on the progressive radar for years. In 2006 he was first introduced to a national television audience as host of a nightly program on Headline News. He managed to quickly build the network's second-largest audience behind attorney Nancy Grace. By 2008, Beck had six and a half million listeners of his national radio show and had won the Marconi Radio Award for Network Syndicated Personality of the Year. With his avid TV and radio following, he was viewed by liberal interests as an influential and dangerous opinion leader in conservative politics: a clear and present danger to the left. Media Matters' trackers began monitoring his every word and attacking him for his socially inappropriate commentary. For example, Media Matters publicized the March 21, 2007, edition of *The Glenn Beck Program* in which Beck referred to comedian Rosie O'Donnell, of ABC's *The View,* as a "fat witch . . . [O'Donnell has] . . . blubber . . . just pouring out of her eyes . . . Do you know how many oil lamps we could keep burning just on Rosie O'Donnell fat?"

Once settled in at Fox, Beck began to use his program to publicly trace the money connections among Media Matters, George Soros, and their affiliated groups and sympathizers. That's when Beck became a prime target, excoriated for his rhetoric about women and President Obama, among other offenses. As with Imus, there was truth behind the smear: Beck had indeed rattled off a long litany of offensive remarks about women and other groups. As we've established, many smear targets are undeniably guilty of making highly objectionable comments. What character assassins do is amplify such comments for political goals. The real reason Beck became a target had less to do with his commentary and more to do with the way he poked at the soft spots of the powerful and influential, including the president. On top of that, the left had decided it needed a villain to keep its base happy and its donors motivated. The campaign orchestrated against Beck became another fascinating blueprint for smears to come.

The origins of the campaign to wreck Beck can be found in a September 2009 internal memo written by Media Matters communications director and Democratic strategist Karl Frisch. He'd brought his ideas from the world of campaign politics. He'd served on the team that tried to get Howard Dean elected president in 2004 and was press secretary to New York congresswoman Louise Slaughter and the Democratic Senatorial Campaign Committee. In a Media Matters internal memo, Frisch presents an elaborate idea for a "Fox Fund" to exclusively target Beck's network with a "well funded, presidential-style campaign to discredit and embarrass . . . making it illegitimate in the eyes of news consumers."

"[T]he progressive movement is in need of an enemy," Frisch writes in the 2009 memo, later obtained by the *Daily Caller*. "George W. Bush is gone. We really don't have John McCain to kick around any more. Filling the lack of leadership on the right, Fox News has emerged as the central enemy and antagonist of the Obama administration, our Congressional majorities and the progressive movement as a whole."

How far is Media Matters willing to go to accomplish this smear? Pretty far, according to the remarkable memo. Everything from stalking to spying.

Step One: Launch

In his memo, Frisch recommends a shocking tactic: he says that Media Matters should hire private eyes to probe into the personal lives of Fox News anchors, hosts, reporters, prominent contributors, and senior network and corporate staff. He also suggests hiring a major law firm to find legal actions to take against Fox News, "from a class action law suit [*sic*] to defamation claims for those wronged by the network." Frisch postulates, "I imagine this would be difficult but the right law firm is bound to find some legal ground for us to take action against the network."

Frisch has other creative ideas for surreptitiously exerting pressure. He suggests Media Matters launch "an elaborate shareholder campaign" against Fox News' parent company, including "a front group of shareholders" or "massive demonstrations . . . at shareholder meetings." He proposes enlisting left-wing director Michael Moore to make a negative documentary about the network. He wants to hire "a team of trackers" to stake out public and private events attended by Fox News talent and senior staff. He proposes Media Matters do "opposition research" on Fox employees, attack them on social media, put yard signs in their neighborhoods, and put a "mole" inside Fox.

The incredibly broad strategic suggestions give the clearest public insight to date into the mind-set of the expanding Media Matters network and its efforts to destroy its enemies. Many of the questionable tactics proposed in the extraordinary 2009 memo have since been used in practice. In this fashion, Media Matters separates itself from the competition. Certainly, right-wing groups aim to be as effective as Media Matters. But none has been able to accomplish the caliber and breadth of smears that Media Matters has executed.

Frisch left Media Matters after five years and went on to found a nonprofit called Allied Progress, which he said would operate like an oppo research group "that uses hard-hitting research and creative campaigns to hold powerful special interests accountable and empower hardworking Americans." To this day Frisch remains proud of the Media Matters smears he devised. Though few Americans have ever heard of him, his current biography touts he's "perhaps best known for his work of nearly five years" at Media Matters, "the nations [*sic*] premier progressive media watchdog." He also boasts that he "developed the organization's long-term strategy to target Fox News as a political actor and was instrumental in building the backbone of the organization's rapid response communications structure, establishing a state of the art operation that has since become a model of best practices for progressive organizations throughout the country." That skill set is worth its weight in gold in Washington, D.C.

On October 20, 2010, a year after Frisch outlined his ambitions in that internal memo, Media Matters received a cash commitment from Soros, specifically to go after Beck. Ironically, the Soros–Media Matters partnership proves the very financial ties Beck warned about on his Fox News program.

Step Two: Distribution

In an unusual joint press release in October 2010, Media Matters announces the Soros funding—a cool million. The announcement suggests that nothing less than civilization is at stake. Soros and Media Matters posit themselves as saviors of the world, promising to do anything it takes to suppress Fox News "in view of recent evidence suggesting that the incendiary rhetoric of Fox News hosts may incite violence." Their crusade is justified, they claim, because Fox could actually lead to people getting hurt.

"I am supporting Media Matters in an effort to more widely publicize the challenge Fox News poses to civil and informed discourse in our democracy," says Soros in the statement. In other words, he's spending big bucks to suppress free speech in a free democracy . . . to *save* democracy. Brock adds that Fox is "a 24-7 GOP attack machine, dividing Americans through fear-mongering and falsehoods and undermining the legitimacy of our government for partisan political ends."

"Worse still, in recent months, Fox has allowed Glenn Beck's show to become an out of control vehicle for the potential incitement of domestic terrorism," continues the Brock-Soros press release. "No American should be quiet about these developments—the degradation of our media and the reckless endangerment of innocent lives."

As a side note, these memes are nearly identical to ones the Hillary camp would use much later against Donald Trump. "It's not just that Trump doesn't know what he's talking about when it comes to national security," Clinton tweeted on August 16, 2016. "His words are dangerous, and they hurt us." And the words are similar to Clinton's rhetoric as she and Brock announced an effort to arbitrate "fake news" after the 2016 election. "Lives are at risk. . . . It's a danger that must be addressed and addressed quickly . . . to protect our democracy and innocent lives," Clinton told reporters.

Back to the Brock-Soros press announcement against Beck. It criticizes the "hidden right-wing billionaire money corrupting our democracy" while praising Soros—a left-wing billionaire—for "quickly and transparently" making his financial support public. Does that mean Media Matters has an open policy of disclosure when it comes to its financiers? No. With rare exceptions, Media Matters doesn't disclose its donors, and it uses third-party fundraisers that obscure the sources.

At the same time, Brock also starts a website under Media Matters called **DropFox.com** to pressure advertisers to boycott Beck's program and Fox News.

For Beck's part, he gives as good as he gets. The day after Soros and Media Matters publicly join at the hip, Beck calls Soros a "spooky dude" on his TV program and suggests that it's Soros and Media Matters who are dangerous.

"Gee, Mr. Soros, you're not inciting violence over there towards me? You're not making me public enemy number one, are you?" says Beck. "I hope not, Mr. Soros. . . . Somebody says something like this and some nutjob could go violent."

Step Three: Outreach

The DropFox.com campaign against Glenn Beck draws in other liberal activist groups, such as People for the American Way, and exploits close ties between Media Matters and Drummond Pike's Tides Foundation. In October 2010, DropFox.com invites readers to copy and send advertisers a form letter that reads, in part:

> *Dear Fox Advertiser,*
>   *I agree with Tides Foundation CEO Drummond Pike:*
>   *"Businesses that pay to broadcast commercials on Fox News are subsidizing Glenn Beck's television show by continuing to pump money into the network. It has become clear that the only way to stop supporting Beck is to stop supporting Fox News."*

Media Matters also quietly funnels $200,000 to a group called Citizen Engagement Laboratory, a political advocacy nonprofit 501(c)(4) that calls itself "a home for social entrepreneurs . . . and a launching pad for new ideas and people powered projects that seek to change the world by leveraging the power of the Internet." The Laboratory is funded in part by grants from Soros's Open Society Foundations. The $200,000 from Media Matters is for a "campaign to expose Glenn Beck's racist rhetoric in an effort to educate advertisers about the practices on his show." In other words, to convince corporations to drop their ads from Beck's Fox program.

Step Four: Escalation

Next, Media Matters begins pushing articles like "15 Whoppers Beck Did Not Get Fired for in 2010," followed by the creatively titled "The 50 Worst Things Glenn Beck Said on Fox News."

The travel website Orbitz becomes an official target of the DropFox blitzkrieg conducted by lesbian and gay organizations, even though Orbitz is considered "gay-friendly"—perhaps *because* of it. The gay community knows Orbitz cares deeply about its patronage and would likely crumple if criticized for advertising on Fox. The smear campaign against Orbitz kicks off on May 16, 2011, with a press release on PR Newswire accompanied by a social media campaign attacking Orbitz on Twitter and Facebook. A boycott isn't very effective if it goes unnoticed; *Huffington Post* quickly assists with an article publicizing it.

Orbitz initially complains it's being subjected to a "smear campaign." But resistance proves futile. After a few weeks of hammering, the travel company cries uncle, issuing a statement that reads in part: "We believe that a discussion about our advertising practices is healthy, important and timely. . . . The question posed to Orbitz by many within the LGBT community resulted in our decision to review the policies and process used to evaluate where advertising is placed."

Steps Five and Six: Demands and Pressure

The money Media Matters funneled to Citizen Engagement Laboratory begins to pay off. Fox is feeling the heat. According to a case analysis later conducted by Presidio Graduate School, the "Drop Glenn Beck" campaign pressured Wal-Mart, GEICO, Verizon, and Chase to drop their ads from Beck's program. "[Citizen Engagement Laboratory] organized and mobilized online and offline communities to help dump Beck. . . . [O]ver 100 companies dropped their support from Beck's show, helping mitigate Beck's political clout and negatively impact Fox News Channel's revenue streams." The Presidio report adds that activists collected more than 280,000 petition signatures asking companies to withdraw their ads; directly contacted more than seventy companies, urging them to renounce support; and "built a multi-media campaign titled, TheRealGlennBeck .com, to serve as a central database of Beck's race-baiting and misinforming praxis."

As you can see, it was a small core of backers that targeted Beck, led by Brock and Soros. They fanned out their money and influence to engage other groups, giving the impression there was broad consensus behind the effort.

Meantime, Media Matters implements the pugnacious tactics Frisch had outlined in his not-yet-public memo. The group announces plans to expand its Fox vendetta to an all-out campaign of "guerrilla warfare and sabotage." The intentions are publicized in an article penned by *Politico*'s Ben Smith (whom a Media Matters insider later praises in a *Daily Caller* exposé as a reporter who writes what they want him to write, which Smith denies). Using the *Politico* article as the tool to deliver its message, Media Matters is basically putting Fox on notice that the smear outfit's staff of about ninety has "all but abandoned its monitoring of newspapers and other television networks" to narrow its focus to "Fox and a handful of conservative websites, which its leaders view as political organizations and the 'nerve center' of the conservative movement." The *Politico* article also serves as helpful publicity for Media Matters, raising its profile among liberal activists and donors.

According to *Politico,* Media Matters has also hired two writers to churn out smears directed at Beck, as well as an activist to spearhead lobbying against advertisers buying time on his program. The group has assembled a legal team to explore hitting Fox with defamation lawsuits and is developing plans to conduct opposition research on Fox employees.

Days after Media Matters reveals its stepped-up efforts in the *Politico* article, Fox News announces Beck is getting the boot: his last day will be at the end of June 2011.

Media Matters takes a victory lap. It formally declares victory and announces its War on Fox News is over in December 2013, saying it had "effectively discredited the network's desire to be seen as 'fair and balanced.'"

Today some conservatives accuse Fox of allowing itself to be co-opted or infiltrated: Media Matters disciples routinely appear as guests and analysts on Fox News, sometimes without the requisite disclosure of their conflicts of interest. During the 2016 campaign, the network sometimes featured debates between Republicans and Democrats who were all against Trump, while he went unrepresented. However, many continue to widely regard Fox as a conservative standard-bearer.

As a footnote, the "Color of Change" subsidiary of Citizen Engagement Laboratory that worked the Beck smear (co-founded by ex–White House "green jobs" czar Van Jones) got a lot of public credit for getting Beck removed from Fox. A former Media Matters staffer later explained, in an exposé in *Daily Caller,* that letting another group receive acclamation for an effort is known as "fingerprint coverage . . . where you know it was the result of your work." Spreading the glory gives the media and public the false impression there's a broader consensus. Today the Citizen Engagement Laboratory website claims credit not only for wrecking Beck, but also for such other initiatives as repealing "Don't Ask, Don't Tell," convincing President Obama to enact the controversial Deferred Action for Childhood Arrivals (DACA) policy for illegal immigrants, and getting CNN to drop conservative business news host Lou Dobbs.

David Brock's growing smear network had now proven it could go far beyond publicly shaming those who were off message. It could steer the narrative. It could draw major donors. It could spread out the money. It could attract sympathetic coverage in the mainstream press. It could coordinate among like-minded groups to start movements. It could take down influential media personalities. Journalists were officially on notice. Media Matters had the power to go well beyond shaping news reports or discrediting a story. A reporter could be ruined.

As Media Matters seemingly cornered the liberal smear market during the first decade of the 2000s, others were catching on. Not just liberals, but also conservatives and corporate interests. They were developing their own playbooks. The dark smear industry was expanding into a Washington, D.C.– and New York–centric powerhouse that would dump billions of dollars into the mix, employ countless operatives, and dominate public messaging in virtually every form it takes.

Chapter Three

|||||||||||||||||||||||||||

The Smear Industrial Complex:
Smear Merchants and Scandalmongers

I've encountered more smear artists than I can count.

In 2010, I'm doing investigative reporting for CBS News when I get a call from a Capitol Hill staffer.

"I'm from the office of [Congressman so-and-so]," says the man on the other end. "I have some important material you really should see."

"Can you email it and I'll take a look?" I ask.

"No, it's better that I see you in person."

We arrange a time to meet at the CBS News Washington, D.C., bureau, on M Street. When I greet him in the lobby, he's accompanied by two other young men, also congressional staffers. One of them carries a folder under his right arm. I take them into the CBS News greenroom. We settle into chairs and I ask what they want to talk about. They hand me the folder. I open it and scan the pages inside. It's a collection of opposition research they've done on a candidate running for office—someone from the opposing party. There's a background report and copies of news clippings. It seems the candidate has gotten caught up in some scandals covered in the local news. It's nothing particularly newsworthy to me, as a national investigative reporter. Besides, I don't typically cover politics.

Nine out of ten times, this is how my meetings end up. You take them because, once in a while, it leads to something important. I politely explain to the trio that this "story" is not for me. As I walk them out, I'm curious.

"What exactly are your job titles?" I ask the Hill staffers.

"What do you mean?" the main one answers.

"Is this your job . . . doing opposition research on political opponents?"

"Yes," he answers enthusiastically. "We have lots more of the same, if you're interested!"

I let the thought swirl around in my head. These men are being paid tax dollars to supposedly serve the public interest working for a member of Congress. Instead, they're using time on the clock to smear political enemies.

What would the public think of their tax dollars financing oppo research? How many are masquerading as Hill staffers while functioning as private eyes and smear artists?

Today's smear artists are sophisticated strategists. Well-paid front men for rich and powerful interests. They research and monitor targets using every available weapon of modern technology. They employ surreptitious tactics to exploit vulnerabilities. Execution is crucial. They must persuade people to form strong opinions. The audience must get angry or become suspicious so they're motivated to take action. The message must be repeated so many times in so many venues, it's unthinkingly accepted without question. It must take root and burrow deeply into the public consciousness. Some smears involve entirely fabricated material. But many believe the most effective smears include an element of fact to provide a patina of credibility. Media Matters had figured that out with its takedowns of Don Imus and Glenn Beck.

As the great smear octopus has grown unchecked, it's proven unstoppable precisely because of the tenets that define our society: free enterprise and free speech. Few ordinary Americans could manage the time and legwork necessary to disassemble various smear efforts. The multibillion-dollar cottage industry attracts both ideologues and hatchet men willing to work for whoever pays the most.

"I'm a contractor for hire," one operator tells me in fall of 2016, when he gets picked up by one of the U.S. presidential campaigns. He's smeared in the past for liberals, conservatives, and corporate interests.

The public has no idea of the extent to which news is influenced by smear merchants. They operate from a byzantine playbook to exploit today's weak-kneed and corporate-owned media. It's one reason why it's increasingly difficult to find fair, in-depth reporting at so many formerly hard-hitting news outlets.

"The best smear artists are sociopaths without conscience, without regret," a player in the game tells me. "They're able to suspend all pretense of fairness and logic." The ends justify the means. Facts exist to be rewritten, twisted, or discarded if they don't fit the agenda.

As it happens, there are countless applicants who fit the job description. That's partly because it pays so well. The smear industry has become a massive enterprise in Washington, D.C., and New York City.

Several players in the field describe to me how they work the system. I'm already intimately familiar with their moves, of course, having been on the receiving end of such efforts, but it's enlightening to hear the operators directly describe their MO.

Step One: Mine and Pump

The wheels are set in motion when political, corporate, or special interests catch wind of a news story that may shed a negative light on them or their agenda. They use a wide range of tactics to obtain as much information as they can about the story in progress so they can identify pressure points. They try to get the reporter on the phone and question him. They'd rather not leave a written email trail. They try to go off the record on the phone, so that they can plant seeds of doubt without being quoted. They provide information, innuendo, and rumor that may be irrelevant, unproven, or false to personally disparage a source the reporter may be using. They have no intention of providing the reporter with an on-the-record interview or any useful information, but they hold out hope like a carrot on a stick as they cajole information from the reporter. *What's your angle?* they demand. *What's the thesis?* Whatever the answer, they set about arguing that it's wrong. Not worthy of a story. Old news. Disproven. Settled science. They find out the names of producers and editors who have influence over the script. They try to determine the date and time the story may be published. This tells them how much time they have to spin and obfuscate. They try to find out who the other "voices" in the story are. *Who are the reporter's sources? Who else is being interviewed and what are they saying?*

Step Two: Connect

Smear outfits often hire ex-journalists for their contacts in the news industry and compensate them generously for connections to their former universe. These ex-journalists know who's weak and who's susceptible to pressure tactics in their former news organizations. Who to call. Who will buckle. Who can they use to discredit the planned story and the reporter who's on it. Smear groups also conduct opposition research to build negative dossiers on opponents. That includes the reporter.

Step Three: Deploy and Discredit

Now they're ready to deploy. For example, PR flacks representing a pharmaceutical company trying to stop a negative story may contact a news outlet's sales department and complain, or threaten to pull advertising. They contact the story editors directly to argue against the story. Their law firms call the news organization's general counsel with threatening rhetoric. They raise rational-sounding objections to the story, though one-sided and often entirely false. They take verbal off-the-record swipes at the journalists pursuing the story, whispering disparaging side comments to chip away at the reporter's reputation in the eyes of his colleagues. They send out missives against the reporter on social media and through partners in the blogosphere. If they can't stop the story, they work to quickly discredit it before it's published. That may include calling upon willing partners in the media to write scathing attacks of the reporter and news item, or preempting the story with a one-sided counterpoint.

An insider from the smear group Media Matters once bragged about how easy it is to yank a reporter's chain by targeting him. "If you hit a reporter, say a beat reporter at a regional newspaper . . . all of a sudden they'd get a thousand hostile emails," said the unnamed source in an interview published in the *Daily Caller.* "Sometimes they'd melt down. It had a real effect on reporters who weren't used to that kind of scrutiny."

Other hired hands reach out to the news organization's anchors, managing editor, senior producers, bureau chief—anyone who might be able to shape or kill the story. They undermine and float veiled threats. Controversialize. Over time, the repeated attacks take their toll.

"I know it's not *your* story," the operators might tell the coworker of a targeted reporter. "And I don't like speaking ill of one of your colleagues, but I'd *hate* for your network to get hung out to dry on bad reporting and I'm afraid that's where you're headed. . . ."

It's a bit like throwing darts and hoping one will stick. These forces need to connect with only one sympathetic ear at the news organization, whether it's in the legal office, sales department, or newsroom. It might be a manager who's risk averse and has neither the time nor stomach to do battle, especially when the adversary is perceived to be well financed or well connected. Suddenly internal roadblocks to the story go up. Today reporters can assume that behind-the-scenes dealings like the ones I've just described are to blame when their bosses are gung ho on a story line for days or weeks—then abruptly lose interest.

In October 2011 it had already grown difficult to get my stories about "Operation Fast and Furious" on the *CBS Evening News*. I'd broken the news several months earlier about federal agents secretly letting thousands of weapons be trafficked to Mexican drug cartels. But the story was subject to the sort of organized pushback attempts I've just described. (In the face of overwhelming documentary evidence and testimony, the Justice Department would later acknowledge the so-called gunwalking campaign and would admit to having given false information to Congress. The story would become the investigative reporting story of the year, receiving an Emmy and the Edward R. Murrow Award.) The Justice Department, which had authorized Fast and Furious, desperately tried to stop my reporting by attempting to pressure me and discredit my work. When that failed, they began searching for a weak link.

On the morning of October 4, 2011, Justice Department PR flack Tracy Schmaler writes a lengthy email to my CBS bureau chief, Chris Isham, arguing that my reporting is inaccurate and unfair. Three minutes later, Schmaler fires off a copy to CBS anchor Bob Schieffer in New York. "Been a few years since last chatted," Schmaler writes Schieffer. "Probably when I was making the rounds w. Chairman Leahy during the SCOTUS hearings. I'm now at Justice. I hope you're well. I'm sorry to be reaching out under these circumstances but feel compelled to flag Sharyl's report last night."

Schieffer replies, "Hi Tracy, I remember you well and we will look into this."

Throwing darts. They only need one to stick.

Another time at CBS News, a broadcast executive once viewed a video story I had ready for air. She said she "loved" it, and that it was "important" and "absolutely vital." But within a week, without explanation, the story fell off the schedule. When I called to ask why, the executive searched for reasons. "Um, well, I'm not sure it's really all that *interesting*," she stammered awkwardly. In a matter of days it had gone from "important" and "vital" to dull and meaningless. I knew that important people had made carefully placed calls.

On another occasion, I was assigned to look into fires that were breaking out on Boeing Dreamliner airplanes due to their lithium ion batteries. It wasn't lost on me that Boeing is America's biggest exporter and the top lobbyist among defense contractors. One battery expert after another that I contacted told me they had been warned by somebody associated with Boeing: don't talk publicly about the Dreamliner fires or else you'll never get another Boeing-related job. Plans for a congressional hearing on the fires mysteriously evaporated.

My producers and I were still able to produce a strong and compelling investigative report about the Boeing Dreamliner fires, which our network lawyers and senior producer signed off on. It drew accolades from those who internally reviewed it. Late the afternoon before it was scheduled to air, I got word that it was being canceled. The decision had been made at a high level without input from me or my producers who helped with the story. We knew the drill. When I pressed for an explanation, one executive told me, "Let's wait and see what the government investigation turns up and report on it *then*."

Other excuses I've heard when a hot story gets shelved?

"Let's wait and cover it when there's a congressional hearing."

"Let's wait until 'everybody' is covering it."

Under the definition of original and investigative reporting, it's neither original nor investigative if "everybody's" covering it. But as a reporter, when you hear these excuses, you suspect somebody got to them. You just don't know who. Unless you have sources inside your own company who murmur these things to you.

One smear operator tells me that "getting a story reined in [at a news organization] is not too hard." He's had success in softening and shaping news narratives. Today, he says, raising doubt about a reporter's impending story can be as easy as picking up the phone and calling the news outlet.

"It helps to call," he remarks. On the call, when he casts doubt about a story or a reporter, "the general counsels get really, really skittish. So sometimes it's best to skip the editor and go right to the lawyers." In fairness, the way he sees it he's simply defending his clients from smears by others.

"I think that's fair game. You're in the crosshairs and somebody's trying to ruin your life. You have the right to petition," he tells me. "You call the [news division's] attorney, you call the general counsel, and you say 'Do you understand what you're doing?' And you rein in some irresponsible actors. We've killed several stories by using that method."

Of all the smear artists I've met, and the ones I interviewed for this book, I've wondered what makes them tick. Do they have common personality traits that set them up to be successful in this nebulous sphere of influence?

For one, I've learned they're people who like being in-the-know or feeling as though they're on the inside. In much the same way that journalists are addicted to being the first to learn the news, these influencers have a deep desire to be privy to behind-the-scenes dealings. That may include secret meetings with members of Congress or their staff. It could mean a private phone call with the editor of an online publication. Or maybe it's being among the first to get clued in on a developing political scheme or strategy.

Another common trait of smear artists: they're polarizing figures who often find themselves in conflict with others on the same team. I know more than a few who've worked paid positions for one interest only to vehemently oppose that same interest at their next gig. One operator (who doesn't want to be identified in this book) had a committed and well-paying engagement with a political interest that he felt later "betrayed" him by talking about him behind his back. "I can burn those motherfuckers," he told me. "I just might do it if they don't stop bad-mouthing me."

Some of the most successful character assassins tend to speak and think in paranoid undertones—justifiably so. After all, they operate in a realm where people really *are* out to get one another. They know what's possible. Although they often appear to be deeply committed ideologues, they're willing to adjust their belief systems to fit to circumstances that are most advantageous to themselves. You could call it opportunist pragmatism.

And lastly, smear artists often share a compulsion to take credit for their handiwork. Although they often operate under the radar, they sometimes can't help but take credit for a job, even when it's ill-advised to do so. Several operators who didn't want to be attached to some of their dastardly projects by name for this book nonetheless wanted to make sure *I* knew they were responsible for the various deeds.

Swift Boating

During the early 2000s, some of the best-known character assassinations come from political campaigns. Perhaps the most famous of these occurs in 2004, when the Swift Boat becomes a ship that launches a thousand smears.

At the time, Senator John Kerry, a Democrat, is running against incumbent president George W. Bush. Kerry's supporters believe his military service in Vietnam uniquely qualifies him to be commander in chief, versus an opponent who served during the same war in what critics portray as the less prestigious—and less dangerous—Air National Guard reserve force. Kerry had served on a Swift Boat, a fifty-foot-long navy patrol boat, on the way to three Purple Hearts, awarded to soldiers wounded or killed in action.

But Kerry has some ghosts in his service background. First, upon his discharge from the military, he returned to the United States and became an antiwar demonstrator. In 1971, he announced he had thrown symbols of his service, his award medals or ribbons, over a fence in front of the U.S. Capitol in protest.

"In a real sense, this administration forced us to return our medals because beyond the perversion of the war, these leaders themselves denied us the integrity those symbols supposedly gave our lives," Kerry said at the time. (As a senator, he later claims he was always proud of his war awards.) Second, critics question the circumstances surrounding his awards, and the extent of his service-related injuries, which garnered him prompt discharge.

Interests supporting Bush hatch a plan to disparage Kerry's Vietnam-era service in the media. If they can twist Kerry's military advantage into a liability, Bush wins. The smear vehicle of choice is a nonprofit called Swift Boat Veterans for Truth.

It begins with hundreds of Vietnam Swift Boat sailors signing a caustic public statement accusing Kerry of exaggerating his service and misrepresenting the military's Vietnam effort. How were all those Swift Boat sailors located three decades after the fact to sign the statement? As the porn king Flynt had done in going after Clinton's critics in the 1990s, the Swift Boat group had hired an ex–FBI agent private eye, according to the *Dallas Observer*. His directive was "to locate swift boat vets and to dig up whatever he could regarding Kerry's service record."

The Swift Boaters call a press conference. Then they release a book, TV ads, and a documentary. All of them hammer away at Kerry's service record and controversial anti–Vietnam War activities. *Is he a patriot who honorably served the country? Or an ungrateful flip-flopper who rejected his service?* On Vietnam and other topics, Kerry's image as a war hero is magically transformed into that of a weak waffler. The meme is reinforced by video that captures Kerry windsurfing off the coast of Nantucket. Bush strategists quickly incorporate the video into an attack ad.

"Kerry voted for the Iraq War, opposed it, supported it, and now opposes it again," says the ad's narrator as Kerry's surfboard changes direction with the wind. "He bragged about voting for the $87 billion to support our troops before he voted against it . . . John Kerry. Whichever way the wind blows."

To this day, there's debate over how much of the Swift Boat smear was true. Regardless, it proved to be so damning, so effective, so brilliant, so horrible—depending on your view—it gave rise to a new verb: *swiftboating*.

The Swift Boat smear's role in Kerry's subsequent defeat leaves a lasting impression on both sides. One lesson learned is that a quick, coordinated response and counteroffense are essential in today's Web-centric environment. Mounting resources after the attack is too late. Waiting even a day is too long. Operatives would soon devise plans to have crisis response teams in place, ready to strike within minutes of a threat. In the future, these teams would also be tasked with anticipating attacks in advance, responding to them—or deflecting from them—before they're uttered. Or preventing them entirely. That kind of operation takes money. The war chest has to be full.

Blumenthal Redux

Meantime, Sidney Blumenthal has remained in the mix long after the Clintons' time in the White House. Following a stint at left-leaning Salon .com, Blumenthal goes back on the Clinton payroll as a senior campaign adviser for Hillary in 2008, helping her spin and smear as she seeks the presidency.

Known as "Sid Vicious" among some of his detractors for his ruthless techniques, Blumenthal's unofficial job description on the 2008 Hillary campaign requires smearing Senator Barack Obama. The mission sends Blumenthal on an obsessive search to locate something referred to as the "whitey tape," according to Mark Halperin and John Heilemann in their 2010 book, *Game Change*:

> The "whitey tape" was a persistent rumor in 2008 that a videotape existed of either Barack or Michelle Obama making racially incendiary remarks, referring to whites as "whitey," that would irreparably damage Obama's presidential bid. Blumenthal was obsessed with the "whitey tape" and so were the Clintons, who not only believed that it existed but felt that it might emerge in time to save Hillary. "They've got a tape, they've got a tape," she told her aides excitedly.

No such tape ever surfaces.

No matter. According to the *Huffington Post,* Blumenthal maniacally emails around anti-Obama rumors, no matter how "batshit." He even distributes conservative gossip and innuendo.

"The original source of many of these hit pieces [against Obama] are virulent and sometimes extreme right-wing websites, bloggers, and publications," declares a *HuffPo* writer. "But they aren't being emailed out from some fringe right-wing group that somehow managed to get my email address. Instead, it is Sidney Blumenthal who, on a regular basis, methodically dispatches these email mudballs to an influential list of opinion shapers—including journalists, former Clinton administration officials, academics, policy entrepreneurs, and think tankers—in what is an obvious attempt to create an echo chamber that reverberates among talk shows, columnists, and Democratic Party funders and activists."

Some credit—or blame—Blumenthal with forwarding the original "birther" smear of Obama. According to McClatchy news bureau chief James Asher and one of his reporters, it was Blumenthal who suggested in 2008 they check out rumors that Obama was born in Kenya, which would disqualify him as a presidential candidate. Clinton and Blumenthal have denied any role in stoking the conspiracy theory, which would later persist throughout Obama's presidency though it's largely considered debunked.

Blumenthal is also linked to efforts in 2008 to publicize Obama's relationship with controversial Chicago pastor Rev. Jeremiah Wright. During the campaign, videotapes of Wright's racially charged sermons surface on the Internet. Of the 9/11 terrorist attacks, Wright said "America's chickens are coming home to roost." He also blamed the U.S. government for spreading AIDS among African Americans, claimed "God damn America" was written "in the Bible," and referred to the United States as the "U.S. of K.K.K. A." Blumenthal also circulates material highlighting Obama's supposed ties to radical activist Bill Ayers, founder of the domestic terrorist group Weather Underground.

In the end, Blumenthal's efforts don't get Hillary to the White House in 2008. And they come back to haunt him when Obama ends up president. Obama appoints Hillary as secretary of state and she wants Blumenthal to be one of her top aides. But high-ranking Obama officials threaten to quit if Blumenthal is allowed into the administration after what he's done to disparage Obama in the primary. The White House bans Hillary from hiring Blumenthal.

Shut out of the administration, Blumenthal is promptly installed as a paid consultant to the Clinton Foundation, according to *Politico,* and later collects paychecks for his work as a consultant to various pro-Hillary smear groups. He maintains a close association with Hillary while she's secretary of state, defends her missteps, and continues attacking her political enemies.

One such instance comes in 2011, after Secretary of State Clinton successfully pushes President Obama to intervene militarily to topple Libyan dictator Muammar Qaddafi. When the strategy appears to be successful, Blumenthal is a cheerleader for Hillary and sees a political windfall. He emails her, "First, brava! You must go on camera. You must establish yourself in the historical record at this moment. . . . You are vindicated." (The emails are revealed later in a congressional investigation into Clinton's email practices.)

Yes, Libya is Clinton's baby and she would tout it as a success story. *Her* success story. But it would soon become one of the most monumental foreign policy disasters of the decade. Obama and Clinton had no effective plan for post-Qaddafi Libya. In the ensuing vacuum, ISIS was born and Libya became a failed state. A breeding ground for Islamic extremist terrorism. Not only do the subsequent September 11, 2012, terrorist attacks against Americans in Benghazi, Libya, threaten to spoil President Obama's perfectly good campaign claim that he's sent terrorists on the run, but they also stand to derail Hillary's presidential hopes and dreams. The services of a professional smear artist are desperately required.

Clinton and other Obama officials initially respond to the Benghazi attacks by misleading the public as to their nature and origins. They push the false narrative that Muslim terrorists aren't at fault. They blame and smear a Christian immigrant from Egypt who made an anti-Muslim-extremist YouTube video.

Deny everything. Accuse someone else.

Selling this fabricated narrative to the public requires Blumenthal's mastery. Clinton is delighted when, three days after the Benghazi attacks, Blumenthal emails her an article that his son, Max, has written for the British *Guardian* newspaper, focusing attention on the false narrative that blames the video. It's titled "Inside the Strange Hollywood Scam That Spread Chaos across the Middle East."

"Your Max is a mitzvah!" replies Hillary, indicating Sid's son has done a good deed.

"Max knows how to do this and [is] fearless," Blumenthal concurs. "Hope it's useful and gets around, especially in the Middle East."

He then advises Hillary to maintain her defense of the disastrous outcome of the Arab Spring, democratic uprisings across the Arab world beginning in 2011 that largely devolved into chaos and opportunities for Islamic extremist terrorists to gain a foothold.

"Keep speaking and clarifying," Blumenthal prompts. "Your statements have been strong. Once through this phase, you might clarify history of US policy on Arab Spring, what has been accomplished, US interests at stake, varying relations with Libya & Egypt, etc."

Next, Blumenthal launches a trademark, vicious diatribe against Republican presidential nominee Mitt Romney.

Romney, of course, is contemptible on a level not seen in past contemptible political figures. His menace comes from his emptiness. His greed is not limited simply to mere filthy lucre. The mixture of greedy ambition and hollowness is combustible. He will do and say anything to get ahead, and while usually self-immolating, he is also destructive. Behind his blandness lies boundless ignorance, ignited by consistently wretched judgment.

He signs off with a tender kiss and hug "xo Sid."

The biggest victim of the post-Benghazi smear is Nakoula Nakoula, producer of *Innocence of Muslims,* the YouTube video the Obama administration incorrectly blamed for sparking the Benghazi assaults. Shortly after the attacks, when Clinton briefly meets with families of the American heroes murdered in Benghazi, they say she doesn't pledge to catch the terrorists responsible. Instead she reportedly tells them, "We're going to find the maker of that awful YouTube video."

There's nothing illegal about making a video, and Clinton never explained what crime she thought Nakoula could be charged with. But he was subsequently arrested and jailed in California for an unrelated probation violation. Many observers theorize he never would have ended up behind bars if it weren't for the fact that Obama and Clinton had made him into a villain.

In 2013, I spoke to Nakoula on the phone when he was awaiting release from a halfway house. He told me that the attacks against him and his video were so vicious, he and his family received regular death threats. He told me he'd arranged that upon his release he would be taken to a secret, secure location where he'd have to live in hiding for his own safety.

The Smear Industrial Complex

As we've seen, the smear is nothing if not versatile; a shapeshifter that can be transformed accordingly for use against targets identified by corporations, competitors, governments, politicians, or candidates for elected office. As the influence of the Internet expands in the early 2000s, the power of the smear grows exponentially. Each player in the smear industrial complex is anxious to build upon tactics of the recent past and pioneer new strategies for the future.

You may ask, *How big is this smear industry of which you speak?* It's impossible to quantify with precision. But we do know it employs tens of thousands of people and is an economy of billions upon billions of dollars. The remarkable scope is extrapolated by considering a few of the sectors that hire agents to operate as scandal mongers.

PR Firms

When it comes to public relations firms in the smear game, there are thousands of powerhouses controlling incredible sums of money. The biggest PR firm in the world in 2016, Edelman, collected $854 million in fees in 2015 and employed six thousand people. And for most PR firms, an important fee generator is the smear. The actual duties might be filed under the headings of "crisis and risk," "strategic communications," "rapid response," "public engagement," or "reputation management." Each one of the top twenty public relations behemoths brings in $100 million a year or more. We can learn something of how they operate from instances where their surreptitious roles were exposed in astroturf or smear campaigns.

In 2006, a YouTube user posted a spoof critical of the global warming documentary *An Inconvenient Truth,* created by former vice president Al Gore. The two-minute-long parody is titled "Al Gore's Penguin Army." It's the one and only video posted by a someone calling himself "toutsmith." The *Wall Street Journal* does a little detective work and traces routing information in an email from toutsmith to a computer registered to Washington, D.C., PR firm DCI Group. DCI Group wouldn't answer whether it was responsible for making the penguin video on behalf of a client.

Also in 2006, PR firm Edelman Communications is caught manufacturing "news" on behalf of Wal-Mart, without disclosing the sponsorship. It starts with a supposedly grassroots blog called *Wal-Marting Across America,* ostensibly written by a couple of ordinary Joes who chronicle their travels in an RV parked in Wal-Mart parking lots. But in a matter of weeks, the blog is exposed as a promotional tool for Wal-Mart's "Working Families for Wal-Mart" campaign, launched by Edelman.

In 2009, PR and lobby firm Bonner & Associates is outed for sending letters to a member of Congress under the fabricated letterhead of the National Association for the Advancement of Colored People (NAACP) and a Hispanic nonprofit called Creciendo Juntos. The letters urge Congress to vote against a bill to curb greenhouse gas emissions. Once discovered, Bonner & Associates blame the forgeries on a temporary employee and say the person was fired.

DCI Group also figures into a cloaked attempt to kill financial reforms after the big bank bailouts in 2010. Even a Massachusetts Institute of Technology economist, Simon Johnson, is suckered in. Johnson tells reporters he was originally approached by DCI Group to take part in a conference call with an organization called Stop Too Big To Fail. Based on the name, he says he believed the group, like him, opposed taxpayer bailouts of giant Wall Street banks that were in financial trouble after their risky and sometimes fraudulent loan practices. After the conference call, Stop Too Big To Fail posts Johnson's photo on its website, as if he were a supporter, to confer legitimacy to their "consumer movement." Johnson says he is shocked to learn Stop Too Big To Fail is actually part of a $1.6 million ad campaign by a financial industry front group called Consumers for Competitive Choice. When he learns their real agenda is to discourage financial reform, he tells reporters, "These guys made the KGB look like amateurs, and I used to work in Russia quite a lot." In a previous iteration, Consumers for Competitive Choice used to be Consumers for Cable Choice, a front group funded by telecom giants such as Verizon, fighting to deregulate the cable industry.

Another example of a PR firm working in the background is an online newspaper called the *Richmond Standard*, which blends real news with features like one titled "Major Inaccuracies in KPIX 5 Story on Chevron Richmond Modernization Project." Readers may not know it, but the California-based publication is the product of a PR firm for oil and gas giant Chevron. Its newsroom reportedly consists of an account executive from the PR company who functions as both reporter and editor. A subsection called "Chevron Speaks" is devoted to articles that advance Chevron's interests, "introduce" Chevron employees to the public with flattering profiles, and attack reporters who do investigative reports on the company.

The corporate nature of the *Richmond Standard* is the subject of critical reporting by a blog called *DeSmog*, which is itself a website led by a PR professional and is dedicated to clearing "the PR pollution that is clouding the science on climate change." DeSmog says the *Richmond Standard* has grown dramatically in readership since it began in 2013 and that "its successes are now garnering attention from other fossil fuel companies." In a public statement, a Chevron official defends the PR newspaper, saying it "was widely panned when it was first started, it was called corporate journalism . . . I mean, it was highly criticized. . . . But now it's to the point it gets more traffic than the *San Francisco Chronicle*." Chevron adds that its corporate sponsorship is transparent. "And we believe the content speaks for itself and invite people to read it for themselves and draw their own conclusions," says a spokesman.

During its second term, the Bush administration became embroiled in a scandal over using tax dollars to pay a PR firm to surreptitiously advance a political agenda and secretly track reporters who were off message. The controversy involved the administration paying public relations company

Ketchum Communications $700,000 to "rate" journalists on the tone of their reporting about the No Child Left Behind education law, and to produce a video that was used by some TV stations as if it were real, independent news. The administration also got caught paying conservative syndicated program host and columnist Armstrong Williams to promote the No Child Left Behind agenda. PR firm Ketchum brokered the deal and acted as middleman for nearly a quarter million dollars in payments to Williams under a contract with the U.S. Department of Education. As part of the agreement, Williams's company produced radio and TV ads featuring the education secretary and publicly supported the law, without disclosing his financial ties. Once exposed in 2005, Williams apologized for the conflict of interest but insisted he did nothing wrong.

In 2011, PR firm Burson-Marsteller gained notoriety in a covert smear campaign called Whisper-Gate. At the time, Internet giants Google and Facebook were competing in a $28 billion online advertising market. A PR agent from Burson-Marsteller reached out to a tech blogger named Christopher Soghoian and asked him to write a critical op-ed about a Google product. Recounting the story Soghoian says Burson-Marsteller offered to "draft" the op-ed for Soghoian and get it published in a "top-tier" outlet like the *Washington Post, Politico,* the *Hill, Roll Call,* or the *Huffington Post.* In other words, Burson-Marsteller wanted to use Soghoian as a stooge to publish a critical piece about Google. Soghoian deduced Burson-Marsteller's client was a Google competitor. It's a shady way for a PR firm to operate.

In an email, Soghoian asks Burson-Marsteller, "Who's paying for this (not paying me, but paying you)?" The Burson-Marsteller agent replies, "I'm afraid I can't disclose my client yet." Soghoian smells a rat and goes public with his outrage. Burson-Marsteller later admits it was working on behalf of Facebook.

"No 'smear' campaign was authorized or intended," insists the PR firm.

This clumsy attempt at a disguised smear should make you think every time you read an op-ed. Op-eds are often nothing more than cloaked propaganda efforts generated by paid or political interests, published under someone else's name.

One infamous conservative PR character in the dirt industry is consultant Rick Berman, known for his stealthy tactics on behalf of corporate clients. In 2007, *60 Minutes* correspondent Morley Safer profiled Berman, beginning with some unflattering adjectives.

"Sleazy. Greedy. Outrageous. Deceptive. Ineffective, except when it comes to making money for yourself," says Safer, as Berman listens patiently. "Corporate lackey who is one of the scariest people in America. . . . [T]he booze and food industry's 6'4", 64-year-old weapon of mass destruction . . . You're a hired gun."

Berman's catchiest nickname of all is Dr. Evil, as in the *Austin Powers* comedy flick whose lead villain has a ludicrous penchant for shooting the messenger. Berman's PR goal is to destroy the reputation of those delivering the wrong message. "Shooting the messenger means getting people to understand that this messenger is not as credible as their name would suggest," Berman explains to Safer.

Will Tucker, of the Center for Responsive Politics, tells me Berman is an expert smear artist who's learned how to navigate the system to his clients'—and his own—advantage. Tucker provides some insight into how Dr. Evil operates.

"Berman starts his own nonprofit groups that have their own credible-sounding names and their donors are kept secret," says Tucker. "[He works by] confusing voters and muddling policy debates by throwing hyperbolic misinformation into the media mix."

Berman's clients and supporters have reportedly included Coca-Cola, Outback Steakhouse, Tyson Chicken, and Wendy's fast-food restaurants. Like some other smear artists, he operates a network of nonprofit "educational" groups that attack ideological enemies like Mothers Against Drunk Driving, or MADD. Who would be against MADD? Berman's American Beverage Institute (ABI), a restaurant trade association that supports "the protection of responsible on-premise consumption of adult beverages." ABI has worked to discourage people from donating to MADD, claiming the nonprofit is guilty of waste and diversion of funds.

Berman has profited handsomely from his network. His PR firm reportedly made nearly $900,000 in 2008 from his own Enterprise Freedom Action Committee, a dark-money nonprofit where he serves as president and director. His five nonprofits together reportedly paid his for-profit business $15 million from 2008 to 2010. The practice of nonprofits doing big business with related for-profit companies owned by the same person isn't illegal, but it is controversial. Berman's nonprofits have been the subject of numerous "Donor Advisories" issued by the charity watchdog Charity Navigator. One states that in 2011, more than half of the functional expenses for Berman's Enterprise Freedom Action Committee went to his own for-profit management company.

"We find the practice of a charity contracting for management services with a business owned by that charity's CEO atypical," reports Charity Navigator. It goes on to say it has issued donor advisories for other Berman-affiliated nonprofits: American Beverage Institute, Employment Policies Institute Foundation, Center for Union Facts, and Center for Consumer Freedom. Berman has defended the arrangements between his business and his nonprofits, saying they are disclosed, reviewed, and approved annually by independent officers and directors; they "comply with conflict of interest policy"; and the "financial statements are audited each year by an independent CPA." He also counters criticism by insisting he argues using facts and is simply defending entities who have themselves been targets of unfair smears.

In 2016, Berman is linked to a new PR campaign called "China Owns Us." It's run by the Center for American Security, under one of Berman's nonprofits. The effort opposes Chinese purchases of American movie theaters and other assets. Part of the campaign includes posting billboards calling movie theater company AMC "China's Red Puppet," writing op-eds, and posting videos on YouTube warning of China's insidious influence on American culture. Berman is evasive when asked who's funding the push. In a *Washington Post* article, he refers to two unnamed "wealthy donors."

Super PACs and Dark Money

After the PR industry, a second influential sector to consider in the smear universe is made up of super PACs and dark money groups. Both categories of groups raise money for political candidates and causes. Their donors might not be disclosed, or their donation trails can be murky or hidden: "dark." They employ teams of opposition researchers, campaign trackers, and character assassins that operate around the clock to deflect, distract, and attack. By mid-December 2016, 2,408 super PACs reported raising nearly $1.8 billion in the campaign cycle, according to the Center for Responsive Politics. The largest single super PAC by far, in terms of cold, hard cash, was the pro-Hillary Priorities USA Action, which attracted more than $192 million in the 2016 election cycle. Priorities USA Action reportedly spent more than $69 million on media buys, including TV, radio, and Web ads, in the 2016 campaign. Coming in second place in terms of money was the conservative Right to Rise, backing Republican Jeb Bush. In what may go on record as the most epic fail of a single super PAC when it comes to bang for the buck, Right to Rise spent all that money only to have Bush plummet from front-runner to flameout by March 2016.

Super PACs are a powerful campaign funding vehicle made possible through the January 2010 Supreme Court decision known as *Citizens United*. Unlike a candidate's official fundraising operation, super PACs are not permitted to coordinate directly with a candidate, but they can collect unlimited political donations. What's more, the Supreme Court ruled corporations and unions can make super PAC donations.

A staple of these groups is negative advertising; they do the dirty work while the candidates maintain a more positive public façade. The huge sums they spend is one indication of just how massive (and lucrative) the smear industry is. In the 2014 election cycle, the total number of campaign ads topped 2.2 million and the vast majority were negative: more than 70 percent of the pro-Republican ads in Senate races, more than 90 percent on the Democrats' side.

One infamous super PAC smear in 2012 was a pro-Obama campaign ad attacking Republican candidate Mitt Romney for his work at private equity firm Bain Capital. Priorities USA earmarked $20 million for the effort, which included a controversial ad suggesting Romney was responsible for a woman's cancer death. In the television commercial, a widower tells how his wife, the cancer victim, died "a short time after" Romney's

Bain Capital shut down the steel plant where the man had been employed, leaving him with no health coverage. FactCheck.org found claims in the ad misleading, and PolitiFact determined the ad to be false. An even larger Priorities USA campaign devoted $30 million to ads disparaging Romney's performance as governor of Massachusetts.

For his part, Romney had a super PAC called Restore Our Future on his side. Major backers included Las Vegas casino billionaire Sheldon Adelson and one of the conservative activist Koch brothers, Bill. The super PAC's staff included the man behind the "Willie Horton" ad, which successfully scuttled the candidacy of Democrat Michael Dukakis for president in 1988. Dukakis had supported a prison furlough program that inadvertently freed Horton, a convicted murderer. Horton went on to rape and assault new victims. The campaign manager for Republican candidate George H. W. Bush was quoted as saying, "By the time we're finished, they're going to wonder whether Willie Horton is Dukakis' running mate." Since Horton was black, Democrats called the ad campaign racist.

In 2012, Restore Our Future plopped down a huge sum of money during the final week of the Obama vs. Romney presidential campaign: more than $20 million. The ad buy included commercials challenging President Obama on his economic record. One was an ominous offering titled "Flatline" and featured a heart monitor.

"If you saw this line in the ER, you'd be panicked," says the ad. "Well, this flatline is Barack Obama's economy. . . . If you don't jump-start America's economy now, your economy stays dead four more years."

Following the money in this environment can be a near-impossible task. Take the example of three Republican social welfare groups: 60 Plus Association, the American Future Fund, and Americans for Job Security. Under federal law, such groups must disclose the source of donations for any cash earmarked for political activities such as ads. In 2010, the three groups failed to disclose that money for some ads they bought came from an organization financed by the conservative Koch brothers. The funding was unmasked in a news interview when a Koch official admitted he not only decided which races the money would be spent on, but also subcontracted to produce and develop some of the commercials. In 2016, the

Federal Election Commission fined the groups, saying they should have disclosed the Koch donations.

Nonprofits, Think Tanks, and LLCs

After PR firms and dark-money groups, the third major sector to consider when measuring the size and scope of the smear industry is the nebulous universe of tax-exempt nonprofits, including "charities," limited liability companies (LLCs), and think tanks that engage in smears, often funded by conservative and liberal billionaires or corporate interests who prefer to stay in the shadows. The revenue from these organizations has expanded vastly since the 1990s—more than doubling—partly due to their utility as mechanisms for propaganda and smears, according to insiders who use them for those purposes. The structures of the organizations provide multiple advantages, from lax federal oversight to great flexibility in purpose and appeal. And since many get tax-exempt status, you help pay for them. As with PR firms, these entities don't publicly report how much they spend on smears. But even a small portion can be a significant sum when you consider there were 1.41 million registered nonprofits in 2013, with a combined $1.73 trillion in revenue.

A typical nonprofit involved in a smear campaign might begin by issuing a press release or "news article" with an epigrammatic title to grab attention and define the parameters. In just a few words, the headline tells who or what you should question or turn against—and why. The article gets distributed via email and social media to reporter lists. A few well-placed calls are made to alert key journalists to the "story." Partners in the blogosphere disseminate the requisite talking points and quote "experts" who agree that the public should be angry. Or suspicious. Or question. Or hate. The experts have been trained, and sometimes paid, by smear groups. They gladly provide the necessary speculation and opinion. They quote one another and call it proof that their claims against the chosen target are true. The "experts" are hired guns, but some in the news media will blindly accept.

Volume and speed are pivotal to creating the impression that it's all a grassroots reaction. The movement must appear to be organic. No fingerprints. Pretty soon there are memes, hashtags, and pithy one-liners advancing the smear. It takes on a life of its own. People see the fuss on social media, on TV, and in popular online publications. They're convinced that they're receiving special insight on the topic that makes them part of an exclusive group. A smarter group. *People just like you and me agree.* . . .

If nonprofits aren't always what they seem to be, neither are think tanks. To most Americans, think tanks are mysterious groups whose work is given a great deal of weight by politicians and the media. Think tank experts and their reports are quoted in news articles and used as ammunition on Capitol Hill to argue for or against policies. Think tanks are passed off as independent research bodies that confer legitimacy to the topics about which they publish and speak.

There are countless think tanks in Washington, D.C., and together they make up their own industry. The State Department goes so far as to list fifty-nine "useful" foreign policy think tanks, such as the Brookings Institution, Cato Institute, RAND Corporation, Nixon Center, and Heritage Foundation. They are places many ex-diplomats, politicians, generals, bureaucrats, and administration officials end up when their government jobs end. The hand of government washes the hand of the think tanks, and vice versa. Like many associations in politics, the relationships are mutually beneficial.

Many think tanks do produce worthwhile investigation and analysis. But, as you might imagine, special interests have increasingly figured out ways to get their nose under this tent, too. They've learned how to execute smears by exploiting the legitimacy that think tanks confer, surreptitiously shaping public opinion, policies, and laws to the advantage of special interests. Critics say some think tanks have put their prestige and influence up for sale.

In 2002, the George W. Bush White House apparently assisted in a bizarre effort to smear its own Environmental Protection Agency (EPA) with the help of a think tank. The revelation came in an email exchange obtained by the London *Observer*. One of the email parties was Bush official Phil Cooney, a former oil industry official. In the email, Cooney is communicating with Myron Ebell, director of the oil-industry-funded think tank Competitive Enterprise Institute (CEI). The two are devising ways to discredit an undesirable EPA report that supports the notion of global warming (while the Bush White House opposes it).

"Thanks for calling and asking for our help," Ebell writes to Cooney. "[W]e made the decision to do as much as we could to deflect criticism [of the EPA report] by blaming the EPA for freelancing. It seems to me the folks at EPA are the obvious fall guys and we would only hope that the fall guy (or gal) should be as high up as possible. . . . Perhaps tomorrow we will call for [EPA administrator Christine Todd] Whitman to be fired."

It would seem they found their "fall gal." Whitman soon resigned after seventeen months on the job, becoming the shortest-serving EPA administrator to date in the agency's thirty-year history.

The Bush administration further worked to smear the EPA report in question by allegedly engaging in "a secret initiative" to sue *itself* over the findings, but under the name of the Competitive Enterprise Institute, according to Connecticut attorney general Richard Blumenthal, a Democrat who demanded an inquiry by the White House. White House officials and the CEI denied any inappropriate behavior.

"We do not have a sweetheart relationship with the White House," insisted a CEI official at the time.

Around the same time, emails show Bush officials heavily engaging multiple conservative groups involved in messaging, lobbying, propaganda, and smears—and not only on the topic of global warming. The administration reportedly sends representatives to attend at least two regular, weekly meetings of various conservative coalitions. Conservative strategist Grover Norquist, head of the lobby group Americans for Tax Reform, leads the 10 a.m. Wednesday meetings and is pleased by the high-level White House interaction. "There isn't an 'us' and 'them' with the Bush administration," Norquist remarks publicly. " 'They' is 'us.' 'We' is 'them.' " The Wednesday meetings are followed by weekly lunches with a second group of conservative influencers, also attended by Bush officials. An executive at the conservative Heritage Foundation think tank boasts that he consults with Bush political adviser Karl Rove a couple of times a week. And the head of the conservative think tank and lobby group Family Research Council brags, "We are afforded access to the highest senior officials."

Think tanks also sometimes assist their corporate donors in ways that aren't fully transparent and, in this way, become part of the subtle mechanisms that sway public policy and advance narratives of the powerful. In August 2016, the *New York Times* and Center for New England Investigative Reporting wrote about the impossibly blurred lines between some think tanks and the projects they launch on behalf of corporate donors. One example they gave was that of a home building giant that donated $400,000 to the Brookings Institution. Internal documents show Brookings offered "a productive, mutually beneficial relationship" including offering a prestigious Brookings "senior fellow" slot to one of the donor's executives. Brookings then worked on think tank initiatives that ended up advancing the company's $8 billion revitalization project. Responding to allegations of conflict of interest, a Brookings official told the *Times,* "We do not compromise our integrity. . . . We maintain our core values of quality, independence, as well as impact."

The *Times* also examined the Brookings relationships with Microsoft, Hitachi, and JPMorgan Chase (which shelled out a massive $15.5 million contribution). Brookings sometimes provided assurances that donors would receive "'donation benefits,' including setting up events featuring corporate executives with government officials," reported the *Times*.

Another case the newspaper examined is the Atlantic Council think tank's partnership with FedEx. After FedEx donated to the Atlantic Council, the think tank issued a policy report driving home the very same points FedEx had raised to promote a beneficial free-trade agreement. These think tank reports are often used to lobby lawmakers and regulators because they're widely viewed as independent and are therefore more persuasive than information coming directly from a corporation.

Yet another think tank, the Center for Strategic and International Studies (CSIS), received donations from drone manufacturers Boeing and Lockheed Martin, then produced a report that supported the industry's desires, according to the *Times*. CSIS even helped set up meetings with, and convince Pentagon officials and congressional staff, to promote its recommendations. CSIS says its efforts did not amount to lobbying.

It's easy to see how the priorities of ordinary Americans often get lost in Washington. Agendas are set by those who can bring their persuasive arguments before power brokers. They advance their own interests and attack their enemies, becoming particularly convincing when they use third-party nonprofits and think tanks perceived as being independent.

Lastly, LLCs, or limited liability companies, are an emerging tool in the political smear trade. They don't have to disclose the names of their donors and can conduct any sort of political activity, so they're convenient for those who want to fund political efforts but keep their names secret. The downside to LLCs is that, as for-profit enterprises, they must pay taxes on the contributions they receive—something super PACs and other tax-exempt nonprofits don't have to do. LLCs also have to spend more than half their time on non-election-related activity, and their primary purpose must be something other than election spending, or else they become a political committee in the eyes of the law and have to disclose donors.

LLCs are playing an increasingly important role in campaign financing for both Democrats and Republicans. "The way LLCs are intersecting with money and politics right now is that we are increasingly seeing contributions coming from LLCs to super PACs," says Will Tucker of the Center for Responsive Politics. That's totally legal, he says, as long as the LLC isn't just a paper company. If, however, it's set up to take money and then direct that money to a super PAC, "that becomes really problematic," he says. "Lawyers consider that to be a straw donation. A straw donation is when a donor gives money to another donor to give money for them, keeping their name off of the campaign reports."

Tucker says LLCs especially deserve a skeptical review when they're set up in places like Delaware or Wyoming. "Both of those states have really lax laws on disclosure for their companies, which makes it really attractive for people who want to hide those kinds of transactions."

An example of a smear artist operating both LLCs and super PACs is Republican communications strategist Liz Mair. (When you hear that somebody's title is "communications strategist," they're probably in the smear game.) Mair's résumé shows she was once online communications director at the Republican National Committee. There she led what she calls a "groundbreaking online media outreach effort aimed at electing John McCain, Sarah Palin and Republicans across the country."

More recently, her website says, she advised Republicans Carly Fiorina, Rick Perry, and Rand Paul. And for a split second, she worked for Scott Walker in his brief run for president. (A day after her hiring by Walker was announced, Mair was forced out of her job for tweets that disparaged Iowans—those who would decide the first presidential primary contest.)

Mair's company, Mair Strategies, is an LLC. In November 2015, she helped start up an anti-Trump LLC called "Trump Card." According to the *Wall Street Journal,* Trump Card LLC was intended to be a "'guerilla campaign' backed by secret donors to defeat and destroy" Trump's candidacy. "I certainly know donors who are very happy that their fingerprints will be kept off things," Mair told the *Journal.* However, Trump Card LLC seemed to quickly fizzle out. (Mair didn't respond to my numerous requests for an interview and information.)

Mair then launched an anti-Trump super PAC called Make America Awesome. It boasted of using "unconventional and cost-effective tactics." It was a smear group. Mair was cagey about who, exactly, paid and directed her. The law doesn't require her to disclose that.

Mair's online job description says a lot about how operatives like her employ social media to use journalists to advance narratives. "About 90% of journalists get story ideas from online media, or use it to conduct research or fact-checking. Getting information out through the blogosphere means it gets an audience with mainstream reporters organically," Mair writes on her website. "Many voters continue to rely on Google search results for information impacting their votes, and Google continues to treat blog and 'non-traditional media' results very favorably in its results. There is no easier (or cheaper) way to deal with search engine optimization than to get favorable coverage out there at a consistent rate."

She goes on to say that Internet, social media, and blogs reach "activists" who "influence politicians to an outsized degree" and "treat online media as one of two vital sources of news and information."

Now that we have an idea of the tactics and players in the smear industrial complex and a sense of its scope, we can move on to the smear's post-2010 coming of age.

Chapter Four

IIIIIIIIIIIIIIIIIIIIIIII

Media Matters
(but Money Matters More)

For all of Media Matters' takedowns and media manipulations through the first decade of the 2000s, there was about to be an elemental shift in the political landscape that would enable the tentacles of the smear octopus to stretch to new lengths in the 2012 national election campaign.

The shift was made possible by the 2010 U.S. Supreme Court decision in a case called *Citizens United v. Federal Elections Commission*. Until that point, U.S. election law imposed strict limits on how much a person could donate to a political campaign. The idea of the restrictions was to limit the ability of wealthy special interests to "buy" candidates who'd be beholden to them above all else. But the *Citizens United* case ruled that the government cannot limit donations to nonprofits for so-called independent political expenditures that help political candidates. Even corporations and unions—barred from giving directly to candidates—can now give unlimited funds to these nonprofits. This suddenly altered who could put how much money into elections.

Before long, a new vehicle for unlimited political contributions was devised: tax-exempt social welfare groups called super PACs. As described earlier, they can raise and spend any sum of money as long as they don't coordinate directly with the candidates that they support (a caveat that critics say has little practical impact). Today, as a result of the changes after *Citizens United,* super PACs raise incredible amounts of money and spend much of it on opposition research against candidates and on nasty negative campaign ads. We'll see how a major beneficiary of this change was David Brock. After *Citizens United,* Brock vastly expanded his Media Matters frontier, establishing himself as a dominant figure in the game as he continued to reinvent the mainstream political smear.

American Bridge

One of Brock's first moves after *Citizens United* was to start the anti-Republican super PAC **American Bridge 21st Century** in 2010. He also developed close ties with the new liberal nonprofit Priorities USA and its super PAC, Priorities USA Action (taking a seat on its board of directors), also formed after *Citizens United* by former White House staffers working to reelect President Obama.

The *New York Times* broke "news" of Brock's American Bridge super PAC venture. He'd gathered $4 million in pledges from the likes of Rob McKay, heir to the Taco Bell fortune, and Robert Dyson, head of a New York acquisitions firm. Brock said he hoped American Bridge could become the left's answer to recently formed conservative leviathans like the American Crossroads super PAC, cofounded by Republican operative Karl Rove.

"My donor base already constitutes the major individual players who have historically given hundreds of millions of dollars to these types of efforts," Brock said at the time. "They just need to be asked, and I have no doubt they will step up at this critical time."

American Bridge 21st Century raised $12 million during the 2012 election cycle to defeat Republican Mitt Romney, seal Obama's reelection, and keep Democrats in the majority in the Senate. Its war room included seventeen trackers armed with high-def cameras to deploy anywhere, anytime, capturing every move of Republican candidates, and feeding material to a long list of hungry reporters. Sometimes, it paid off big.

In 2011, an American Bridge tracker was following around Republican attorney general Jon Bruning of Nebraska while Bruning was running for U.S. Senate. In Papillion, Nebraska, Bruning delivered a homily about welfare, telling his audience the story of a road construction project interrupted by the presence of endangered beetles. The beetles, said Bruning, were captured in a bucket trap each night and released safely up the road. That is, until raccoons discovered the delectable insects conveniently collected in the buckets—and began helping themselves.

"The raccoons, they're not stupid, they're going to do [it] the easy way if we make it easy for them, just like welfare recipients all across America," Bruning tells his audience. "If we don't incent 'em to work, they're going to take the easy way out."

American Bridge and its partners peddled the video excerpt as a caught-on-tape moment. They claimed Bruning had disparaged all welfare recipients by calling them lowly, scavenging raccoons! Dozens of news outlets picked up the spin and reported it accordingly. Bruning tried to explain that he was trying to make the case for spending cuts, but he never really had a chance. He ended up apologizing for his "inartful" remarks and subsequently lost the primary.

Also in 2011, American Bridge targeted Republican up-and-comer Senator Scott Brown of Massachusetts. Brown was running for reelection, facing off against the Democrat's darling, Elizabeth Warren. American Bridge researchers combed through Brown's record, appearances, speeches, and writings and discovered his website had lifted a passage from former senator and cabinet secretary Elizabeth Dole.

"From an early age, I was taught that success is measured not in material accumulations, but in service to others," read the suspect passage. "I was encouraged to join causes larger than myself, to pursue positive change through a sense of mission, and to stand up for what I believe."

When confronted, Brown said that the verbatim repeat of Dole's passage was an accident, and blamed his website creators, who had used Dole's Web template. But to American Bridge, it was plagiarism worthy of national outrage. It published five "articles" in three days hammering away at Brown. The predictable bunch of news outlets that could typically be relied upon to advance Media Matters' agenda followed suit. *HuffPo* declared the month to be Brown's "October of Controversy." *Politico* and *Daily Kos* jumped on the media bandwagon with their own negative articles. *New York* magazine asked, "Can we ever trust Scott Brown again?" American Bridge took credit for the story getting picked up by New England Cable News and TV stations WFXT and WHDH. Associated Press used the American Bridge research for a story distributed to hundreds of news clients.

The political nature of the selective outrage was obvious. The "tell" is how American Bridge and its allies easily overlooked Democrats embroiled in similar plagiarism scandals. In 2008, the liberal website *Slate* defended an Obama case of copycatting material as "Obama's own relatively innocent lifting of rhetorical set pieces from his friend [then–Massachusetts governor] Deval Patrick, which occasioned a brief flap." Conservative-turned-liberal media mogul Arianna Huffington was also once embroiled in a plagiarism scandal for allegedly copying material from a biography by John Ardoin and Gerald Fitzgerald for her book *Maria Callas* (1981). The claims were settled out of court. And of course, Vice President Joe Biden had his own admitted past with plagiarism when it was discovered that a biographical paragraph in his stump speech was lifted from a similar speech by British Labour politician Neil Kinnock. But as far as American Bridge was concerned, the Democrats' transgressions are bygones, while Brown's was a national scandal. He subsequently lost the election to Warren.

By late May 2012, American Bridge's videographers had recorded 1,300 hours of tape and organized it into a system that enabled them to rapidly locate damning images of Republicans for use in attack ads or distribution on social media. One of those clips showed GOP congressman Steve King of Iowa at a town hall meeting using the term "pick of the litter" as he argues the United States should admit only the best immigrants to America. Democrats quickly distributed the video and formulated it into a smear, suggesting King had likened immigrants to dogs. (In this case, King won reelection, anyway.)

In August 2012, an American Bridge tracker was present when Republican Senate candidate Todd Akin of Missouri made the remark that "legitimate rape" victims don't get pregnant because "the female body has ways to try to shut that whole thing down." Outrage over the comment crossed party lines and even GOP loyalists couldn't defend it. The video was posted on the super PAC's website and quickly went viral. Akin lost badly to incumbent Democrat Claire McCaskill.

Meanwhile, Brock moved smoothly between his work at American Bridge and Media Matters. In October 2012, a month before the presidential election, he joined up with fellow smear artist Sid Blumenthal to spin the press on the Obama administration's Benghazi debacle. First, Media Matters went on the offensive against Representative Jason Chaffetz, the Republican chairman of the House Oversight Committee, who stood to conduct the most aggressive investigation into the recent Islamic extremist terrorist attacks against Americans in Benghazi, Libya. Brock also disparaged Mitt Romney, who was criticizing the Obama administration (including then-Secretary of State Hillary Clinton). The Brock smears employed classic tactics and lingo to advance the theme that Benghazi was somehow a "myth." And though the primary sources on Benghazi missteps were Obama officials—many of them lifelong Democrats—Media Matters used its sharpest propaganda tricks to portray the whole scandal as a debunked fabrication conjured up by partisan Republicans.

As the Obama administration's narrative on Benghazi quickly unraveled, Blumenthal emailed Clinton Brock's Media Matters blogs attacking her critics.

"H: Got all this done," Blumenthal writes in the email dated October 10, 2012. "Complete refutation on Libya smear. Philippe can circulate these links. Sid." "Philippe" refers to Clinton's personal aide at the time; "circulate these links" likely means emailing them to the malleable news media. Friendlies in the news media can be counted on to quote from the Media Matters propaganda or use it as sourcing for their own stories. A month later, Obama wins a second term and Clinton's own presidential aspirations are preserved. At least for the moment.

Preparing for the next presidential campaign in 2016, Brock's American Bridge is in it for Hillary all the way. It acts as a dirt subcontractor, supplying a steady stream of opposition research against Republicans to the pro-Hillary super PAC Priorities USA Action. Targeted candidates listed on the American Bridge website include Republican presidential candidate and senator Ron Paul, South Carolina governor Nikki Haley, former congresswoman Michele Bachmann, Indiana governor (and later vice presidential nominee) Mike Pence, New Mexico governor Susana Martinez, Ohio senator Rob Portman, and former U.S. ambassador to the United Nations John Bolton. There's no pretense of evenhandedness or bipartisanship.

In June 2015, the *Free Beacon* website alleges that American Bridge operatives engineered a smear of the wife of Republican presidential candidate Marco Rubio. According to the article, the operatives accessed Florida court records, uncovered a rash of traffic violations by Rubio's wife, and shopped around the discovery to the press. Even the *New York Times* reported them as if they were big news. (The *Times* denied relying on American Bridge for material. The newspaper said it obtained the information on its own after hearing other reporters were seeking it.)

But it's an internal memo that turns out to be the most telling when it comes to the breadth of American Bridge's reach and media influence. In October 2016, WikiLeaks publishes the super PAC's self-proclaimed summary of accomplishments in the 2016 campaign so far, as emailed earlier to Clinton campaign chairman John Podesta. Focused on winning a Democrat majority in the Senate at the time, American Bridge explains in the memo that it set up "war rooms" for the first time, on the scene, in states where its trackers monitored Republican candidates so that it could "interact with reporters on site, and to cut and move footage more efficiently so we can break news before anyone else." American Bridge also uses its vast resources to produce one-sided investigative "news" and then peddle the product to reporters. Apparently it works. The American Bridge memo states that its war room in Wisconsin collected negative clips about Senator Ron Johnson and managed to get coverage in *Talking Points Memo,* the *Milwaukee Journal-Sentinel,* the *Capital Times,* the *Hill,* and *Roll Call.*

The American Bridge memo also boasts that CNN was receptive to its outreach. It reads, "CNN recently ran a feature story on our use of livestream technology." And American Bridge takes credit for publicizing "Jeb Bush's comments on privatizing Social Security (June 2015), Bush's comment that 'all lives matter' (July 2015), Chris Christie jumping on Jeb Bush's 'work longer hours' bandwagon (July 2015), and Rick Perry slamming Jeb's economic growth record in Florida (July 2015)." The memo says that several video clips of the candidates were "cut, and shared on social media and/or by press release while the candidates were still delivering the same speech." American Bridge also claims to have "placed" negative stories about Bush with CNN, the *Washington Post,* Associated Press, *New York Times, Wall Street Journal,* and "several key Florida outlets. . . . Our tracking operation has also been key in undermining Jeb through a constant barrage of rapid response attacks."

American Bridge Corrects the Record

When it comes to the funding for American Bridge, once again George Soros is in the mix as its largest donor, giving $1 million in 2012, another $1 million in the 2014 election cycle, and $1 million in the 2016 campaign. That's on top of at least $10.5 million Soros gave to pro-Hillary Priorities USA Action.

But not all the money that went to American Bridge stayed with American Bridge. The group reportedly made healthy six-figure contributions to other liberal groups, including another super PAC called America Votes Action Fund and the outside spending group Planned Parenthood Action Fund. It also circulated money to several other Brock groups. And as the money goes round and round, both Brock and his chief fundraiser, Mary Pat Bonner, are major beneficiaries. Brock collected $467,864 from American Bridge from January 2013 through mid-December 2016. Bonner pulled in $4.57 million in fundraising commissions from American Bridge between 2011 and mid-December 2016.

Shortly after founding the American Bridge super PAC, Brock started a companion 501(c)(4) nonprofit called **American Bridge 21st Century Foundation**. Needless to say, that meant another salary for Brock ($177,134 over three years), more commissions for Bonner (nearly a million dollars), and further opportunities for donor money to be transferred around in ways that obscure the original source. For example, from 2014 to 2016, the American Bridge foundation raised millions from undisclosed donors and then shuttled millions of it to the American Bridge super PAC.

A second component under American Bridge was **Bridge Project**, yet another Brock group that claimed to utilize "comprehensive research, video tracking, and rapid-response communications" to "dismantle false attacks on progressive policies and shine a light on the moneyed special interests behind the conservative agenda." Bridge Project then added a third subpart: the searchable database **ConservativeTransparency.org** to track funding behind right-wing groups.

A fourth element under the American Bridge umbrella ranks as more significant than the others. It's **Correct The Record**, which started up in 2013 with $400,000 in American Bridge funds to become a "rapid response" strategic research website and daily email blast. Then, just two years after its start, in the run-up to the 2016 election, Correct The Record became focused on one goal: defending Hillary Clinton and defeating her enemies. To accomplish this, Brock converted it into a third major pro-Hillary super PAC. Super PACs are generally barred from coordinating with campaigns, but this new propaganda powerhouse intended to test the limits of campaign finance laws, becoming the first to openly announce a direct relationship with a political campaign—Hillary's.

Here's how that worked. In 2006, the Federal Election Commission (FEC) passed rules stating that "the vast majority of Internet communications are, and will remain, free from campaign finance regulation." The super PAC version of Correct The Record claimed it planned to primarily operate on the Web and, therefore, was exempt from campaign finance rules. To lead Correct The Record, Brock brought in Democratic operative Brad Woodhouse from American Bridge. In an interview with the *Atlantic,* Woodhouse said, "We're constantly thinking of ways to deliver messages that don't require slick television ads. . . . Being quick and pithy and smart and snarky in the digital space is just as important as anything else."

Correct The Record quickly took the lead in publicly smearing Clinton's opponents early and often, placing quotes and research with reporters, deploying additional trackers to spy on the enemy, and issuing "press release" attacks. A typical offering on Correct The Record's website included features such as "David Brock Calls on GOP to Disavow Trump," "Trump Rally, Again, Glorifies Violence," "Trump/Fox News Lies About Clinton Foundation Investigation," "Donald Trump's History of Discrimination, Racist Comments, and Support," and "Hillary Clinton's Accomplishments as Secretary of State." (And that's just one day.)

Internal emails later published by WikiLeaks show some Clinton insiders feared a backlash from the public and press over Correct The Record's unprecedented and questionable coordination with the Clinton camp. Neera Tanden, head of the pro-Clinton Center for American Progress, received an email from the editor of her group's Think Progress blog. "This makes zero sense to me," comments the editor about Correct The Record's controversial path. Tanden forwards the note to Clinton campaign chief John Podesta, adding her own comment: "this does seem shady."

"Brock $ machine!" Podesta replies.

"That's fine," Tanden retorts. "But skirting if not violating law doesn't help [Hillary] INMHO."

Correct The Record's plan for direct coordination with Hillary moves forward nonetheless. Five days later, on May 18, 2015, Clinton campaign manager Robby Mook emails Clinton a memo discussing options for her campaign to go even further: to also coordinate directly with the Priorities USA super PAC. The memo notes the law bars super PACs from coordinating with political campaigns on ads that "express advocacy," but it theorizes there might be a way to get around that prohibition. It all hinges on how one defines "express advocacy."

"The advertisements [which the Hillary campaign could coordinate with Priorities USA] would focus on a public policy issue; praise your position on the issue or criticize an opponent's; and urge viewers to take an action in support of your position (or in opposition to your opponent's)," reads the memo to Clinton. "The advertisements would not focus on your qualifications or fitness for office, and would not refer to elections, candidacies, political parties, or voting by the general public. . . . While we believe that such a program is legally permissible, it would be breaking new ground—more so than what [Correct The Record] is doing." The memo goes on to caution, "As evidenced by the press scrutiny of [Correct The Record's] announcement, the media reaction to such a program could be toxic."

The Clinton campaign memo further notes that the conservative super

PAC American Crossroads petitioned the FEC to conduct similar activities in 2011, and the commission divided three-to-three on the request. "The FEC cannot find a violation [of law] without the support of four commissioners," continues the Clinton campaign memo, "so the ongoing deadlock reduces (though by no means eliminates) the likelihood of adverse action [against us] by the FEC" if the Clinton campaign were to coordinate directly with Priorities USA on campaign ads. It's unclear whether the Clinton campaign moved forward with the idea. A conservative watchdog group called Foundation for Accountability and Civic Trust filed an FEC complaint in May 2015 arguing Correct The Record was violating federal law by coordinating with the Clinton camp. But there's no indication the federal government concluded the super PAC did anything improper.

As Correct The Record broke new ground with Hillary campaign ties, it continued the vertiginous money connections that define much of the Brock smear machine. It collected $400,000 from Brock's American Bridge super PAC in 2013 and another $58,000 in 2016. It received $1 million from Priorities USA Action, and $275,000 from Clinton's official campaign committee. Then Correct The Record turned around and transferred $407,000 back to American Bridge. It also provided almost the entire budget, $466,776, for yet another Brock-created super PAC, called Franklin Forum.

Correct The Record also meant another six-figure paycheck for Brock. That's five salaries for him so far, if you're counting: Media Matters, Media Matters Action Network, American Bridge Foundation, American Bridge super PAC, and Correct The Record. Meanwhile, Bonner collected $647,271 in additional fees from her fundraising for Correct The Record.

Finally in the organizational tree, there's a fifth component to American Bridge, subpart Correct The Record: a joint fundraising project with Priorities USA called **American Priorities 16**. According to FEC records, American Priorities 16 first emerged in 2012 as **American Priorities Joint Fundraising Committee** and was funded entirely, with $250,000, by one person: attorney Daniel Berger. Berger was a Barack Obama fundraising bundler who also gave substantial money to American Bridge and other Hillary causes. American Priorities 16 was intended to be another conduit to raise big money from liberal donors. The cash was to be split between the two Hillary super PACs: Correct The Record and Priorities USA Action. But a check with the Center for Responsive Politics in late 2016 showed no income to speak of at American Priorities 16.

Message Matters: Talking Points Specialist

Brock's plate may already seem full, but he continued to develop parallel splinter projects to advance the progressive narrative. Such was the case with **Message Matters**, a talking points specialty shop.

There was a time when talking points were to be heard but not seen. In other words, the public wasn't supposed to know the messenger was using propaganda to drive a narrative. But somewhere along the way, talking points have become so prevalent, so audaciously accepted, they're used openly with no semblance of shame. Message Matters help set that trend.

Originally, it appears Brock created Message Matters around December 2011 as a project under the Media Matters umbrella. Positioned to impact the 2012 campaign, its website provided an instructive glimpse behind the curtain and laid bare its propaganda tactics: "We develop messaging by aggregating, analyzing and distilling polling, tested messaging, and expert recommendations, and monitoring the media to identify what is and isn't working." Message Matters said that it equipped "leaders" to "Drive the conversation and go on offense . . . Speak to shared values in the way people actually talk; and Advance shared progressive goals, ideas and values." Message Matters became a veritable talking points machine and continued on past the 2012 campaign.

Those "expert recommendations" came from a who's who of left-wing activists; nearly a hundred groups were listed on the website. "One-pagers" were issued for left-wing pundits so they could fan out on TV network Sunday talk shows with coordinated messages—which explains, in part, the syndrome of news programs devolving into little more than look-alikes, with pundits and experts on both sides forwarding the narratives of paid interests.

A Message Matters one-pager issued in May 2013 instructed liberal interviewees on how to herald a good Obama jobs report or defend a bad one, as the need arose. In either case, the strategy involved claiming liberal policies were responsible for everything positive; conservative policies were to be faulted for everything negative. Liberal messengers were advised to divert the conversation to "other good economic news" and then "go on offense."

Another subject of Message Matters talking points was Obamacare. Any criticism of the troubled health care initiative was deemed to be an "attack" for which "responses" were suggested. Liberal messengers were advised to defend Obamacare by focusing the audience on a "core message": how Republicans were refusing to deal with health care costs. A list of strategies appeared under the subtitles Connect, Define, Explain, and Illustrate. Note how the recommended responses divert from the question at hand.

> ATTACK: *"Obamacare increases health care costs."*
> RESPONSE: We passed Obamacare because no family should have to choose between putting food on the table and visiting a doctor.
> ATTACK: *"Letting Medicare bankrupt the country is stealing from our children and grandchildren."*
> RESPONSE: Children are not better off if their parents and grandparents are worse off. Should the debate really be about pitting family members against family members—or politicians putting the wealthy ahead of people who work for a living?
> ATTACK: *"We should raise the eligibility age for Medicare."*
> RESPONSE: If you're a wealthy politician who doesn't worry about affording health care for himself or needing to retire after a lifetime of manual labor, sure, it's no big deal to you.

A final example from Message Matters shows just how dishonest its messaging could be:

> ATTACK: *"Health reform is pushing employers to not offer health insurance benefits at all."*

RESPONSE: With the health law in place, 98 percent of workers who get coverage through their work are expected to keep their plans.

In fact, the claim that 98 percent of workers would be able to "keep their plans" was wholly false—and the administration knew it. As I reported for CBS News in November of 2013, Obamacare planners long ago projected the Affordable Care Act would "collectively reduce the number of people with employer-sponsored health coverage by about 14 million." Even those who were able to keep their work plans often saw their costs grow and benefits shrink as the policies were transformed to comply with Obamacare rules.

Despite the many successes of Media Matters and its numerous subgroups, the tangled web of entities has also produced some notable missteps. In 2012, a top Media Matters Action Network official was accused of making anti-Semitic remarks. Shortly thereafter, it appeared the Media Matters Action Network's main Web page became inactive. But according to IRS records, Brock continued to collect a salary from the Media Matters Action Network and it remained a conduit for hundreds of thousands of donor dollars passed to other Brock groups.

There was another self-inflicted controversy and more negative publicity among the Brock groups in May 2013. This drama began when Message Matters spoke up on behalf of the Obama Department of Justice's improper, secret monitoring of Associated Press (AP) reporters' phone records. Message Matters published a set of talking points encouraging liberal pundits to *defend* the government's spying. They were emailed to three thousand "progressive talkers and influentials." As a result, Democrats, Republicans, and journalists bombarded Media Matters with criticism. Journalist Glenn Greenwald, who broke the Edward Snowden story about the U.S. government's mass operations to spy on Americans, tweeted a sarcastic comment: "Media Matters helpfully distributes talking points to those who want to defend DOJ's attack on AP."

Brock appeared taken aback and initially addressed the ridicule by faulting Media Matters' sister organization, Media Matters Action Network. Though Media Matters and Media Matters Action Network share Washington, D.C., offices and personnel, and both were started and are headed by Brock, he tried to portray them as entirely separate entities as he passed off the blame. "People did not understand what we were trying to do," Brock explained in an interview about the controversy at the time.

After the dust settled, Brock announced plans to spin off Message Matters into a detached group, to keep Media Matters separate as a supposedly pure and unbiased fact-based organization. The last editorial entry on the Message Matters website is dated May 16, 2013.

Meanwhile, the Media Matters Action Network was busily spawning its own subparts, including **Political Correction Project** to attack conservative politicians and advocacy groups, and **EqualityMatters.org,** a website started in 2010 to promote "gay equality." (In December 2015, six months after the U.S. Supreme Court legalized gay marriage, the Equality Matters website ceased being updated.)

No matter the project, the Media Matters Action Network and its affiliates employed the same trademark tactics as other Brock groups: identifying and smearing perceived enemies through "strategic communications, research, training and media monitoring."

Brock's New CREW

Brock's strategy wasn't limited to starting his own new groups. In 2014 he took over several notable existing groups, some of which had stronger nonpartisan veneers than anything he'd created. That would lend more mainstream credibility to the narratives he pushed.

Such was the case with Brock's ironic conquest of **Citizens for Responsibility and Ethics in Washington** in 2014. CREW is a 501(c)(3) founded in 2003 to police the ethics of politicians. CREW had tilted left even before Brock's takeover, but nonetheless it had been regarded by some as an often-fair watchdog of political missteps by both Democrats and Republicans. Its most popular feature was the annual "Most Corrupt Members of Congress" list. Over nine years, the list was heavy on Republicans—sixty-three—but it did include twenty-five Democrats. CREW once even demanded resignations from congressional Democrats Anthony Weiner (who texted lewd photos of himself to a woman he hardly knew) and

Charles Rangel (who was caught evading taxes while heading up the House tax law committee).

But all of that was before the shocking shakeup of August 2014, when Brock was named chairman of CREW's board of directors. Shortly after the announcement, a spokesman addressed reporters about CREW's new leadership.

"Transparency and good government are progressive values," spokesman Mark Glaze told journalists. "I think the organizations associated with David [Brock] have been working on those issues in different ways for years, and CREW and its professionals will bring an additional tool in that toolbox." CREW—a new tool of Media Matters and its radical left smears.

CREW founder and executive director Melanie Sloan was replaced by Noah Bookbinder, who'd been chief adviser to Senator Patrick Leahy, a Democrat. When reporters asked Brock if his version of CREW would continue lodging complaints against both Democrats and Republicans, Brock replied, "our experience has been that the vast amount of violations of the public trust can be found on the conservative side of the aisle."

Brock's favorite raiser of funds was also heavily vested in CREW. In the three years prior to Brock's takeover, Mary Pat Bonner had raised $2.12 million for CREW and collected a windfall of $203,000 in fees for her company. I asked both Brock and CREW to provide the amount of Brock's compensation, if any, after Brock officially joined CREW, but neither would disclose it. At the time of this writing, CREW had not filed tax forms for 2015 or 2016.

A glance at the CREW website in 2016 confirms the devolution of the once-respected group. It was now filled with familiar partisan attacks on Brock's usual targets: Karl Rove, the Koch brothers, and the National Rifle Association. Later, as Trump rose to prominence in the presidential race, CREW put him in the crosshairs, filing a bribery complaint over his contribution to Florida's attorney general, and IRS complaints against him and his Trump Foundation. News organizations obediently followed the narrative, picking up the partisan CREW filings as "news" and elevating the Trump controversies to national headline status. CREW had been reimagined as another tool to amplify the Media Matters agenda. But to the uninitiated, the influence of Brock and Media Matters was largely invisible.

To journalists, including me, who'd reported on CREW's investigations in the past, the new, intensely political CREW was a stark departure. In October 2016, I first emailed to ask a spokesman for the amount of Brock's compensation, if any, and asked to see the group's latest tax filings, which the organization is required to make available for public inspection. CREW spokesman Jordan Libowitz didn't provide the information but gave an oddly defensive response. "Isn't it a breach of journalistic ethics to misrepresent yourself on the phone to hide the fact that you are a reporter?" he wrote in an email, though I had not misrepresented myself. He continued, "If you are going to threaten legal action against an organization, it helps to have the IRS regulations correct, which you did not," though I had not threatened legal action. When I told him I didn't know what he was referring to, he ominously replied: "We have caller ID." Of little surprise, Libowitz's bio shows him to be a Democratic political operative who worked on the losing "Sestak for Senate" campaign in Pennsylvania. Now masquerading as a fair arbiter of political ethics at CREW.

Meanwhile, CREW suspended its popular bipartisan "Most Corrupt Members of Congress" feature. On another occasion, when I called to ask whether it would return, a CREW spokesman told me, "It may come back, in some form or another," but explained, "it's incredibly resource heavy, so it's really a matter of getting a lot more done in terms of researching dark-money groups and digging deeper into complaints."

According to a Bloomberg news analysis of CREW's work after Brock's takeover, the watchdog "mothballed a number of projects related to government transparency, congressional corruption, and so-called Astroturf lobbying campaigns that purport to represent grassroots movements but are primarily the product of a few wealthy donors." A CREW cofounder, Louis Mayberg, resigned from CREW's board in 2015 under its new direction with Brock at the helm, stating, "I have no desire to serve on a board of an organization devoted to partisanship."

Once Brock began commanding CREW, he fathered yet another offspring: **American Democracy Legal Fund**, a 527 political organization under the IRS tax code. According to the Federal Election Commission, a 527 is "defined generally as a party, committee or association that is organized and operated primarily" to affect an issue or a candidate's selection for public office. A 527 can raise unlimited funds from individuals, corporations, and unions.

Brock again called upon his pal Brad Woodhouse to run the American Democracy Legal Fund while Woodhouse simultaneously served as president of the liberal advocacy group Americans United for Change and headed up the super PAC Correct The Record.

Shortly after its creation in fall of 2014, American Democracy Legal Fund launched a DropFox.com-type campaign to pressure Fox to drop Republican Mike Huckabee's weekly program from its lineup. At the time, Huckabee was a potential 2016 challenger to Hillary Clinton. The American Democracy Legal Fund wrote Fox chief Roger Ailes and, like other Brock groups, seemed to hold itself out as an independent ethics watchdog, giving no hint of its liberal slant or Media Matters ties. The letter read in part:

> On behalf of the American Democracy Legal Fund (ADLF), which was established to hold public officials and candidates for office accountable for possible ethics and/or legal violations, I want to bring to your attention two legal complaints our organization has filed with the Internal Revenue Service (IRS) and the Federal Election Commission (FEC) against Governor Huckabee and a nonprofit organization he created. . . . These are not the kinds of things a cable television host normally does. Governor Huckabee is obviously preparing to run for president at the same time he is working as an on air personality for Fox News, which has rightly frowned on such activity from on air personalities in the past.

Less than two months after that letter, Huckabee's Fox program ended.

By March 2016, American Democracy Legal Fund had lodged ethics complaints against most of the Republican presidential candidates, as well as other key conservative targets: Jeb Bush, John Kasich, Ben Carson, Donald Trump, Rand Paul, Huckabee, Scott Walker, Ted Cruz,

Chris Christie, and the chairman of the House Benghazi committee, Trey Gowdy. It also filed a separate complaint against a group of twenty-three House Republicans and eleven of the presidential candidates.

American Democracy Legal Fund shows relatively few donors and expenditures. It appears to be a low-cost way to advance smears and generate headaches, distractions, and expenses for conservative targets in much the same way as Media Matters operative Karl Frisch had advised in his strategy memo back in 2009.

I conducted numerous searches for tax records and was unable to find documents for the American Democracy Legal Fund. When I asked, Brock declined to provide information on where the material could be found, or what the group's specific tax designation under the 527 heading is. Neither would Brock disclose his salary, if any.

While Brock's American Democracy Legal Fund was devising attacks on national Republican politicians, its parent, CREW, continued targeting Republican groups. In June 2016, CREW filed complaints against ten conservative or libertarian dark money organizations with the IRS, Justice Department, and FBI. Fellow liberal groups amplified the message by spreading news of the complaints, then the media reported on them. One media outlet described CREW as a "nonprofit" and "Washington ethics advocacy group," failing to disclose Brock's takeover or CREW's political ties for context to readers.

Despite CREW's best efforts to crush Republicans in 2016, Trump won and Republicans maintained their majority control of both the House of Representatives and the Senate. In December 2016, Brock announced he was stepping away from CREW to focus more fully on his opposition research super PAC American Bridge and head up a new effort to fight "fake news." More on that later.

Besides CREW, another Brock takeover occurred in 2014, this time at the **American Independent Institute**. This group was first founded in 2006 as a 501(c)(3) nonprofit as the Center for Independent Media. It held itself out to be an independent investigative news outfit "dedicated to investigating and disseminating news that impacts public debate and advances the common good." But from the start, the institute was anything but independent in terms of mission and politics. Its website alluded to its political advocacy mission. It proudly declared that it set itself apart by its "reporting" because it "not only covers the news but also shapes it."

"This is the defining value of investigative journalism in the 21st century: the recognition that outcomes matter, that reporting the news well is no longer enough," read the website.

Brock first entered the picture as president of the institute in 2012. The next year, Media Matters was a large contributor, giving the institute $100,000. Analyses of American Independent Institute conducted during this time period by the Project for Excellence in Journalism of the Pew Research Center found the group to be among the most consistently ideological nonprofit news outlets examined. Pew said the news group didn't "reveal much about who's paying their bills," and its work "skews clearly in one direction." (The other nonprofit "news" group pegged by Pew as "consistently ideological" is the mirror image of the American Independent Institute: the conservative nonprofit Watchdog.org, which also holds itself out as "committed to creating non-partisan journalism.")

When Brock took over CREW in 2014, he announced plans for a "relaunch" of American Independent Institute. More money flowed in from Media Matters. American Independent Institute handed out grants to liberal writers to smear conservative issues and people in the name of journalism. "Reporters" included partisans and writers from famously liberal organizations. There were Paul Glastris, onetime assistant and speechwriter for Bill Clinton (who has written for the *New York Times, Washington Post, New Republic,* and *Slate*); Haley Sweetland Edwards (*Time,* the *Atlantic*), who wrote an article about "how conservatives have effectively lobotomized Congress"; Christopher Ketcham (*Vanity Fair, GQ,* the *Nation, Salon, Mother Jones, Harper's Magazine*); and Eli Clifton (*Salon, Huffington Post, Slate, Gawker*), who wrote an article attacking Rush Limbaugh. Brock's media pals published the liberal-funded results.

My initial search of tax records did not reveal information for the American Independent Institute, and again Brock would not provide any when I asked. As was the case with CREW and American Democracy Legal Fund, he declined to say whether he receives compensation from the group. I eventually found records filed under a slightly different name: The American Independent, a 501(c)(3). They reflect $180,000 in payments to Brock over three years for roughly 3.5 hours of work a week. That works out to a payment rate of $329 an hour.

As you can see, Brock was branching out far beyond his original missions of publishing blogs that criticized the media, training liberal messengers to dominate airtime on the news, tracking conservative candidates for elected office, and smearing enemies of the progressive agenda. Now he was quite literally creating and funding news, paying writers to "report" favorable narratives as stories to be gobbled up by Internet news outlets thirsty for content and the progressive narrative. He used CREW and American Democracy Legal Fund to advance seemingly independent stories about Republican unethical behavior, and advanced chosen news narratives with "reporters" from American Independent Institute whose work was bought and paid for. He was becoming a one-stop shop for the needs of the smear. *Why work so hard to convince news reporters to report your narrative when you can have total control: manufacture the story, supply the news items, and hire the "reporters" yourself. And there's an added bonus: the "real" news will often end up copying your story.*

The Franklin Groups

The Franklin groups are another of Brock's fascinating collections. He's listed as chairman of **Franklin Education Forum**, a 501(c)(3) "civil liberties advocacy group," at its creation on June 19, 2013. Brock said it was "spun off" from Media Matters. Like other Brock groups, it provides "message development and speaker promotion, to strengthen top progressive messengers and messaging." It also trains liberal disciples who go forth and preach the gospel in the media. He also starts up a 501(c)(4) arm, the **Franklin Forum**, which also says it provides education and public speaking training for liberal messengers, including Democrats running for elected office.

"We provide intensive media training boot camps for rising and seasoned progressive pundits and equip high-impact leaders with messaging that drives the debate and goes on offense against right-wing frames," reads the mission statement. Among its advertised specialties: "the physics of persuasion, reaching your audience, and masterminding non-verbal presence (what you say with posture, gesture, space, face, and voice)."

Then there's a third Franklin component: the **Franklin Forum PAC**, which counts on some familiar backers. They include Paul Egerman, Barbara Lee, and Stephen Silberstein, big donors who also give generously to American Bridge and Correct The Record—the same players donating money to groups with different names but run by the same people, with the same ultimate goals.

In May 2016, Brock adds a fourth component to the Franklin Group, an LLC called **Franklin Strategies**.

The dizzying financial interconnections continue. Franklin Education Forum's start-up budget, $452,000, is provided by Media Matters, and Brock's fundraiser, Bonner, gets a slice of the action: $56,500 in fundraising fees. Most of that cash is promptly transferred again: $338,527 of it to the 501(c)(4) Franklin Forum. The next year, 2014, Bonner collects another $124,250 in commissions from Franklin Education Forum. In the 2016 election cycle, Brock's pro-Hillary super PAC Correct The Record gives Franklin Forum $466,000, and Franklin Forum both gives to and receives money from American Bridge. And, as you may have guessed, the Franklin Group provides Brock another salary: his sixth that we know of. He receives $72,000 a year for a four-hour workweek, according to tax forms, or about $346 an hour.

True Blue

In late 2015, Brock begins launching another group. It starts with a new Delaware-based LLC called **True Blue Media.** Brock would later say that he envisioned True Blue Media as the left's answer to *Breitbart News.* Placed at the helm as CEO is former Hillary Clinton adviser Peter Daou.

Coincident with the start-up of True Blue, in November 2015, Brock takes control of liberal news site *Blue Nation Review*, purchasing an 80 percent stake. He's taking his efforts to control the news narrative to its logical next step: buying his own news distributor, in this case providing Hillary Clinton her very own media outlet.

In explaining the purchase, Brock tells the *Huffington Post* that his current network just isn't enough. "The need for alternative sources of information and independent reporting has never been greater," he says in a statement. It's unclear how *Blue Nation Review* could possibly qualify under any definition of "independent" reporting.

"With the 2016 campaign now fully underway," Brock continues, "the time is right for the rise of a new liberal standard-bearer and *Blue Nation Review* is poised to assume that role."

The website's home page discloses *Blue Nation Review*'s clear liberal bent but doesn't mention its pro-Hillary or Brock ties. "BNR is a project of True Blue Media, bringing you political coverage and commentary that reflects the values and principles of Blue America," reads the website. A check of its "news" in March 2016 showed all of the articles are pro-Hillary, anti–Bernie Sanders, and/or anti–Republican candidates. With the election around the corner and Hillary in the middle of a nasty primary fight, Brock now has a seemingly "unbiased" liberal website in his pocket to push pro-Hillary stories.

In September 2016, BlueNationReview.com executes its "next phase" in True Blue Media's goal "to build the premiere [*sic*] media platform for people who share Blue America's worldview": a new website called **Share-blue**. It promises to maintain its "rigorous editorial standards"—like the ones apparently applied to articles like "Spike Lee Bursts Out Laughing at Trump's Outreach to Black Voters," "Republicans Want to Stop Minorities from Voting," and "Is Trump's New 'America First' App Designed to Connect White Nationalists?"

With the creation of Shareblue, True Blue Media also announces intentions to introduce a "new [as-yet-unnamed] polling and predictive modeling destination."

The day of President Trump's inauguration in 2017, Brock announces the hiring of journalist David Sirota to head True Blue Media. Less than three weeks later, Sirota backs out of the deal, implying he'd thought it would be focused on nonpartisan accountability journalism. In announcing the reversal of his job acceptance, Sirota issues a statement saying, "the circumstances of the job subsequently changed."

It's unclear whether Brock takes compensation from any of the True Blue entities, and he would not disclose that information when I asked.

Brock's Take

Think what you will about David Brock, but he's got to be the hardest-working man in tax-exempt politics. You could say he profits nicely from his nonprofits, apparently getting paid up to hundreds of dollars an hour at times. In 2004, his Media Matters compensation alone was about $121,325. By 2015 he was earning substantially more from his flagship: $305,266.

According to tax records, Brock worked nearly full-time for Media Matters, more than thirty-one hours a week, to earn that $305,266 in 2015. That works out to about $189 an hour. He also finds time to earn six figures more at Correct The Record ($153,763 in the 2016 election cycle) and receives an additional six figures from his American Bridge super PAC. He's still got hours left in the day to pull in compensation from Media Matters Action Network, Franklin Forum, American Bridge Foundation, and the American Independent Institute (where his $60,000 salary for 3.5 hours per week works out to roughly $329 an hour). On top of all that, he has given time and expertise to CREW, American Democracy Legal Fund, and Priorities USA. I asked Brock for a breakdown of his compensation and how much time he spends a week on average on each organization. However, as mentioned, Brock declined my interview requests and would not confirm his hours or compensation from his groups. Media Matters, CREW, and American Bridge also declined to provide requested information.

Compiling what I could from public information, I found that in 2014, Brock claimed to work sixty-four hours a week, at a total of seven organizations. That doesn't count the time he spent on three pro-Hillary super PACs, where he earned several hundred thousand dollars more, but the number of work hours is not disclosed. And the same year, he started up the American Democracy Legal Fund.

Sharing his time among the organizations might be made easier because so many of them are located in the same office building. According to tax filings, all of the following Brock-connected entities have, at some point, listed their address as the same twelve-story high-rise in the Mount Vernon Triangle of Washington, D.C.: 455 Massachusetts Avenue.

American Bridge 21st Century Foundation
American Bridge 21st Century Super PAC
American Democracy Legal Fund
American Independent
American Priorities Joint Fundraising Committee
American Priorities 2016 Joint Fundraising Committee
Bonner Group (fundraiser)
Citizens for Responsibility and Ethics in Washington
Correct The Record Super PAC
Franklin Education Forum
Franklin Forum
Franklin Forum PAC
Franklin Strategies, LLC
Media Matters
Media Matters Action Network

After poring over tax documents and cross-referencing the information among Brock's various groups, here's what I found in terms of compensation for the Brock-Bonner duo:

Brock's known compensation from his network:
$2,811,464   Media Matters for America (2003–2014)
$157,083   Media Matters Action Network (2004–2014)
$177,134   American Bridge 21st Century Foundation (2011–2014)
$467,864   American Bridge Super PAC (2014 and 2016 election cycles)
$108,000   Franklin Education Forum (2013–2014)
$153,763   Correct The Record (2015–2016)
$184,923   American Independent (2012–2014)
$3,875,308   Total

Bonner Group's known commissions from Brock network:
$7,513,315   Media Matters for America (2005–2014)
$890,233   Media Matters Action Network (2008–2014)
$923,221   American Bridge 21st Century Foundation (2011–2014)

$4,568,814	American Bridge Super PAC (2012–2016 election cycles)
$647,281	Correct the Record Super PAC (2016 election cycle)
$102,500	Citizens for Responsibility and Ethics in Washington (2014)
$35,625	Franklin Forum 501(c)(4) (2013)
$180,750	Franklin Education Forum (2013–2014)
$217,536	The American Independent (2012–2014)
$134,947	Progressive Media USA (2008)
$15,111,722	**Total**

The end result of the empire Brock built is a smear engine unrivaled in its organization, reach, and influence, working its way toward a cymbalic crescendo in the madcap 2016 campaign.

Chapter Five

||||||||||||||||||||

Plausible Deniability:
Conjuring an Astroturf Reality

The two men look at each other and shift in their seats. They look back at me and one of them shrugs.

"I guess we're part of the problem."

They're high-level operators in the smear game, and I've just told them I'm investigating manipulation of public opinion through use of social media accounts with fake identities. We're having lunch at the elegant Hay-Adams hotel in the nation's capital. People like them frequent places like this. We're not in the chic restaurant upstairs on the entry level. We're in the aptly named subterranean bar Off the Record.

These men are among the untold thousands who draw lavish salaries at Washington, D.C., law firms, public relations companies, crisis management agencies, lobby groups, and strategic firms that are, for all intents and purposes, smear operators. They may not consciously think of themselves that way, but deep down they know that's what they are. They tell themselves and their clients that they're just protecting their self-interests, defending smears from the other side. Maybe they're right. If you don't fight for yourself—if you don't fight back—you'll be destroyed.

"An entire movement can be organized using phony social media accounts," remarks the younger operator, wearing a boyish haircut and a crisp navy business suit. He used to work on the Hill. He tells a story about how sports teams are known to be among the first to use Facebook accounts under bogus names to observe what their star athletes were posting online. The athletic teams, says Boyish, created false personas of beautiful women to befriend the athletes. Through those accounts, the teams quietly monitored the extracurricular activities of their players.

"These guys would never accept a friend request from one of their team managers," adds Boyish. "But a pretty girl? Yeah."

They're describing a strategy known as "astroturf."

Astroturf is a close cousin to the smear. It's a vehicle that allows the smear industry to conduct some of its most influential work in complete disguise. The idea is to keep the public from ever knowing exactly who is behind a particular effort to sway opinion.

As social media has become an unavoidable part of modern life, it's proven the perfect conduit for mass astroturf campaigns. But in truth, astroturf has been a part of the smear playbook for years. Plainly speaking, astroturf is when political, corporate, or other special interests disguise themselves and try to represent their causes as being genuine groundswells of support by ordinary people. Astroturfers write blogs, use social media, publish ads and letters to the editor, pay people to form protests or demonstrate as crowds, or simply post comments online to try to fool you into thinking an independent or grassroots movement is speaking. They use college professors and scientists; nonprofits; government; doctors and university researchers; public officials; news and scientific publications. If there's a way to co-opt a mode of communication or a group of communicators, they've figured out how to do it.

The whole point of astroturf is to try to give the impression there's widespread support for or against an agenda when there's not. Astroturf seeks to manipulate you into changing your opinion by making you feel as if you're an outlier when you're not. It magically transforms the media into propaganda agents. In short, what do you do when you don't have an actual grassroots campaign for your cause? You buy it—or manufacture it—with astroturf.

Today fake accounts and pseudonyms are tools of trade for propaganda and smear groups, corporations, and special interests. They covertly inundate and dominate the social media landscape, with assistance from strategic planners and special software. Data and technical firms specialize in this technical skill set for hire.

The people who populate these jobs are former federal officials, retired members of Congress, past politicians, ex-military officers, lobbyists, onetime Capitol Hill staffers, quasi-journalists, and spouses or children of the well connected. People pay a lot of money to hire people with that kind of access. As we've learned, they're part of a large subculture that has quietly developed in Washington, D.C. It operates below the radar of ordinary Americans yet influences nearly every image and idea they're exposed to.

Sitting at the Hay-Adams and listening to these two high-level players in the smear game talk to me about their work in the astroturf field, I find myself thinking about the increasingly artificial reality presented to the public in the news and online. I can't help but remember the 1998 film *The Truman Show*. It's a dark comedy about an orphan, Truman Burbank, unwittingly raised by a corporation in a simulated reality broadcast as a TV show around the world. Everyone is aware of the ruse except Truman, played by Jim Carrey. In the film, his natural surroundings are actually sets. Hidden cameras document Truman's daily travails. Unbeknownst to him, the people he believes are his family and friends are hired actors. A bit like Truman, in our daily lives, *we're* confronted with artificial realities that aren't what they seem. They're carefully constructed narratives forged by unseen special interests designed to manipulate our opinions.

"People don't realize that *nothing happens by accident*," one operator tells me. "When people go about their daily lives, it's like a movie. There's no scene that isn't meant to be there. There's no dialogue that's random. People and companies spend a lot of money to place these ideas before you to achieve an objective, and they're willing to make any expense to achieve it."

If the smear community is a tight-knit club that operates on a different plane of consciousness than the rest of us, then you can think of astroturf campaigns as the calling cards of the various players. They recognize and admire one another's handiwork. They know that when common themes emerge in the news, it's because of their peers. A meme goes viral because someone designed it to advance an agenda. A public figure gets eviscerated by blogs using strikingly similar terms because the idea was planted. A motif is widely circulated on social media because paid agents made it happen. The right results turn up high in Google searches because data nerds know how to game the system.

As I look across the table at the two smear merchants in front of me, it's easy to see how technology has fundamentally changed the smear game, while simultaneously raising its stakes. The older one in the pair (who has a military background) remarks offhandedly that technology has made it easier to covertly control and manipulate information on the Web.

"The military does it all the time. They can delete somebody's tweet or their entire Twitter account," he says. "Did you know that? Like it never even existed!"

Internet Secrets

We like to think of social media as a place where ideas are freely exchanged. Where controversial voices and ideas can be heard. A fast-paced, Wild West dynamic where manipulation of the message would be difficult to accomplish. But a peek behind the curtain exposes a reality that's far different. And the plain fact that people don't think they're as easily fooled on social media . . . makes them easier to fool. In reality, the Internet and social media have given astroturf campaigns the opportunity to flourish. While ideas and discussions may flow freely online, they are often anonymous, with no true sense of who's actually behind the accounts. *After all, it's easier to smear someone when you never have to show your face, or, as it often turns out, you don't even have one.*

There are countless examples of astroturf campaigns taking root online in recent years. In 2015, Twitter made plans for an #AskPOTUS town hall with President Obama to compete with rivals like Reddit, which was drawing a lot of attention for its interactive Q&A sessions with well-known people. But the Twitter session was not the freewheeling event some might have expected. According to a former Twitter senior employee who spoke to *BuzzFeed,* the head of Twitter, Dick Costolo, had ordered employees to build an algorithm to filter out any abusive tweets that might be directed at Obama. A source said Twitter also manually censored the #AskPOTUS tweets because the automated system was inconsistent. The decision to control the message was kept secret from some senior employees for fear they would object. Some who did find out were said to be upset because they believed the censorship defied Twitter's supposed commitment to free speech. All this subterfuge from a company that had once boasted of itself as "the free speech wing of the free speech party."

Facebook has its own demons, according to former insiders at the social media site. They claim some news on Facebook is presented or withheld for biased reasons. In May 2016, an ex–Facebook employee was anonymously quoted on Gizmodo, a design, technology, and science fiction website, saying he was part of a project that "routinely suppressed news stories of interest to conservative readers from the social network's influential 'trending' news section." Several people who were reportedly employed at Facebook as "news curators" told Gizmodo they were "instructed to artificially 'inject' selected stories into the trending news module, even if they weren't popular enough to warrant inclusion. . . . Depending on who was on shift, things would be blacklisted or trending." One former curator said suppressed topics included former IRS official Lois Lerner, who took the fifth before Congress after being accused of targeting conservative groups, and popular conservative news aggregator the *Drudge Report*. Facebook denied the allegations.

Online manipulation can be found on news and quasi-news sites as well. In January 2016, there's an Internet smear directed against a Hollywood film based on a true-life story. The film is *13 Hours: The Secret Soldiers of Benghazi*. It tells the personal stories of three CIA operators who heroically helped fight off Islamic extremist attackers on September 11, 2012. This is a movie that supporters of presidential candidate Hillary Clinton, by necessity, must smear. Clinton was secretary of state during that night's tragic events. Dozens of Americans in Benghazi had waited for an outside U.S. military rescue that never came. Obama was missing in action. The military blamed Hillary's State Department for not giving the green light to launch a rescue option. Four Americans, including U.S. ambassador Christopher Stevens, were killed.

It will be difficult for the administration and Hillary Clinton interests to directly impeach the heroes in the film. So some seek to controversialize the movie itself. To try to keep people from seeing it. Convince the potential audience that it's boring. Tedious. A flop. And so, even before the movie's release, there's a suspicious stampede of negative reviews. Whether intentional or not, they lead to an astroturf smear campaign.

Vox, the left-wing website headed by a liberal blogger named Ezra Klein, pans *13 Hours* in an extensive blog based solely on the trailer, if you can believe it, not the actual film.

"Even the trailer for Michael Bay's Benghazi movie is patronizing and dishonest," writes *Vox*'s Max Fisher. He then goes on to incorrectly portray as a "myth" the idea that military rescuers were prevented from quickly helping.

On the website *Deadline Hollywood,* Anthony D'Alessandro claims that *13 Hours* opened "lower than expected." Gary Susman of Moviefone claims it "struck out at the box office." The *Hill* agrees in a blog post titled "Benghazi Film Flops at the Box Office." *Salon*'s hit job is titled "Audiences Reject '*13 Hours*': Big Blow for the Right's Desperate Quest for Clinton's Benghazi Smoking Gun—It's Just Not There." (Yes, that's the actual headline.) Alyssa Rosenberg, a left-wing culture blogger for the *Washington Post,* portrays *13 Hours* as "boring" and sprinkles her review with tried-and-true astroturf language such as "conspiracy theories" and "obsessed," suggesting she's spreading propaganda. *Flavorwire,* too, claims the film "tanked."

Washington Post gossip blogger Erik Wemple also advances the narrative of *13 Hours* as a conservative movie—apparently hoping the label will discourage viewers from wanting to see it, or at least from admitting publicly how much they like it. Proving the effectiveness of Media Matters' nonpartisan veneer, Wemple even quotes Media Matters in his blog without disclosing its conflict of interest: it's a liberal smear group tied to Hillary Clinton.

"An analysis by Media Matters found that in the 20 months following the [Benghazi] attacks, the leading cable news network ran nearly 1,100 segments on the topic," Wemple writes.

If you hadn't seen the movie for yourself, you might read these "reviews" and think it *is* a terrible movie and a box-office flop. But let's look beyond the smear.

13 Hours was actually the number-two-grossing new movie release in the United States its opening week, second only to *Ride Along 2*. It was the number-four movie in the United States overall and by early February was the number-three movie of the year. Its opening weekend, *13 Hours* closed in on Paramount Pictures' projection of $20 million in earnings, taking in more than $19 million for the four-day weekend. Of the opening, *Variety* stated, "The wartime drama took in a respectable $900,000 at 1,995 locations on Thursday night." By way of comparison, at the same time the propagandists were calling it a dud, the *13 Hours* opening was in the same range as *The Wolf of Wall Street* and surpassed *The Big Short,* which was released a month earlier. Neither was considered to be a flop at that stage. As for audience popularity, the majority of reviews for *13 Hours* were overwhelmingly positive, hovering around 87 percent on RottenTomatoes.com. Compare that to 58 percent for *Ride Along 2.*

Is it just coincidence that while *13 Hours* is enjoying a respectable weekend box-office opening and rave audience reviews, there is a singularly negative, false narrative being furthered by the liberal media? There's no better example of astroturf.

On the other hand, when the antagonist portrayed in the film comes forward to slam the movie, much as an accused thief claims innocence after his fingerprints appear on the jewels, the media treats *his* claims as the definitive truth. He was the CIA chief in Benghazi who allegedly delayed the CIA operators from helping their comrades under attack.

"Baloney," declares NBC News, taking the side of the CIA official accused of bad behavior. Staying on narrative, the network further states "the movie has generally gotten lousy reviews," and claims "conservatives have been touting [it] because it portrays State Department officials— who were taking orders at the time from then–Secretary of State Hillary Clinton—in a bad light." While it may be true that conservatives pounced on the Benghazi example to criticize Clinton, it is incorrect to suggest that all the news reporting fell in this category and that there weren't legitimate, serious issues to consider.

You may ask: Why do I regard this as an example of astroturf and a smear, rather than just a consensus about a bad movie? There are a series of "tells." First: the players. They include a familiar group of media outlets well known for advancing liberal narratives and, often, whatever happens to be on the Media Matters agenda. Whether they formally organize to do so or are simply receptive to the particular narrative, they're clearly helpful soldiers in the astroturf wars. Second: their information is misleading and, in some cases, inaccurate, indicating their mission is to further a narrative rather than simply reflect the truth. Third: some of the efforts appear disingenuous. For example, slamming a movie on the basis of viewing a trailer isn't the work of a reporter, or even a sincere reviewer. It's a product of the agenda-driven. Fourth, the "reviews" use well-recognized astroturf language. Taken together, it's hard to draw any other conclusion than that the "consensus" against *13 Hours*—at least among these "reviewers"—was rooted in an astroturf smear campaign.

In the end, astroturf succeeds if it does nothing more than distract from the truth by throwing so much confusing information into the mix, ordinary Americans throw up their hands and disregard all of it. As Brock once said in an interview, "[O]ften the goal is just to confuse people, and to take the political opponent off his or her game, and to not let them talk about what they want to talk about."

"I Became a Target"

Politicians aren't the only targets of brutal astroturf campaigns. Social media allows most anyone to become victim of these seemingly "organic" efforts.

In October 2016, Scott Adams, creator of the office humor comic strip *Dilbert,* wrote a very serious blog post titled "The Week I Became a Target." In it, he claimed he'd been targeted by Hillary Clinton interests because of his support for Donald Trump. The campaign against him employed classic facets of astroturf, including attacks against him on social media, in the news, and even on a book review site.

"This weekend I got 'shadowbanned' on Twitter," Adams writes. "It lasted until my followers noticed and protested. Shadowbanning prevents my followers from seeing my tweets and replies, but in a way that is not obvious until you do some digging. Why did I get shadowbanned? Beats me. But it was probably because I asked people to tweet me examples of Clinton supporters being violent against peaceful Trump supporters in public. I got a lot of them. It was chilling."

Adams reveals that the week before his "shadowban," his Twitter feed "was invaded by an army of Clinton trolls leaving sarcastic insults and not much else on my feed. There was an obvious similarity to them, meaning it was organized." At around the same time, coincidentally, liberal website *Slate* published a hit piece on Adams. "It was so lame that I retweeted it myself," he says. "The timing of the hit piece might be a coincidence, but I stopped believing in coincidences this year."

Adams mentioned two more "coincidences" in his blog. The one and only speaking engagement he'd booked for 2017 was suddenly canceled, the host citing a desire to "go in a different direction." Then people began posting negative reviews of one of his books on Amazon.

"I wouldn't want to buy anything from an author who feels he's too rich and gets taxed too much," writes one of the reviewers. Another adds, "Adams thinks he's the smartest guy in the room. SPOILER: He isn't. Not by a long shot. Adams also believes he pays too much in taxes. And Donald Trump is a genius. Save your money and save Scott Adams the grief of paying more taxes."

"All things considered, I had a great week," concludes Adams after weathering multifaceted attacks. "I didn't realize I was having enough impact to get on the Clinton enemies list. I don't think I'm supposed to be happy about any of this, but that's not how I'm wired. Mmm, critics. Delicious :-)"

The week I read Adams's account, I knew a fresh smear campaign against me was likely being hatched in clandestine corners over this very book. I had recently contacted Brock to ask for an interview and for information on his network of groups. That's definitely going to stir the pot. But those of us who recognize astroturf tend to be better equipped to defy it.

What happened to Adams demonstrates the many simultaneous paths a smear can travel to marginalize a target, from harassment on social media to cutting into one's livelihood. An operation like that takes connections, and the smear artist has them. Adams's story reminds me of a respected ex-member of Congress who had a great job for years at a Washington, D.C., law firm and lobby group until he dared to publicly criticize President Obama and Hillary Clinton on national security issues. For the first time ever, he told me, his firm tried to shut him up and instructed him to cancel scheduled television appearances. He was told that top people at his firm in New York were supporters of Clinton for president and weren't happy about his analyses. When he continued his TV appearances despite the warnings, he got a perfunctory email telling him to collect his belongings. He'd been fired. Powerful people have many ways to silence critics, whether it means getting them fired, having their speeches canceled, or controversializing them in the news. Sometimes an astroturf character assassination is successful in silencing a voice entirely. Such was the case with University of Colorado professor Roger Pielke Jr., who used to write about climate change. In March 2014, he wrote his first piece for the website *FiveThirtyEight:* "Disasters Cost More Than Ever—But Not Because of Climate Change." From the viewpoint of global warming activists, Pielke's views had to be crushed.

The liberal website *ThinkProgress* publishes a hit piece discrediting Pielke, calling him a "controversial hire" for *FiveThirtyEight* and claiming he'd used "deeply misleading data." Pretty soon, *Salon, Slate,* and the *Huffington Post* echo the criticism, putting the squeeze on *FiveThirtyEight* editor in chief Nate Silver. "Silver is still backing the wrong horse, and the sooner he dumps Pielke, the better," *Slate*'s David Auerbach declares.

Before long, *FiveThirtyEight*'s Silver buckles, publishing a mea culpa rebuttal to the original Pielke story and stating, "All journalism relies on trust. . . . Any time that trust is undermined, it's a huge concern for us. We thank you for your continued feedback. We're listening and learning." And with that, Pielke stops writing about climate change.

More than two years later, in 2016, emails released by WikiLeaks provide a window into the effort to controversialize Pielke. *ThinkProgress* editor Judd Legum is writing megadonor Tom Steyer, a hedge fund billionaire and global warming activist, and takes credit for stopping Pielke.

"I think it's fair say that, without [*ThinkProgress*'s blog], Pielke would still be writing on climate change for 538," Legum postulates.

In response to these revelations Pielke tells reporters, "It spells out in black and white . . . that there was an organized, politically motivated campaign to damage my career and reputation, based on a perception that my academic research was thought to be inconvenient." On Twitter, Pielke then posts a graph showing the frequency of attacks orchestrated by *ThinkProgress*'s parent, the Center for American Progress.

"[The Center for American Progress] wrote 160+ articles about me, many misrepresenting my views and calling me a climate skeptic and denier," Pielke told reporters. "With their megaphone, propaganda worked. . . . I'm surprised I lasted as long as I did." He also said, "They were ultimately successful in removing an academic from working on a topic . . . [there's] nothing like a political witch hunt to help you focus on career priorities."

The Center for American Progress is a think tank founded by John Podesta, who was President Clinton's chief of staff, leader of President Obama's transition team, and head of Hillary Clinton's 2016 campaign. The center said it was simply correcting Pielke's misinformation.

Comments for Hire

And so, when you want to find information that's not posing a hidden agenda—what's left? If you think there's more transparency over at the op-ed pages of major news publications, then you haven't been paying attention.

"I write op-eds in the name of other people," a noted player in the field confesses to me. "I'm advocating for large clients. Communicating somebody else's idea. I've written five of them in four days on different topics I know little about."

His signature is never at the bottom of his work; it's always somebody else's. Someone who's paid for use of their name. Maybe a university doctor, physician, or economist. A current or retired public notable. It's like money laundering, only instead of hiding the origin of ill-gotten gains, it masks the source of paid opinions. The ghostwriter never gets credit. He gets a paycheck.

"Most people think op-eds are written by their neighbor or an interested party who just feels strongly about a topic," I tell this ghostwriter.

"I know. I used to think that, too," he replies. "After working in D.C. so many years, even *I'm* surprised at how so few write their own material, even impressive elected officials. I mean, really well-known people."

Another player who dabbles in this business is a trial lawyer and Democrat activist.

"I get letters published in newspapers all the time for my clients. And you know what? No newspaper editor ever asks if the client really wrote it," he tells me incredulously. "Can you believe that? They don't even *ask*."

An internal memo written by the Clinton super PAC Correct The Record boasts that between May 15, 2015, and December 1, 2015, it "helped write and place 36 op-eds across the country in a number of publications including *Politico, Times Union, Huffington Post,* CNN, *Washington Blade,* and New Jersey's *Bergen Record.*"

Comments on the Internet are also prime astroturf real estate. Paid interests disguised as ordinary people troll assigned topics, news sites, reporters, blogs, and social media for the purpose of posting comments that spin and confuse. You already knew that. But there's another comment arena that's being manipulated under the noses of ordinary Americans: the *Federal Register.*

The *Federal Register* is where federal agencies publish proposed regulations so the public can comment on them before they're enacted. It's a process required by a law called the Administrative Procedure Act. Agencies are supposed to respond to the public feedback.

As I write this, I'm betting most of you have never submitted a single official comment about any of the millions of federal regulations enacted over the years. So who *is* filling up these comment sections? You guessed it: insiders and paid interests. Those who want to stop regulations or have them passed or amended in their favor. One player in the field tells me that he spends a great deal of time and effort filing comments on behalf of paid clients.

"I do a lot of work in beating back bad regulations by using the comment period, by driving comments into the government," he says. It's effective and it doesn't cost a penny.

As you can see, complacency in the media combined with incredibly powerful propaganda and publicity forces means the public sometimes gets little of the truth. Special interests have unlimited time and money to figure out new ways to spin opinion while cloaking their role. Surreptitious astroturf methods are now more important in influencing opinion than traditional lobbying of Congress.

Fake Personas

In December 2015, the Department of Justice announces the shocking arrest of nineteen-year-old Jalil Ibn Ameer Aziz. The teen allegedly used Twitter accounts and fake personas to operate a network that spewed violent, Islamic extremist rhetoric. All from the comfort and safety of his parents' Pennsylvania home. The feds say Aziz employed a manifold of Twitter accounts to promulgate his vile doctrine and magnify its impact under fifty-seven names, including @KolonelSham, @WiseHaqq, @AnsarUmmah, and @MuslimBruh0. During the raid of his home, police found an alarming cache of high-powered ammunition. Aziz was charged with advocating violence against U.S. troops, chatting online about buying a seventeen-year-old female slave, and recruiting for the terrorist group ISIS. An unhinged teenager was able to amplify his dangerous message by using social media to give the impression he was many people. Imagine what the pros in the smear game can do with similar tools and tactics!

Emails revealed by the collective "Anonymous" network of Internet hackers prove the government is in the game. They provide a window into the feds' shocking efforts to deceive the public using secretive social media tactics. The emails come from computer security company HBGary Federal, which bid on a job to advance the U.S. government's astroturf efforts. The project called for designing "persona management" software, creating an "army" of fake social media profiles maintained by actors. The software would allow one actor to be able to pretend to be many different people online. Each individually created identity would be assigned its own virtual machine or thumb drive to help the actor keep his various identities straight, depending on which he was using at a given time. Each persona would have a unique email and social media accounts. The accounts could be constructed to appear as though they'd existed for a long time. Read part of the contract solicitation yourself:

> [We] *will create a set of personas on twitter, blogs, forums, and myspace under created names that fit the profile. . . . These accounts are maintained and updated automatically through RSS feeds, retweets, and linking together social media connecting between platforms. [O]nce you have a real name persona you create a Facebook and LinkedIn account using the given name, lock those accounts down and link these accounts to a selected # of previously created social media accounts.*

It's a sophisticated scheme allowing government agents to fool regular people into believing multiple individuals are posting original content. The fake accounts can be cleverly set up to post automated content that maintains the façade. In this next excerpt from the contract solicitation, HBGary speaks of helping the government by "gaming" to hide the true location of its actors, and of using "tricks" to "add a level of realness."

> *Using the assigned social media accounts we can automate the posting of content that is relevant to the persona. In this case there are specific social media strategy website SS feeds we can subscribe to and then repost content on twitter with the appropriate hashtags. In fact using hashtags and gaming some location based check-in services we can make it appear as if a persona was actually at a conference and introduced himself/herself to key individuals as part of the exercise, as one example. There are a variety of social media tricks we can use to add a level of realness to all fictitious personas.*

Besides these hacked HBGary emails, we can glean further insight into the artificial realities invented and maintained by the U.S. government by digging through federal contract solicitations online. One from 2010 seeks software to allow "government agencies and enterprise organizations" to "manage their persistent online personas." The contracting office was the U.S. military's MacDill Air Force Base, in Florida. The government was using your tax dollars to create a stable of phony online social media identities "without fear of being discovered."

Fake personas aren't just a trick used by government. They're also deployed by corporations and special interests. Take the controversy over the Dakota Access Pipeline, or DAPL, in 2016. At the time, a Twitter account under the name of Dannielle Mcardell is among a group publicly going after protesters of the oil pipeline, including members of the Standing Rock Sioux Indian tribe. Dannielle's profile photo is that of a beautiful young woman with bare shoulders and sensuous, model-like good looks. One of her attack tweets reads, "Taking kids to a violent protest the #NoDAPL people hosted is negligence. Someone call child protective services." After doing some digging, the blog DeSmog alleges that "Dannielle" isn't a real person at all, but a persona created by an industry front group that used at least sixteen fake social media accounts to smear pipeline opponents.

Cheap, Easy Stunts

"The only people saying you have to raise billions and buy a bunch of negative ads are the people vested in the old way," Christian Josi tells me. He's a conservative operator in the political and corporate smear universe. "You don't have to do ads. You do stunts. And they work." Josi is a guy who fights most of his professional battles under the radar but emerges on social media with bared claws from time to time. In November 2016, he posts a Facebook entry that reads, "Am told David N. Bossie [of the conservative group Citizens United] recently referred to me as a 'drug-riddled asshole' at Trump Tower. Half true. Never done drugs, am asshole. Fuck you, Dave. Remember how good I have been to you over the years? . . . Reagan Award? Asking me to be Executive Director of Citizens United? Fuck you dickhead. I will stomp your weak disloyal ass."

But I digress.

The universe in which Josi operates is a brave new one where cheap and easy stunts can do the trick. One example is a T-shirt caper against Obamacare architect Jonathan Gruber, who was hauled before Congress in December 2014 after videos surfaced of him calling the American public "stupid."

"We made T-shirts with Gruber's picture on it that said 'I'm with

Stupid' and flooded the Hill with them," Josi says. "*Drudge* and *Fox and Friends* picked it up and it went viral immediately."

Josi describes another T-shirt project he helped arrange for the Tea Party in order to marginalize Kevin McCarthy, the handpicked successor to unpopular Republican Speaker of the House John Boehner. It boiled down to creating a memorable meme.

"We made a bunch of T-shirts and did a caricature of Boehner with a yellow face and cigarettes, and handed them out at the capital metro," he says. The shirts labeled McCarthy as "McBoehner" and depicted him with a drink and cigarette in his left hand, and an artificial tan. In other words, Boehner's clone. The caper got free publicity through mentions in the *Hill* and the *Wall Street Journal*. McCarthy ended up withdrawing from consideration as Speaker.

"We took out Kevin McCarthy with a plane ticket and four hundred T-shirts we handed out at the South Capitol Metro station. It was picked up immediately on *Drudge* and Fox," Josi proudly recounts.

In 2016, Josi mounts a third T-shirt stunt in partnership with conservative operators radio host Alex Jones and Roger Stone. Josi tells me the goal is to reintroduce to a generation of millennials Bill Clinton's womanizing past, including allegations of rape (for which Clinton was not charged or prosecuted).

"We wanted to bring that debate back up to people who have no idea, to refuel the resurgence of interest in Bill Clinton's lifelong behavior, not because of him but because of the way Hillary enabled him and terrorized his victims and continues to do so," says Josi.

So the plan is hatched for the "Bill Clinton RAPE" T-shirt. It features an image of Clinton with the word *RAPE* written underneath. Josi says the design of the shirt wasn't his idea, but he was hired to help devise ways to get it publicized. The first step, it's decided, is for Stone to parade the T-shirt in front of the media gaggle at the Republican National Convention on July 21, 2016. The hope is that the news media would snap a photo and publish it.

It works like a charm.

"*Time* magazine took the bait and did this headline: 'Roger Stone Just Showed Up to the RNC in a Bill Clinton 'RAPE' T-Shirt," says Josi. Free publicity for the smear. "We used the *Time* piece for months to sell the shirts and launch a broader effort."

The point wasn't to make money, he says, but to "be a wedge and start that conversation. It worked beautifully for a surprisingly small amount of money." From there Josi used social media to encourage anti-Clinton activists to post pictures and video of themselves wearing the T-shirt.

"One kid put on a shirt and videotaped himself trying to get into the United Nations," Josi tells me. "They made him turn the shirt inside out. We also have asked supporters to wear a shirt into the Clinton Library while videotaping it."

In October 2016, a man wearing a Clinton "RAPE" T-shirt interrupts Hillary's vice presidential nominee, Tim Kaine, at a rally. "Bill Clinton is a rapist!" the man shouts until he's escorted out by security. "We don't know this guy," says Josi. "But we love him and how grassrootsy it is. You can do stuff on a dime in the era of social media."

T-shirts fall under the category of public stunts rather than secretive dirty tricks. But as we've learned, much of the smear artists' work goes on in the unspeakable, recessed corners of society.

Cognitive Dissonance

Even the president of the United States can engage in astroturf. He can use the bully pulpit and the good ol' bandwagon appeal to give the impression there's more widespread support for an idea than actually exists. In his final State of the Union address, in January 2016, President Obama uses these tactics to make global warming skeptics feel like odd men out.

"Look, if anybody still wants to dispute the science around climate change, have at it," lectures the president. "You'll be pretty lonely, because you'll be debating our military, most of America's business leaders, the majority of the American people, almost the entire scientific community, and two hundred nations around the world who agree it's a problem and intend to solve it."

But that's not what a Pew survey found two months before. It concluded that Americans are among the least concerned on the planet about climate change. A majority of those polled in the United States (55 percent) did *not* think it's a very serious problem. A majority (59 percent) did *not* believe it's harming people now. A majority (70 percent) was *not* very concerned that climate change would harm them personally.

"You'll be pretty lonely," insists the president, quite incorrectly. Technically, it's lonelier on *his* side of the climate change planet. In confidently stating his false claim, President Obama is not only using the classic bandwagon appeal as a persuasion technique; he's also employing vintage repetition tactics. To paraphrase Hitler's propagandist, Goebbels: *It would be possible to prove, with sufficient repetition and a psychological understanding of the people concerned, that a square is in fact a circle.*

The president hopes to make something true by convincing you of something that's not. If people are persuaded to believe that 99 percent of their neighbors think global warming is a very serious problem, then maybe 99 percent of the people will come to believe that global warming is a very serious problem. Or at least the majority who disagree will keep their mouths shut because they've been effectively smeared.

I always think one of the best ways to sniff out possible use of astroturf in a smear is simply by trusting your common sense. Pay attention to those stark moments of cognitive dissonance. That's when a theme, meme, or supposed majority opinion is entirely at odds with what you believe to be true.

Fact-Checking Fact-Checkers

As astroturf has grown more pervasive and deceptive, and its practitioners more adept at blending it into the media landscape, the role of fact-checkers has become increasingly important. As you might guess, that's made them a target of astroturf themselves. Even the fact-checking landscape has been co-opted by attempts to sway public opinion and smear enemies of selected ideas. As the *Wall Street Journal* has reported, these days the business of fact-checking often turns on matters of the fact-checker's opinion.

For example, there's a big discrepancy in the way PolitiFact views veracity of Democrats and Republicans. One study found the fact-checker rated a majority of statements by Democrats, 54 percent, to be mostly or entirely true, but only 18 percent of Republican statements to be accurate. The study was done by the George Mason University Center for Media and Public Affairs, headed by S. Robert Lichter.

"PolitiFact.com has rated Republican claims as false three times as often as Democratic claims during President Obama's second term, despite controversies over Obama administration statements on Benghazi, the IRS [targeting of conservatives] and the AP [government spying scandal]," writes Lichter.

U.S. News & World Report also examined the biased fact-check phenomenon in an article titled "Fact Checkers Biased against Republicans." Author Peter Roff writes, "It was Obama who said you could keep the health care you had if you liked it. . . . It was Obama who said Benghazi happened because of a YouTube video. It was Obama's IRS that denied conservative political groups had been singled out for special scrutiny. And it was Obama who promised that taxes would not go up for any American making less than $250,000 per year." Roff concludes that the tendency for fact-checkers to rate Democrats as much more truthful than Republicans probably has more to do with "how the statements were picked and the subjective bias of the fact checker involved than anything remotely empirical." He argues fact-checkers are needed "to check the facts being checked."

Of course, when Americans detect they're being fed a narrative and want to separate fact from myth, they can always dig deeper. Perhaps they'll consult the popular website authority Snopes, which considers itself "the definitive Internet reference source for urban legends, folklore, myths, rumors, and misinformation." What many people don't know is that sprinkled in among Snopes's helpful myth-busting features is incorrect and biased information about all kinds of topics, including medical, political, and scientific ones. In debates over the Ultimate Truth, Snopes can often be found siding with establishment and corporate interests, even when it's contrary to the facts.

I first noticed this years ago when I ran across an item in Snopes calling the suspected link between breast cancer and antiperspirants a "myth." Indeed, that's the narrative the cosmetics industry and industry-funded American Cancer Society were peddling at the time. But as I reported on CBS News, peer-reviewed published studies suggested a possible link, the National Institutes of Health was promoting additional research to investigate the relationship, and the Food and Drug Administration had been investigating the matter seriously for several years. Snopes was incorrect. At some point after my reports, Snopes eventually changed its information to correctly reflect the scientific studies I'd reported on.

Snopes also sometimes takes sides on political issues that are far from factually settled. An article by Peter Hasson in the conservative *Daily Caller* noted in 2016 that Snopes recently "tried to pose as a political fact-checker" but that its fact-checking "looks more like playing defense for prominent Democrats like Hillary Clinton."

Hasson suggests there's a reason for that. Snopes's political fact-checker Kim LaCapria is a liberal who has referred to Republicans as "regressive" and afraid of "female agency." He says prior to Snopes, LaCapria worked at the *Inquisitr,* a website that's had to retract hoaxes or misleading stories. She trashed the Tea Party as "teahadists," accused the Bush administration of criminal wrongdoing in the September 11, 2001, Islamic extremist terrorist attacks, and dismissed the idea of food stamps being used to buy alcohol or guns as the stuff of Republican fantasy. Hasson says once hired at Snopes, LaCapria wrote "fact checks" that read more like an opinion column. One argued against Donald Trump's proposed Muslim immigrant moratorium. Another defended Hillary Clinton for saying "we didn't lose a single person in Libya," though four Americans were killed in Benghazi, Libya, on September 11, 2012. (LaCapria argued that Clinton was referring only to the U.S. invasion of Libya, not what followed.) LaCapria also wrote stories arguing that although the Islamic extremist responsible for the Orlando, Florida, nightclub terrorist massacre was a registered Democrat, he might not really be a Democrat; defending Hillary Clinton after outrage over her wearing a $12,495 jacket while discussing raising wages and reducing inequality; and insisting that Facebook censorship of conservative news was just a rumor.

Many Americans are starting to get wise to the blurred line between fact-checkers and facts, according to a survey by Rasmussen Reports. It finds 62 percent believe news organizations skew fact-checks to help the candidates they support. Eighty-eight percent of Trump supporters said they believed news organizations skew the facts, while a 59 percent majority of Clinton backers said they trust media fact-checking.

Fact-checking would come to take on new meaning in the 2016 campaign and beyond as code for discrediting Donald Trump. Democrats would open new war rooms devoted to "fact-checking Trump in real time." They would coin the term *factivist* and successfully pressure journalists to adopt aggressive tactics that result in almost never proving Trump correct (and almost universally declaring him wrong), even when the truth is a matter of opinion rather than fact. Indeed, fact-checking has become one of the more important fronts in astroturf campaigns as smear merchants look to add credibility to what they're selling.

Another indispensable front in modern smear campaigns is, of course, the media itself. Putting the media to use, whether to advance astroturf or act as "factivists," is the cornerstone of a good smear. And it all starts with good relationships.

Chapter Six

||||||||||||||||||||

Transactional Journalism:
The Black Market Information Trade

It's March 2016. I'm speaking at a meeting on Capitol Hill attended mostly by congressional staffers. Groups of Democrats and Republicans routinely invite me and other journalists to speak. Sometimes I go because it helps me to get to know the players. They try to pick my brain. *Why do journalists do such-and-such? Why can't we get a fair shot from such-and-such news organization?* There's an understandable desire within both political parties to use the media to their advantage. In terms of who has the organization, leadership, strategy, and infrastructure to take better advantage, Republicans tell me they know that going into the 2016 campaign, it's the Democrats. They ask me how they can get the same edge. I tell them I'm not a political adviser, just an observer.

At this particular March meeting, a hand shoots up in the back of the room during Q&A. I mentally note that the average age of the staffers seems to be dropping. Once they make enough connections to be considered marketable in Washington's K Street world, they tend to leave elected politics and move on to the big money. They become consultants, advisers, and associates at lobby firms, PR companies, think tanks, strategy groups, and smear operations. Most political staffers don't grow old in public service.

The young man with the question hasn't worked on the Hill very long. But he already has ideas about how things work. He stands up and flashes a friendly grin.

"If we wanted to give you—for lack of a better word—'dirt' on somebody, and if you looked at it and didn't want to use it, how could we get you to agree to keep it confidential so we can give it to somebody else? How would we go about that?"

The question is revealing. It tells me that the practice of public officials shopping "dirt" to reputable journalists has become so common, this twentysomething I've never met before has no compunction about raising it openly in front of his colleagues. He thinks his job, as he collects a salary from taxpayers, is to conduct and spread opposition research against political enemies. He thinks my job, and that of other reporters in Washington, is to sift through the dirt we're handed and decide whether to use it or take a pass. It tells me this must happen all the time.

I politely explain that "dirt" really isn't my thing. I tend to cover issues and angles that are underserved, but generally not because someone is peddling muck. He apologizes for his use of the word. But there's no need.

"I know how it works," I tell him.

It's not his fault. It's my industry's. We encourage the worst practices by allowing ourselves to be used. The result is transactional journalism.

Transactional journalism refers to the friendly, mutually beneficial relationships that have developed between reporters and those on whom they report. It's when the relationships cross a line beyond chumminess and the players strike clandestine business deals, whether formally or implicitly, to report on people and topics a certain way. Reporters may offer favorable treatment in exchange for getting a "scoop." They may agree to let an interview subject dictate terms when it comes to topic and timing of publication. They may promise to ask some questions and avoid others. They may carry on cozy relationships that allow their reporting to be influenced in ways they don't disclose to the public. Usually reporters afford the most favorable treatment to those with whom they are ideologically in synch. All of this crosses an ethical line, in my opinion.

Transactional journalism results in a perverted dynamic. Public officials manipulate the press into competing to be first to receive government and political propaganda—self-serving rumors or press releases promoting agendas or smearing opponents. The reporter who's first to publish these handouts gets a hearty pat on the back from colleagues.

"Great get!" they say.

In the news business a "great get" used to mean that you, as a reporter, got an exclusive story as a result of your ingenuity, shoe-leather journalism, and persistence. Today it simply means you're the recipient of a White House or political party leak. As one national journalist tells me, "When you're one of the top dogs in the 'handout chain,' you get the info first. And the total shills are feeding the material. The political operatives use [the media] . . . build them, break them down, or bust them when they need to or want to."

Transactional journalism has become key to a smear artist's ability to formulate a *Truman Show*–esque alternate existence all around us. As with astroturf, it's a vehicle to create a smoke screen, making narratives appear to be organic, hard-nosed journalism when they're the exact opposite. Much like astroturf, this is a world in which little happens by accident. Topics and people make news because it's all been prearranged, preplanned, agreed upon.

About Those Exclusives . . .

When I first started reporting at a national level, I listened as colleagues and managers spoke in awe of many stories broken by certain noted journalists and publications. The rest of us were often sent chasing after their "exclusives." After a few years, I learned that many of these stories were not the result of hard work and digging, at least not on the part of the journalists. The reporters were simply willing repositories for propaganda planted by operators and smear artists. They're the sympathetic ear on the other end of the phone, as sought by political operatives make it their business to seek out like-minded journalists. Instead of recognizing these so-called news exclusives for what they really are—handouts from players advocating for their interests or smearing opposing views— we in the news media covet them, perpetuate them, and encourage the syndrome.

How is [publication X] getting all those stories? our managers anxiously ask. Their question carries the implication that if only *we* were a little better at reporting, a little more plugged in, *we'd* have the exclusives. Work in Washington, D.C., long enough and you get wise to what's really happening. You try to tell your managers. The objects of their desire are little more than press releases that special interests want publicized for their advantage. Some managers get it. But some tune out . . . they just wish *you* had those exclusives.

And it's not just in this country. A U.S. smear operator who worked on a foreign election campaign tells me how he discovered, to his delight, that many news publications overseas are overtly in the tank for one political candidate or another, actively shaping the artificial reality the public sees. Their attempts to influence votes go far beyond a typical endorsement or comment on the editorial pages. They use their news stories to construct a desired reality.

"Two [foreign] newspapers called me and basically said, 'Tell us what you want us to report, give us the information, and tell us when you want us to publish it,'" the operator tells me. Obviously, that kind of service was good for him and his candidate. "It was to my benefit," he says, "but even *I* thought it was kind of outrageous."

More than ever, the sort of "reporting" conducted as a result of such efforts, both on the conservative and liberal sides, passes for news and is rewarded with clicks from readers and kudos from media managers. It's everything today's quasi-semi-news media seeks: quick, easy, low-cost, low-risk, requiring little effort and drawing lots of attention from the right people.

As smear artists feed reporters "news," there's a disconcerting outgrowth of the dynamic: reporters reporting on ourselves and on the reported. This "inside baseball" reporting began in opinion columns and blogs and now permeates nearly every corner of the news. We report on internal info fed to us by opposing interests to advance their agenda. We report on one another. We report on each other reporting on these interests. The resulting stories are aggregated, circulated, and regurgitated among the same relatively small circle of players. They're retweeted on Twitter, shared and liked on Facebook, and distributed on Google News.

They draw positive feedback from our managers, generate validation from peers, and capture the attention of important insiders. Instead of bringing meaningful news to viewers and readers, we copy, impress, or best one another with stories of interest to no one but each other.

During the 2016 presidential campaign, an acquaintance who's also a national news journalist calls me from the road.

"Whatever happened to journalism?" this reporter asks rhetorically. "Everyone's reporting meaningless inside bullshit. I overhear live shots on the campaign trail and the reporters are saying, 'My inside sources tell me . . . ' And they don't have inside sources. They're pretending they have some secret, inside track when it's someone from a campaign handing them information the campaign wants put out. And it's stuff the average Joe doesn't really even care about."

We're being led by the nose as we attempt to pull the audience in a given direction. We're giving a command performance while fooling ourselves into believing it was our idea. And we're leaving ordinary Americans out of the equation. On a Venn diagram, there would be three circles: The news media and insiders we report on would be two circles that wholly overlap. Regular people would be in a third circle far away that doesn't intersect the other two.

Consider the weirdly prominent national news coverage given to a smack down between two pro-Hillary super PACs during the 2016 campaign. The groups were competing for the same big liberal donors. The rivalry was of little interest to anyone except the political elite. Yet the "story" prompted dueling hatchet jobs feverishly covered by the national press as if it were a burning issue in the minds of millions.

In early February 2015, the whole super PAC feud comes to a head. Hillary ally David Brock quits in a tiff from the board of one of the pro-Hillary super PACs, Priorities USA Action, accusing colleagues of orchestrating a "political hit job" against him and the other super PAC, which he founded, American Bridge. Brock gets his side of the story published in *Politico. Politico* brags that it's obtained Brock's actual resignation letter! In it Brock claims Priorities USA has launched a "specious and malicious attack on the integrity" of his own organizations. "Frankly," Brock grouses, "this is the kind of dirty trick I've witnessed in the right-wing and would not tolerate then."

What an exclusive! What great reporting!

On a scale of one to ten, a neutral assessment would put the news-worthiness of all this at about zero. But each stakeholder in the story has his favorite go-to reporters. And so the drama is extensively covered by *Politico,* the *New York Times,* and the *Hill.* The media is being used. After all the dirty laundry is aired, the two super PACs quietly make their peace and return their joint focus to the business of smearing Hillary's opponents.

In 2016, many in the news media stop even trying to pretend to be fair or neutral. Smear artists constructing their own desired realities have the phone numbers of all the right reporters. One Republican operative describes his simple strategy for success. He doesn't work directly for the official GOP party but gets picked up for projects on behalf of conservative interests and candidates. He says it's easy to get sympathetic journalists from certain outlets to report what he wants.

"I have always made it my business to find out where reporters' sympathies lie and I pitch accordingly." As if it is an afterthought, he adds, "I'm not saying it's a nice, clean, happy business."

The Email Proof

Thanks to the persistent nature of email, we have documentary evidence of this ugly reality. Emails that expose the black market information trade. The transactional nature of relationships between newsmakers and the media. Every day, deals are being cut in secret. Backs are scratched. One hand washes another. It makes it easy for special interests to advance an agenda or accomplish a smear. The past nine years, there's been a breakneck acceleration in this disturbing trend. There have always been questionable dealings between some reporters and the interests they cover, both Democrat and Republican. But Barack Obama's presidency comes at a time when key factors conducive to transactional journalism converge in an explosive way. Obama is the first Democrat elected to the nation's highest office since the invention of Facebook and Twitter, the first since the Internet became firmly established as a means for journalists and their interests to frequently communicate in real time, and the first since the explosion in quasi-news outlets online, which are often used to plant and feed narratives. Many left-leaning reporters who predominate at major news outlets weren't interested in advancing the agenda of Obama's predecessor, George W. Bush. But they eagerly establish dubious relationships with Obama agencies and officials, including then–secretary of state Hillary Clinton.

Proof of these relationships is contained within several collections of internal emails. Some of them were released under Freedom of Information Act requests and lawsuits. Others were published by WikiLeaks in 2016. They reveal an unseemly coziness among prominent journalists and government officials. Once upon a time, reporters caught engaging in such behavior could expect to be ostracized or even banished from the field of journalism. Today these relationships draw little more than snickers and a silent sense of relief from colleagues. Relief because they're glad that *their* emails weren't exposed.

The emails offer us the chance to become voyeurs, peering in on private dealings between reporters and propagandists. A form of commerce never meant to be seen by outside eyes.

Emails dating back to Obama's first months in office unmask transactional journalism conducted by Washington reporter Marc Ambinder from the *Atlantic*. He's also written for *New York Times, New Yorker, Washington Post, Vice, Hotline,* ABC News, and CBS News. This particular transaction takes place on July 15, 2009, as Secretary of State Clinton is set to make a speech. Under normal circumstances, Clinton aide Philippe Reines might have to work pretty hard to convince reporters to cover the speech at all; it's not of much interest to average folks. But in today's dynamic, an advance copy of the Clinton speech will be heralded as a "great get," and Ambinder wants it. The question is, what's he willing to do to get it?

In an email exchange, Reines says there are certain "conditions" Ambinder must meet in order to get the text of the speech. Ambinder replies "ok." Reines then dictates his terms in a numbered list.

1) You in your own voice describe [Hillary's words] as "muscular"

2) You note that a look at the [audience] seating plan shows that all the

envoys—from Holbrooke to Mitchell to Ross—will be arrayed in front of her, which in your own clever way you can say [is] certainly not a coincidence and meant to convey something

3) You don't say you were blackmailed!

Ambinder responds, "got it."

It's a remarkable scenario. Reines is a Clinton aide who's paid by taxpayers yet functioning much like a private PR agent. It's the same at many federal agencies. Their press departments use their public positions to forward the agendas of their political bosses, all on our dime. In this instance, Ambinder poses as a journalist but agrees to serve the interests of the politician, all to get his hands on a speech that serves the interest of the politician.

Here's an excerpt from Ambinder's final article *(emphasis added):*

When you think of President Obama's foreign policy, think of Secretary of State Hillary Clinton. That's the message behind a muscular *speech that Clinton is set to deliver today to the Council on Foreign Relations. The staging gives a clue to its purpose:* seated in front of Clinton, subordinate to Clinton, in the first row, will be three potentially rival power centers: envoys Richard Holbrooke and George Mitchell, and National Security Council senior director Dennis Ross.

The article delivers everything Reines had demanded. Once these emails become public in February 2016, the *Atlantic* issues a statement that reads, "This is not typical, and it goes against our standards." For his part, Ambinder insists the emails don't capture the totality of his communication and aren't indicative of his normal reporting techniques. He explains, "The way Reines had described the [Clinton] speech, it *was* muscular. So I found the adjective appropriate. So: muscular was my word. The decision to characterize the envoys was mine. No one fed me anything. Period."

It must be coincidence, then, that other reporters thought up the exact same unusual adjective when describing the Clinton speech. Washington fixture Mike Allen, of *Politico* and formerly of the *New York Times* and *Time,* also calls the speech "muscular" and notes the seating arrangement as Reines had instructed Ambinder to do. Likewise, the headline at *New York* magazine uses the word *muscular,* and the article shows a cartoon of Clinton with bodybuilder arms. Happenstance? You decide. But when you notice the news media or pundits all seizing upon similar terminology, it's reasonable to suspect there's an orchestrated effort.

After the Clinton speech, it seems as if Ambinder becomes part of a veritable Clinton admiration society. On July 26, 2009, when the secretary of state appears on NBC's *Meet the Press,* Ambinder emails Reines adoringly, "she kicked A." In November 2010, after a Clinton press conference, Ambinder gushes in an email, "This is an awesome presser. She is PITCH f#$*& PERFECT on this stuff."

In other emails, Reines seems to convince ABC News reporter Dana Hughes to take a jab at her colleagues on Hillary's behalf. Reines asks Hughes to add a line to a story she'd published, to take "a small poke at 'BuzzFeed and others.'" He adds he would be "very appreciative" of the favor. Hughes complies with the request and adds to the article.

There's more secret collusion between news reporters and federal officials buried in emails between the CIA and Ken Dilanian, an AP reporter who had previously covered the spy agency for the *Los Angeles Times.* The emails from 2012 reveal a surprisingly "deferential" and "collaborative" relationship, according to the *Intercept,* which obtained the emails in 2014 in response to a Freedom of Information Act request. Dilanian's interactions with the CIA include him "explicitly promising positive news coverage and sometimes sending the press office entire story drafts for review prior to publication." This is a stark departure from normal ethical practices for journalists. *Can you imagine Bob Woodward or Carl Bernstein running their unpublished Watergate stories past the Nixon White House?*

"I'm working on a story about congressional oversight of drone strikes that can present a good opportunity for you guys," Dilanian writes to a CIA press official in April 2012, adding that the story will be "reassuring to the public." Later, Dilanian sends the CIA press office a draft of his story and invites them to weigh in.

"This is where we are headed," he writes, asking if they want "to push back on any of this."

Next, Dilanian emails a softer version of his story, according to the *Intercept,* and asks, "does this look better?"

The next month, he sends the CIA yet another story draft.

"Guys, I'm about to file this if anyone wants to weigh in," he writes.

And in May 2012, Dilanian again emails the CIA a story outline.

"This is what we are planning to report, and I want to make sure you wouldn't push back against any of it," he writes.

Dilanian later concedes to the *Intercept* that it was a mistake for him to send unpublished stories to the CIA. "I shouldn't have done it, and I wouldn't do it now," he says. "[But] it had no meaningful impact on the outcome of the stories. I probably should've been reading them the stuff instead of giving it to them."

In September 2012, there's a fascinating email exchange between reporters and Clinton aide Reines shortly after the Benghazi, Libya, terrorist attacks. CNN has just reported that it's found the diary of murdered U.S. ambassador Christopher Stevens in the burned-out rubble of the compound where he'd come under attack, and the diary chronicles his worries about lax State Department security. That contradicts the narratives Clinton and other Obama officials are spinning: they claim there was no way they could have predicted that Stevens and the other Americans in Benghazi would be at risk. Reines attempts to discourage other journalists from reporting on the Stevens diary by launching a kill-the-messenger campaign. He fires off an extraordinary email blast to more than one hundred reporters, accusing CNN of violating the privacy of Stevens's family by reporting on the diary contents.

There's record of only one reporter in the whole bunch pushing back: the late Michael Hastings of *Rolling Stone* and *BuzzFeed* (who died nine months later in a fiery, single-car crash). In an email to Reines, Hastings defends CNN's reporting and asks why the cable news network rather than the State Department recovered Stevens's diary from the U.S. compound. Hastings implies if U.S. officials were sloppy enough to overlook a diary, they might have also left behind other sensitive, valuable intelligence.

"Your statement [about] CNN sounded pretty defensive," Hastings writes to Reines. "[D]o you think it's the media's responsibility to help secure State Department's assets overseas after they've been attacked?"

Reines replies: "As far as the tone of my email [about CNN] I think you're misreading mine as much as I'm misreading yours as being needlessly antagonistic."

"No, you read my email correctly—I found your statement to CNN offensive," Hastings counters.

Hastings is an exception. Other emails to and from Reines indicate it was far more common for reporters to shower him with adulation and flattery. In May 2010, Rebecca Cooper, then host of a local Washington business news TV program, emails Reines, "I heart you."

In June 2010, Jeremy Peters of the *New York Times* is looking for dirt about *Politico*—and seems delighted when Reines comes up with a quote for him: "[*Politico* thinks if] a light bulb is out that's a story."

"That's brilliant," Peters raves. "You should totally let me use that on the record. . . . That's great. Anything else you can recall like that—their greatest hits of non-news—would be great."

The *Washington Post* also turns to Reines for ideas on how to smear *Politico*. The *Post*'s Anne Kornblut emails: "if you get bored in a meeting, want to send me some examples of politico's [*sic*] most flagrant stupidity or errors?" (Why the jihad against *Politico*? It's unclear.)

And under the heading of you-wouldn't-believe-it-if-you-didn't-read-it-yourself, other reporters send emails practically begging Reines to feed them propaganda. Massimo Calabresi, a Washington correspondent for *Time,* turns to Reines for help in producing a fawning "40-under-40 mini-profile" of Clinton confidant Jake Sullivan: "what makes him successful in general." (Sullivan is widely considered a potential pick for a top Clinton post if she makes it to the White House in 2016). Associated Press reporter Beth Fouhy implores Reines for story assistance. "I've been asked to do the Huma [Abedin] story. I really need your help," she pleads. CBS News submits a personal note telling Reines that the network is about to launch a series on people who have achieved "extraordinary success" and made a "significant contribution to society." The CBS reporter wants to include Hillary Clinton, of course.

Maybe you thought the mission of reporters was to seek out original stories of interest to viewers, not smear one other and spread propaganda for favored interests. You thought State Department aides like Reines, paid with your tax dollars, would be spending their time serving the public. Instead, the media is being used as a private news agency creating a product intended for an audience of press and government insiders.

In January 2013, *Politico*'s Mike Allen is back in the picture greasing the skids with Reines. Obama is about to be sworn in to a second term. Clinton is leaving the secretary of state job post-Benghazi and has presidential aspirations. It turns out Allen has his own aspirations. He wants Reines to arrange a high-profile interview with Clinton's daughter, Chelsea. To get it, Allen offers to sacrifice basic tenets of journalism. It doesn't sound like the first time he's dabbled in the black market information trade.

"This would be a way to send a message during inaugural week," Allen types in an email to Reines on January 10, trying to persuade him to make Chelsea available for an interview. "No one besides me would ask [Chelsea] a question, and you and I would agree on them precisely in advance."

Allen continues bargaining by offering up favorable conditions as he imagines how the Chelsea interview would play out.

"This would be a relaxed conversation, and our innovative format (like a speedy Playbook Breakfast) always gets heavy social-media pickup," Allen writes. "The interview would be 'no-surprises': I would work with you on topics, and would start with anything she wants to cover or make news on. Quicker than a network hit, and reaching an audience you care about with no risk."

I know what you're thinking. An interview with Chelsea Clinton doesn't sound like terribly riveting news. But today it's another "great get." Clinton surrogates and supporters would circulate the article to other reporters as if remarkable reportage has been committed. Those reporters would pull snippets and quotes to repeat in their publications and newscasts . . . an echo chamber conferring worth to an essentially worthless story. A few reporters in newsrooms around Washington and New York would state the obvious, that there are better, more important stories to devote ink to. But they're drowned out by oohs and ahs from managers who wonder aloud, *How does he get that kind of access?!* and demand to know, *How can we get it next time?* And each time these questions are asked, the value of transactional journalism rises. Next time even more reporters will compete for the government handout. Like frenetic traders on the New York Stock Exchange driving up the price of a catchpenny stock.

Back to Allen's email. It's an unmitigated ethics violation for a reporter to offer to agree on precise questions in advance, in conference with the interest to be interviewed. At least, it used to be. That's because it results in secretly pre-scripted events that require playacting by both parties.

I'll pretend to ask you a spontaneous question. You pretend you didn't know it was coming and present your rehearsed answer. I'll act surprised. Maybe I'll arch an eyebrow, cock my head ever so slightly, and sit up in my chair when you answer.

Despite Allen's alluring offer, he doesn't get the Chelsea interview. In 2015, the whole email exchange is obtained and publicized by the gossip website *Gawker,* which had sued the State Department to access its internal emails. *Gawker* sardonically comments: "[Chelsea] Clinton ultimately declined Allen's generous offer not to ask her any questions that she didn't already know about." It also notes that five weeks after Allen's unrequited pitch for a Chelsea interview, Allen cowrote a column complaining about President Obama's supposed preference for doing "softball interviews." You know, the kind he had surreptitiously offered to Chelsea.

Politico editor Susan Glasser responds publicly to the Allen email controversy by stating, "We didn't end up doing any interview with Chelsea Clinton and we have a clear editorial policy of not providing questions to our guests in advance." Allen himself replies separately in November 2015 with a brief item in *Politico* titled, "MY BAD!" In it he brushes off the gaffe as "clumsy"; as if he's been misunderstood.

"You may have missed a *Gawker* post last week that rightly took me to task for something clumsy I wrote in an email to Philippe Reines in 2013, seeking an interview with Chelsea Clinton at a POLITICO brunch. In the email, I said I'd agree to the questions in advance. I have never done that, and would never do that," Allen insists.

His explanation seems oblivious to the contradiction. Was he misleading Reines in the email, or is he misleading us now?

Allen continues.

"POLITICO has a policy against it, and it would make for a boring event. As you know from attending our events (or can tell by clicking on any of the videos on our website), they're spontaneous, conversational and news-driven. . . . A scripted back-and-forth would be a snore." He adds,

"We didn't do the interview with Chelsea Clinton, and would never clear our questions. But the email makes me cringe, because I should never have suggested we would. We retain full, unambiguous editorial control over our events and questioning."

That explanation makes me think of Orwellian "doublethink." From *1984*:

> *To know and not to know, to be conscious of complete truthfulness while telling carefully constructed lies . . . The power of holding two contradictory beliefs in one's mind simultaneously, and accepting both of them . . . To tell deliberate lies while genuinely believing in them, to forget any fact that has become inconvenient.*

There's further email evidence of the familiar relationship between Allen-the-*Politico*-reporter and Reines-the-Hillary-spokesman. Reines repeatedly makes suggestions for tidbits to publish in Allen's "Playbook" feature. Allen responds with "awesome" and "miss ya." Allen also includes Reines in a small email group asking them to "confidentially help suggest a name" for a new column about to launch. He later thanks the group. "Thank you for right track/wrong track. Genius! Stealing it and owe you," he writes. In another instance, Allen's Playbook publishes a news blurb favorable to Clinton that's been ghostwritten by Reines. In response to the emails revealing this fact, *Politico* defends printing the unattributed Reines material by saying the information was "worth flagging" for readers and was "condensed into [*Politico's*] signature, bite-sized format with a link to the outside source."

December 2013 emails later published by WikiLeaks provide evidence of another notable journalist making an advance editorial agreement with an interview subject. The *Wall Street Journal's* Peter Nicholas is trying to get an interview with former president Clinton. Clearance for the interview is going through the Obama White House, which apparently wants to be sure Clinton doesn't address any current controversies, whether it's Benghazi or the recent, embarrassingly botched launch of Obamacare. The *Journal's* Nicholas reportedly agrees to stay on topic if he lands the Clinton interview. Clinton spokesman Matt McKenna emails Obama press secretary Josh Earnest that "Peter" (Nicholas) has given "an assurance . . . he won't stray from questions" about the agreed-upon topic. It's widely considered improper for a reporter to agree in advance to limit questions because it opens the door for the press to be used as a propaganda tool to advance a narrative. When reporters strike bargains to avoid addressing obvious controversies, it artificially diminishes the controversies in the public domain.

Pulitzer Prize–winning journalist Jeff Gerth says transactional relationships such as these pose challenges to reporters like him who are engaged in straightforward news gathering. For example, when well-connected politicos catch wind of a potentially damaging article in the works, they simply call upon their close press relationships to undercut it.

"They preempt," Gerth tells me. "They go to a favorable outlet and get somebody to write something they want. That way, they've a) beaten you to the punch and b) framed it the way they want rather than by an objective journalist."

In November 2015, Gerth recalls obtaining a copy of a controversial, paid speech Hillary Clinton made to Wall Street interests, which her campaign was keeping secret. Prior to publishing a story in *ProPublica,* Gerth contacted Clinton's representatives to offer them a chance to respond. Gerth then mysteriously got scooped by left-wing apparatus *Vox,* which published an article praising the same controversial Hillary speech before Gerth could publish his. Was this mere coincidence or did Clinton reps spring into action to influence the message? Gerth blames Clinton strategists. "It's what they do," remarks Gerth.

Think about it. Party officials can count on certain reporters to "play ball." News reporters send yet-to-be-published work to party and government officials for input and approval. That makes some news organizations not terribly different from propaganda outlets. Remember, this is just a small slice of the picture revealed because of WikiLeaks and the Freedom of Information Act.

What is it we *don't* know?

By their own account, David Brock's super PACs are frighteningly effective at using news reporters as tools. Internal memos revealed by WikiLeaks in October 2016 describe the wild success American Bridge and Correct The Record supposedly met with in dictating news narratives and undermining the field of GOP presidential candidates.

According to the memos, American Bridge began plotting against Republicans one month after the 2014 midterm elections, releasing a "primer" to negatively "define the [Republican] field before the prospective candidates could define themselves for the electorate." American Bridge says it was able to undermine Jeb Bush and to market a negative media narrative on Wisconsin governor Scott Walker, leading to his failure as a presidential candidate: "We developed a powerful narrative of cronyism, outsourcing, and looking out for the interests of big business over middle class families, which undercut [Walker's] economic message." The pro-Hillary super PAC also took credit for "forcing the Kochs [conservative billionaire donors] . . . out of the shadows" and said that one of its reports against the Kochs resulted in "a high-profile CNN story."

For its part, Correct The Record offers incredible statistics proving its reach and influence. In the memos, it boasts of having conducted "over 900 on-the-record and off-the-record media interviews" and sending "80 sets of talking points, background materials and briefings on topical issues" to defend Clinton to "372 surrogates including influential and frequent pundits on broadcast and cable news." It sent "media advisories" and "talking points" to "960 members of the national media and 10,756 regional reporters in 28 states," and to "369 televisions producers and bookers." It placed 21 "strategic memos" with the media, "impacting the framework for dialogue about 2016, Clinton, and her competitors." Correct The Record said that its strategic memos "led to stories in a number of news outlets including *National Journal, Politico, USA Today,* MSNBC and *The Hill.*"

By now, if you don't think deals are being made all over Washington between journalists and special interests, to get clicks and win favor, to smear the right people and advance the right narratives, then you haven't been paying attention.

The Targets

James Tomsheck learned firsthand how the government can exploit cozy relationships with the press to help destroy a target. He became victim of a smear after blowing the whistle inside U.S. Customs and Border Protection (CBP)—an agency he insists is riddled with corruption. Tomsheck was an ethics watchdog at CBP with the title of Assistant Commissioner for Internal Affairs. He tells me his department's anticorruption work was extremely important. "I had been in law enforcement in three different agencies for forty years," he explains. "And at no point of it, thirty-one years of which was in federal law enforcement, had I ever encountered anything approximating the level of corruption, misconduct, and excessive use of force." He says his troubles began in 2009 when a man named David Aguilar became deputy commissioner of the agency.

At that time, "there was a concerted effort to obstruct the Office of Internal Affairs and restrict information that we were sharing with our colleagues and the FBI," Tomsheck tells me, "and to diminish the opportunities to work in a fully cooperative and collaborative way with other agencies."

Matters came to a head in the summer of 2010. Aguilar called Tomsheck and his deputy, James Wong, into a meeting and allegedly asked them to do something shocking.

"What we were told to do was 'redefine corruption' in a way that would reduce the actual number of corruption arrests" within CBP, Tomsheck says. Apparently Aguilar wanted the current number of corruption arrests inside the agency, which was on the north side of eighty, to look much smaller.

"Mr. Aguilar actually took a sheet of paper and wrote a number that was twenty-something," Tomsheck alleges. "He never actually turned it towards us, but wrote the number taking up a full eight-and-a-half-by-eleven sheet of paper, and kept tapping it with his pen as he was explaining how we would go about redefining corruption in a way to reduce the number of corruption arrests."

"How would one do that—redefine corruption?" I ask Tomsheck as he recounts his experiences.

"It couldn't be done," he answers, "and more importantly, we wouldn't consider doing it. Mr. Wong and I clearly understood that we were being given an order to cook the books. When we returned to our offices and looked at one another, we both had the same reaction, that we had been in a bad scene in a very bad movie."

(As I researched this account, Wong corroborated Tomsheck's story. Aguilar and the CBP declined comment.)

When Tomsheck refused to cooperate with the alleged request to redefine corruption, he says, the assassination of his character began. Among other pressures, he received a lowered job evaluation. Eventually he was reassigned out of Internal Affairs. And although he says he wasn't provided the rationale for the reassignment, within hours somebody had anonymously given the press an explanation designed to disparage him. It was a false narrative that he'd been removed for not being tough enough in cracking down on use of excessive force at CBP.

Tomsheck knew it was a smear.

"There were media reports, that surfaced hours after my assignment, that I had been removed because I had been insufficiently aggressive in dealing with excessive-use-of-force issues, and had failed to properly discipline Border Patrol agents," he tells me.

"What do *you* think is the reason you were removed?" I ask.

"I don't think there's any question the reason I was removed was because of the aggressive posture that I and my colleagues had taken with regard to corruption, misconduct, and aggressive use of force."

I ask who he thinks leaked the false story to the press about why he was reassigned. He says there's no doubt in his mind it involved high-level government officials. Tomsheck sued the government over his treatment and received a settlement.

As he recounts his experience, Tomsheck speaks to me in a measured tone, but I can sense the anger and frustration he's suffered. He took pride in his job as the ethics cop for Customs and Border Protection, and he was good at it. But those who wanted him out of the way won the day. And they managed to use the press to drag his name through the mud as they pushed him out the door. It's nearly impossible to fight the heft of the government complex and its media partners when they go after you. They can define who you are. They can destroy you.

John Dodson got the same message when he, too, became a government whistleblower in 2011.

"You're, in a sense, drowning where you can't seem to find the surface," Dodson tells me of the massive smear campaign he withstood. "It's not just drowning; you're trapped in this cube of water and you don't know which way is up, which way to get out."

Dodson, a special agent with the federal Bureau of Alcohol, Tobacco, Firearms and Explosives (ATF), blew the whistle on ATF's secret "Fast and Furious" gunwalking program under the Department of Justice (DOJ). Under Fast and Furious the government did the unthinkable: it allowed thousands of assault rifles and other weapons to be trafficked to Mexican drug cartels. Dodson was on the ATF team that was required to execute the case and watch idly as guns were "walked" across the southern border. He'd raised internal objections to the outrageous idea that federal agents like himself were forced to allow traffickers to transport guns to cartel thugs. But his objections just got him labeled as a troublemaker. When a Border Patrol agent named Brian Terry was murdered in Arizona near the border in late 2010 by illegal immigrants armed with some of the Fast and Furious–trafficked weapons, Dodson took steps to expose the government's ill-advised scheme. First, he quietly brought the facts to Senator Charles Grassley. Grassley asked the Justice Department about the allegations. DOJ responded in a letter dated February 4, 2011: it categorically denied Dodson's claims. In essence, the Justice Department was calling Dodson a liar.

"I was hugely taken aback by that," Dodson tells me today. "It was something I never conceived of happening, that DOJ would flat-out call me a liar in an official letter to Congress."

"I was prewarned," Dodson continues. He explains that a staffer in Senator Grassley's office had tried to explain what he'd be up against as a whistleblower against ATF and DOJ leaders. "But even though I was prewarned, I was really surprised when the government's smear of me first started with the February 4, 2011, letter."

As an investigative reporter for CBS News at the time, I connected with Dodson for an exclusive television news interview shortly after that letter was written. The resulting story on the *CBS Evening News* received international attention. It also spurred the government to launch coordinated efforts to publicly smear Dodson—and me, as the reporter pursuing the uncomfortable truth. And government operatives would ultimately use other journalists to accomplish the smears.

"[Then-acting] ATF director Kenneth Melson had a town hall meeting at Baltimore field division within days of the CBS interview," says Dodson. "And when he was asked about [the gunwalking] he simply told the entire Baltimore field division that I was a disgruntled employee, that I screwed up one case so badly that it couldn't get prosecuted." In reality, Melson was not only well aware of the illicit gunwalking; he'd also remotely monitored some of the questionable firearms trafficking activities through a live "pole cam" set up to feed video to his computer in Washington, D.C. Yet he was publicly denying any of it ever happened.

In my early days of reporting on the case, I meet Dodson at his Arizona home. "I want to show you something," he says as he leads me outside to his vehicle, parked on the dusty shoulder of the road in front of his house. He points to tracks indicating someone had been fiddling around with it during the night. There are telltale smudges in the dust on the exterior, indicating, he believes, someone had come to remove a hidden tracking device they'd placed earlier. "I know this," he says. "I do it for a living."

Later, when forensics experts identified unauthorized remote intrusions into my personal and CBS work computers, they were able to see that the intruders had viewed my Fast and Furious–related documents and photos. Someone had even planted classified documents on my CBS laptop. My mind flashes back to Dodson. He'd said the government was trying to frame him as if he'd released classified information. Was that related to the classified documents planted on my computer by unauthorized intruders?

At one point during the Fast and Furious scandal, someone inside the government trying to destroy Dodson leaked to the press a highly sensitive document about his undercover work at ATF—and the press published it. He says it put his life in danger. It was later revealed that the source of the improper leak was none other than Obama's U.S. attorney for Arizona, Dennis Burke, who oversaw ATF's Fast and Furious case. After Burke was exposed as the leaker of the confidential documents on Dodson, he was forced to resign.

Dodson says the Obama administration's effort to destroy him also included assigning private investigators to dig up dirt on him, attempting to frame him for supposedly revealing classified information, blowing his undercover work, and—he believes—reading his personal email and listening in on his phone calls. But one of the biggest smears against Dodson was what I and many others viewed as a hit piece in *Fortune* magazine written by Katherine Eban.

"My ex-wife called me in December [2011]," Dodson recalls. "She said that she had just been contacted by a reporter for *Fortune* magazine who wanted to ask her some questions about me and our divorce. My ex was terrified. She didn't know what to say and gave me the woman's information. I called her directly."

"What did Eban say when you called?" I ask.

"She said she thought I was a fascinating in-depth central character. I told her I thought it was piss-poor journalism for her to make her first call to my ex-wife. I demanded to know how she got [my ex-wife's] name and phone number and she wouldn't tell me.

"I know it was a smear," Dodson continues in his opinion. He tells me that Senator Grassley's office "had pretty much already established thoroughly that the *Fortune* article was a hit piece sanctioned by DOJ and ATF to smear me. That was the sole purpose."

Indeed, the *Fortune* article published in June 2012 incorrectly portrays him—the whistleblower—as the one who was running guns, motivated by anger and incompetence.

"The article was so bad that a joint effort between Senator Grassley and the House Oversight Committee took the time to go through and issue a congressional report rebutting [the *Fortune* story] line by line," says Dodson. "It was completely and utterly full of factual errors, not even in the realm of reason." The oversight committee demanded—but didn't receive—a retraction. The claims of Katherine Eban, the woman who wrote the *Fortune* article, were also rebutted by the findings of an investigation by the Department of Justice inspector general.

After the article and the other smears, Dodson had an uphill battle to rescue his reputation in the court of public opinion. Many in the news media continued to report incorrect talking points about Fast and Furious and Dodson—as provided by the Obama administration and its allies. Ul-

timately Dodson sued *Fortune,* alleging "the article is fictitious in the sense
that it contains facts that Defendant knew to be false prior to publication"
and that Eban "falsely reported that [he] initiated gun walking activity
based on a grudge he had with his superior." *Fortune* eventually settled
Dodson's case on confidential terms and issued a "clarification" stating:
*"The article did not intend to suggest that John Dodson or any other ATF
agent advocated a policy of 'walking guns,' and any inference to the contrary
is incorrect."*

For Dodson, the professional and personal toll of his whistleblowing
and the subsequent smears was immeasurable. On any given day, he didn't
know if he would be followed, fired, or arrested. "The DOJ tried to indict
me at one point [on false charges]," he says.

As the target of a smear, "you want to set the record straight," Dodson tells me. But nobody wants to believe. "Part of it pissed me off. How
dare they call me a liar? How dare they say this when I know I'm right,
telling the truth and can freaking prove it. You go from scared to angry
back and forth."

I ask Dodson how he managed to persevere. He pauses to reflect. He's
been asked nearly every question on the planet about his tribulations of
the past couple of years. But not this one.

"I look back on it now and wonder, How did I manage to get through
it? How did I manage to keep my job and freedom?" he says. "I don't
know, other than blind luck. I'd like to say that right is right and the truth
always comes out, and that when you're telling the truth you don't have to
worry. But you do have to worry because perception is reality and all these
elements, much greater elements than me, are treading in some very dark
deep waters and I was the most expendable person in there.

"It was a bad place to be. And I've been there on the threshold of losing
everything and smeared and completely cast out. And I know the fear and
stress and panic. I was so stressed out I literally grew a hump from just
the knotted-up muscle tissue on my left shoulder. I'm better mentally and
emotionally than before I blew the whistle, but professionally, my career
is in the toilet. I'm a lot better today but I'm disenfranchised about the
government and our system."

I've reported on many whistleblowers who have become targets. But

I've also found myself a target in the transactional journalism game on more than one occasion. Nearly four years after I first filed a Freedom of Information Act request with the Department of Justice (a response was due in thirty days under the law), I finally got a partial reply on February 3, 2017. The documents provided included emails between DOJ and reporters *about* me. In one of them, *Politico*'s Mike Allen—the reporter who'd been so cozy with the Clinton camp in other emails—again appears to act more as a politico disguised as a reporter than as a journalist. The email was dated October 4, 2011. At the time, I'd been breaking news on Fast and Furious. In a routine interview I gave to radio host Laura Ingraham to promote my CBS News stories, Ingraham asked me about the Obama administration's reaction to my hard-hitting reports. As it happens, I'd just been on the receiving end of a rant by White House spinner Eric Schultz, and yelling by Justice Department PR flack Tracy Schmaler.

"[Schmaler] was just yelling at me" in response to my reporting, I told Ingraham. "The guy from the White House on Friday night [Schultz] literally screamed and cussed at me."

"Who was the person at Justice screaming?" asked Ingraham.

"The person screaming was Tracy Schmaler; she was yelling not screaming. And the person who screamed at me was Eric Schultz at the White House," I said.

Those excerpts from Ingraham's radio show were quickly circulated to journalists by Ingraham's executive producer, Matt Wolking.

"Judging from the White House's reaction to [Sharyl Attkisson's] investigation, it seems officials there know they are in deep, hot water," remarks Wolking to reporters in emails containing a transcript and a link to Ingraham's program.

When the email arrives in Mike Allen's in-box at *Politico,* he doesn't even wait fifteen full minutes before forwarding it to Justice Department flack Schmaler with a comment: "Just FYI . . . Never heard of a reporter doing this. . . ." He's apparently referring to me publicly talking about how Obama officials have yelled and screamed at me about my stories. To a reporter like Allen, I'm talking out of school. These sort of ugly dealings are normally keep secret, at least by journalists who want to get—or stay—on the good side of newsmakers. Whether Allen is returning a favor or trying to curry favor with DOJ, his email to Schmaler shows he clearly has an open line of communication with a government PR officer that, in my opinion, extends beyond a news-gathering function.

I have another brush with transactional journalism after the February 2016 release of controversial emails between journalists and Clinton aide Reines. *Washington Post* gossip blogger Erik Wemple writes an article criticizing the smarmy press dealings exposed in the emails. "Corrupt journalism doesn't pay. Nor does abetting it," his headline chides.

But he's about to become embroiled in the very controversy he criticizes. After reading Wemple's blog, Clinton aide Reines fires back in a letter to Wemple. Reines makes it clear that his emails with reporters are being released bit by bit under a Freedom of Information Act lawsuit filed by *Gawker*. Soon, Reines points out, more emails will be released. Reines notes that some of those emails will be from Wemple himself—and could prove embarrassing. He accuses Wemple of lobbing stones at a glass house.

"[Y]ou can't throw a dart at the White House Correspondents Dinner without hitting someone who has been involved in quote approval, ground rule negotiation, source obfuscation—and every other routine thing that goes on every day, on both sides of the aisle, on both sides of the equation," Reines tells Wemple in the email. "And with all due respect, that includes you." (As an act of self-flagellation, Wemple publishes the entire Reines email in his blog, apparently so that Reines can't hold it privately over his head.)

"And right or wrong, this is the norm," Reines continues. "It's the norm in every newsroom—including your own—and every communications shop in the city. So anyone shocked by the gambling going on in the casino is being disingenuous at best. *And they are setting themselves up for a fall when their email is outed*" (emphasis added).

That last sentence strikes an intentionally ominous note and is aimed squarely at Wemple. *What sorts of embarrassing email exchanges had Wemple had with Reines?* Faced with this not-so-veiled threat, Wemple preempts the damage by confessing, in his own *Post* blog, to an ethically questionable exchange he had with Reines in 2013 about—of all things— *me*. Wemple admits he'd approached Reines to ask for "a wide-ranging discussion about then–CBS News correspondent Sharyl Attkisson." He says Reines asked what the ground rules would be for the talk. Wemple acknowledges he did the very thing he'd just criticized other reporters for doing: he replied, "You stipulate!" inviting Reines to call the shots on the "discussion."

So Wemple had turned to Reines, a Clinton surrogate, in seeking smear material to use against me. Why? It's not hard to guess. Wemple often serves Media Matters' interests, and at the time, Media Matters was working hard to controversialize my Emmy Award–nominated reports, which were viewed as damaging to Hillary Clinton and President Obama. Media Matters was also in the process of spinning information over the recently announced intrusions of my computers. These intrusions formed the basis of my ongoing lawsuit against the federal government alleging that unknown federal agents conspired in an extensive clandestine surveillance of me using tradecraft and tactics unearthed through confidential sources and multiple forensics examinations.

As CBS News had reported on August 7, 2013:

> [C]orrespondent Sharyl Attkisson's computer was hacked by "an unauthorized, external, unknown party on multiple occasions," confirming Attkisson's previous revelation of the hacking. CBS News spokeswoman Sonya McNair said that a cybersecurity firm hired by CBS News "has determined through forensic analysis" that "Attkisson's computer was accessed by an unauthorized, external, unknown party on multiple occasions in late 2012. Evidence suggests this party performed all access remotely using Attkisson's accounts. . . . CBS News is taking steps to identify the responsible party and their method of access."

Over the next three years, Media Matters and other propagandists will work together to advance false narratives implying the computer intrusions were the stuff of fantasy. A quintessential smear operation designed to silence reporting contrary to their interests. Unfortunately for them, they are fighting facts, forensic evidence—and a target who understands the smear.

And now, after all this, you have a keen understanding of the environment leading up to the 2016 campaign. Both sides are determined to use every available PR, propaganda, and media tool to their advantage. Everything is on the table. Extraordinary sums will be expended. Untold thousands of people will be part of the effort. The winner could be the side that has the best connections to journalists, is most effective in advancing its narrative in the media, can come up with the most damaging smears, controls the most money to buy oppo research and negative ads, has the deepest organization to command astroturf assets, and has the best vision for how to deploy them.

At least that's how it was supposed to work.

Chapter Seven

||||||||||||||||||||||||||

The Anti-Smear Candidate
(and the Disloyal Opposition)

Donald J. Trump launches into the presidential race on June 16, 2015, nearly naked, with no giant super PAC or other opposition research smear group to get his back. In fact, the very GOP interests that would normally kick in to protect their candidate and attack the enemy take a hands-off approach, turning their backs on the unconventional Trump. Even the conservative activist Koch brothers, who normally dump millions into the presidential mix to boost the Republican selection, sit this one out.

Trump's on his own.

Fighting him are some of the most skilled smear artists known to the netherworld. They get busy the moment he announces. They dump tens of millions of dollars into relentless assaults that get amplified on the news and the Internet. Nobody in modern politics takes more arrows than Trump. He's not only getting hammered by Democrats. He's also taking it on the chin from well-financed Republicans. All that money buys lots of oppo research. Negative ads. Media.

In many ways, this entire campaign season, from the primaries through the general election, becomes the epitome of the smear. The exclamation point on an evolution that's been taking shape for years. It's what all the machinery—carefully assembled and refined over the last thirty years—has been building toward. Every single tactic is deployed—from astroturf, online and in person, to transactional journalism across the media spectrum. Every single group comes suited up to play hardball: think tanks, super PACs, PR firms, LLCs, and operatives who have been smearing for decades on both sides of the aisle—David Brock and Rick Berman, to name a couple. All of them, left and right, have one man in their crosshairs: Donald Trump. Trump is hit with smear after smear—some of them based on truth and some not. Inside of just a few weeks, he's called a mobster, illegal-immigrant hirer, foreigner hater, non-Christian, tax evader, and member of the KKK.

And that's before the campaign really gets ugly.

Fellow Republicans like Mitt Romney join in the fun of disparaging Trump. Romney publicly speculates that there's a "bombshell" hiding inside Trump's withheld tax records. Perhaps, Romney hypothesizes in an interview, Trump isn't as wealthy as he brags he is. Maybe he hasn't donated money to veterans' charities, as he's claimed. Unsubstantiated conjecture that used to be relegated to rumor pages today passes for front-page news.

Yet Trump refuses the demands to apologize, resists the calls to drop out of the race, and defies the pleas to soften his tactics. When his earliest and most ferocious attacks come from the supposedly neutral news, his defense mechanism is to become his own one-stop smear shop. Reporters take heavy casualties, much to the delight of the general public. At every packed rally, Trump gestures with sarcasm and contempt toward the news cameras in the back of the room.

"They won't turn the cameras and show how big the crowd is," he taunts. "The media is *so* dishonest. *So* dishonest!" The audience boos with delight.

By the end of the campaign, Trump rallies regularly break into thousands chanting *"CNN sucks! CNN sucks!"*

The news media proves to be Trump's most powerful, determined, passionate, and pervasive enemy. What they fail to realize is that their actions will make The Donald the B'rer Rabbit of politics, begging not to be thrown in the briar patch when it's really where he wishes to be. Trump scolds the press and protests its treatment of him—but masterfully turns it into a campaign platform, tapping into widespread contempt for the media. It becomes an advantage. A badge of honor. Instead of shrinking reflexively from the perpetual attacks, Trump relishes them, like a hound dog slopping in the mud.

Trump-the-successful-businessman combats his political opponents with a stroke of genius: he employs classic brand strategy to tarnish them with catchy nicknames. "Lyin' Ted," "Little Marco," "Crazy Bernie," "Low-Energy Jeb." He manages to pick them off one by one until it's just down to him and "Crooked Hillary."

Doing his dirty work directly, and owning it, makes Trump a wild card the likes of which establishment smear groups have never seen. The anti-smear candidate.

Donald Trump may be kryptonite to the smear.

The Cash

While Trump begins with limited financial support from the establishment, his opponents are awash in funds. And many of his fiercest adversaries are fellow Republicans. I comb through records and discover a daunting list of so-called outside groups spending incredible amounts of cash to destroy Trump. Much of the money buys opposition research and negative ads.

The top spender on behalf of Hillary Clinton is Priorities USA Action, the pro-Clinton super PAC where David Brock sits on the board. Priorities USA Action first started up in 2011 to support President Obama's re-election campaign. It's reinvented to serve Clinton's interests in 2016. And there's big money from billionaire George Soros in Priorities USA: $10.5 million for the 2016 cycle. Other megadonors to the super PAC include hedge fund mogul Donald Sussman, who kicks in $20 million (almost half in the final months of the campaign); the venture capitalist Pritzker family, which provides more than $14 million; the hedge fund Saban family, which gives $9 million; and the family of hedge fund billionaire James Simons, which chucks in $10 million.

Here's a look at the biggest outside money groups fighting Trump, both liberal and conservative, and the totals they spent:

Biggest Anti-Trump Outside Group Spending

Priorities USA Action	$126 million
Our Principles PAC	$19 million
NextGen California Action Committee	$13 million
Leading Illinois for Tomorrow	$9.9 million
United We Can	$8 million
Club for Growth Action	$7 million
American Future Fund	$6.7 million
Democratic Congressional Campaign Committee	$6.6 million
Women Vote!	$5.9 million
Conservative Solutions PAC	$4.7 million
NextGen Climate Action	$4.6 million
For Our Future	$3 million
House Majority PAC	$2.8 million
Club for Growth	$2.7 million
iAmerica Action	$2.7 million
Planned Parenthood Votes	$2.6 million
League of Conservation Voters	$2.1 million
Senate Majority PAC	$1.8 million
Stand for Truth	$1.8 million
Black PAC	$1.7 million
Fifty-Second Street Fund	$1.6 million
El Super PAC Voto Latino	$1.6 million
Service Employees International Union	$1 million

Source: Center for Responsive Politics

Only at the eleventh hour, when Republicans finally accept the fact that he's all they've got, does Trump begin to receive the sort of financial support other top candidates had enjoyed. In June 2016, a super PAC called Get Our Jobs Back announces an in "in-kind" donation of services worth $50 million. Get Our Jobs Back was started by former *New York Post* owner Steven Hoffenberg, who'd spent time in federal prison for a

Ponzi scheme. Another super PAC, Future 45, kicks in $23.9 million for Trump, almost all of it in a single month, from September 28 to October 28. Twenty million of that total comes from billionaire Vegas casino magnate Sheldon Adelson and his wife.

Biggest Pro-Trump Outside Group Spending

Get Our Jobs Back	$50 million
Great America PAC	$28.6 million
Future45	$23.9 million
Rebuilding America Now	$22.6 million
Make America Number One	$20 million
NRA Institute for Legislative Action	$8.7 million
Republican National Committee	$7.8 million
45 Committee	$3.1 million

Source: Center for Responsive Politics

By the time Election Day rolls around, pro-Clinton super PACs and outside groups report drawing nearly $206 million, compared to around $164 million raised by pro-Trump groups. Add in the funds each campaign raised directly and Clinton ends up with a total of $769 million; Trump has less than half—about $408 million, and that's including at least $66 million that he personally kicked in.

Now on to the one billion dollar race.

Shaping the Clinton Narrative

Before Clinton or Trump officially announces their candidacy, David Brock and his groups are working to shape the Clinton narrative. But there's evidence Brock is running afoul of his own party behind the scenes. After all, he has long stirred suspicion among fellow liberals who find it impossible to fully trust a man who shifted allegiances so dramatically in the past. Some of the rifts are exposed when WikiLeaks publishes hacked emails from accounts belonging to the Democratic National Committee (DNC) and Clinton campaign chair John Podesta. They provide a treasure trove of insight into the surreptitious manipulation of the public (and a willing press) by political operatives and the infighting.

In a February 2015 email, president of the pro-Clinton Center for American Progress, Neera Tanden, emails Podesta discussing Brock and his rainmaker Mary Pat Bonner. "Brock/Bonner are a nightmare," declares Tanden. She seems to think Brock was a source for a *Washington Post* article that reported big liberal donors are holding off on contributing to Hillary's biggest super PAC. "Sometimes HRC/WJC have the worst judgement," Tanden continues, apparently referring to Hillary and Bill Clinton placing their trust in Brock. "I'll be telling mary pat [Bonner] later this week that we aren't renewing her contract—wish me luck!"

A month later, Tanden again emails Podesta about Brock: "I hope Hillary truly understands now how batshit crazy David Brock is." (Brock was publicly feuding in the press with rival Hillary super PAC Priorities USA Action, where he sits on the board.) Around the same time, a *New York Times* reporter emails Podesta: "[I]s this blow up over [Brock's] Media Matters going to make it harder for the Clinton folks to bring in and use effectively the best of the Obama alums?"

"No," replies Podesta, "mostly about Brock's eccentricities shall we say."

In another email exchange, Democrat Andy Spahn, a major Hillary fundraiser and longtime adviser to movie mogul Jeffrey Katzenberg, criticizes the tone of a Brock super PAC ad. Spahn emails Clinton advisers Podesta and Huma Abedin, "Ad is offensive. And ineffective. You should denounce it."

While Hillary operatives and supporters are feuding internally, the Clinton campaign is busy strengthening its transactional relationships with journalists to put out a positive message. In a January 2015 strategic memo about "shaping a public narrative," Clinton officials describe *Politico* reporter Maggie Haberman as an ideal "friendly journalist," willing to generate positive press for the campaign. Under the title "Placing a Story" the memo states:

> *We feel that it's important to go with what is safe and what has worked in the past. We have has* [sic] *a very good relationship with Maggie Haberman of Politico over the last year. We have had her tee up stories*

for us before and have never been disappointed. While we should have
a larger conversation in the near future about a broader strategy for
reengaging the beat press that covers HRC, for this we think we can
achieve our objective and do the most shaping by going to Maggie.

It almost makes it sound as though Haberman is on the payroll of the
Clinton campaign. Interestingly, when the emails are publicized, Snopes
steps up with a questionable "fact-check" to defend Haberman's alleged
collusion with the Clinton camp.

"The fact that some Clinton campaign staffers perceived they had a
good working relationship with a particular political reporter is also not
proof in and of itself of any wrongdoing on the reporter's part," concludes
Snopes's Bethania Palma. But Palma didn't include any response from
Haberman to explain the emails, which would be a normal part of any legitimate fact-check. Instead Palma treats Haberman as an aggrieved party
and implies her critics are the ones who owe answers. Specifically, the
"fact-check" takes on Paul Joseph Watson, of the conspiracy website Infowars, who had accused Haberman of bias based on the emails. "Watson
has not responded to our request for comment regarding his claim," writes
Palma accusingly. When a reporter goes after the person raising questions
to the exclusion of the person accused of wrongdoing, it's reasonable to
suspect there's an astroturf effort under way to shape the narrative.

It turns out that before the Clinton campaign can execute its strat-
egy to place a positive story at *Politico* with Haberman, as outlined in the
January 2015 internal campaign memo, Haberman gets hired away by the
New York Times. No matter. There's another Clinton friendly at *Politico,*
Mike Allen (the reporter who had offered the "no surprises" Chelsea Clin-
ton interview back in 2009), who writes an article that seems to serve the
Clinton campaign's goals. The campaign memo had stated that it wanted
to make the point that Hillary plans to take a "big-tent" approach. As it
happens, the headline of Allen's article on January 26, 2016, reads, "Inside
Hillary Clinton's 2016 Plan: New Campaign Takes Shape, with 'Big-Tent
Mentality.'"

Clinton may want to distribute her "big tent" message, but the Clinton
machine is forced to devote significant work behind the scenes managing

her unfolding email scandal. At the time, voters are just learning that, as secretary of state, Clinton had failed to maintain a public record of her government emails, as required under public records law. Nobody yet knows that she mishandled significant amounts of classified information on her private servers. That comes later. But Americans are finding out Clinton's secret system meant her emails weren't properly searched under Freedom of Information Act requests made by the media and the public over the years. Her campaign devises a scheme to deflect attention; to turn the tables on her Republican accusers. It's a media strategy to get the public to buy in to the notion that it's hypocritical for GOP lawmakers to criticize Clinton for her public records shortfalls, because *their* congressional emails aren't covered under the Freedom of Information Act.

Accuse someone else.

Clinton aide Philippe Reines comes up with the idea to make the point and get the news to cover it by submitting Freedom of Information Act (FOIA) requests to a number of Republican members of Congress, particularly those who are on the Clinton email investigative trail, like Trey Gowdy, Darrell Issa, Jason Chaffetz, and Lindsey Graham. Since Congress is exempt from FOIA, it's assumed the members won't turn over their emails. The Clinton campaign will then peddle the "story" of their hypocrisy to the press. Reines speculates the news would get more favorable media coverage if the FOIA requests came from someone outside the Clinton camp, according to internal emails later published by WikiLeaks. So he appeals to defense attorney and former Democrat counsel Abbe Lowell.

"Here is what we are thinking and hoping you can help us with: this kerfuffle with the Secretary's email is obviously one we are trying very hard to work through and to explain to people," Reines emails Lowell on March 5, 2015. "Obviously, the committee investigating the Benghazi attacks have latched on to this, as well as others in and out of Congress who claim this subverted several processes, including FOIA. We do not agree with that, but in the course of this we've discussed an ironic hypocrisy that we believe the public would benefit in knowing. . . . Obviously, those [lack of FOIA] responses [from Congress] would be very compelling to the news media."

It's unclear whether Lowell actually submitted the FOIA requests for documents from Republican members of Congress. But eight days after Reines came up with the idea, the Associated Press happens to publish a helpful article titled "Congress Doesn't Have Rules for Saving Emails: While Congress demands Hillary Rodham Clinton emails, it exempts itself from open records requirements." AP reporter Erica Werner writes, "the same House Republicans who are subpoenaing Clinton's emails as part of their inquiry into the Benghazi, Libya, attacks are not required to retain emails of their own for future inspection by anyone." She specifically refers to Clinton archnemesis Congressman Gowdy. *U.S. News & World Report* and other national media outlets pick up the AP article. Reines couldn't have hoped for more favorable spin if he'd written it himself!

Smear Redux

About this time, there's a revival of the smear against longtime Clinton foe Jeff Gerth. He's the Pulitzer Prize–winning journalist who wrote the groundbreaking Whitewater article about the Clintons in the *New York Times* in 1992, and coauthored *Her Way: The Hopes and Ambitions of Hillary Rodham* in 2007. In the Clinton crosshairs for twenty-three years, he's writing for the nonprofit *ProPublica* as Hillary's latest run for president gets under way. The Clintons can't afford to have a credible journalist digging up old ghosts or unearthing new scandals. The go-to strategy is the same as before: conjure up controversy over Gerth's decades-old *New York Times* article.

On March 3, 2015, liberal columnist Michael Tomasky publishes a story in the *Daily Beast* that falsely claims "important parts" of Gerth's 1992 article have been "debunked" and "were never independently confirmed." A few days later, Tomasky furthers the narrative on cable TV news. In an appearance on Fox, he reiterates his view that Gerth's article "didn't really hold up." Gerth is taken aback.

Often, journalists choose to ignore smears made against them, even when they include false and arguably libelous information. Engaging those who aren't seeking truth simply tends to feed the monster. But on this particular occasion, Gerth decides to get in the game.

"Tomasky wrote the whole article without speaking to me," Gerth tells me. "Nor did anyone from the *Daily Beast*." His pushback includes hiring an attorney to contact the *Daily Beast* and ask a few simple questions. *Which parts of Gerth's article, specifically, had supposedly been debunked or proven incorrect? Why hadn't Tomasky followed basic tenets of journalism and reached out to Gerth prior to publication of the article?*

Eventually the *Daily Beast* modifies Tomasky's article, taking into account some of the concerns expressed by Gerth and his lawyer.

You might say Tomasky had been "debunked" and "discredited."

But victories in the smear universe can be fleeting. The machine that churns out the dirt is experienced, practiced, and vast. Take a look at Gerth's biography on Wikipedia today. Considering that he's won the biggest recognition in journalism on the planet, one might think that would be the headline: his Pulitzer Prize. But as of this writing, the top line of Gerth's Wikipedia biography—edited by anonymous interests, of course—states simply that he's written lengthy, probing stories "that drew both praise and criticism." It adds that he "came under fire for stories about the Whitewater controversy." Of course, he only came under fire from the interests of the alleged wrongdoers. But in the controlled worlds of Wikipedia and the smear, that passes for truth.

I thought it would be interesting to take a peek at Tomasky's Wikipedia bio for comparison. Funny, but it doesn't mention *his* controversies in the first sentence. Nothing about having made unfounded accusations, violated tenets of journalism, or revised his *Daily Beast* article after it was challenged by Gerth. While I was at it, I checked out Brock's Wikipedia bio, too. By any neutral measure, he's one of the most controversial and discredited figures in the smear game. Yet the opening line of his bio makes no mention of that. He's described innocuously as "one of the most influential operatives in the Democratic party." Dishonest smear artists manage to maintain flattering Wikipedia descriptions, while the targets of smears are tagged with the moniker "controversial."

Most victims hit by a professionally executed smear end up retreating into the dark recesses of society, hoping it just goes away. They give up on trying to set the record straight, clear their name, or live the life they used to. Gerth is one who managed to come out on top after all these years. I recently asked how he did it. He says it comes down to learning to think like they do.

"It's like the game of Go," Gerth postulates. Go is an ancient Chinese strategy game that's more complex than chess, with more tactical possibilities than the total number of atoms in the visible universe—or so it's said. "That's what it's like. You have to plot an infinite number of different permeations and combinations for what they are going to do."

Gerth says the scrutiny he's faced as forces have tried to discredit him makes him go the extra mile to make sure every fact he writes is beyond unimpeachable. When he coauthored a book on the Clintons' Whitewater scandal, it included nearly two thousand footnotes. Though Clinton interests disparaged the book, Gerth says, the facts proved impeccable. "Nobody ever asked for a correction from our publisher." Gerth adds that when he writes an article or book, he goes out of his way to also present the smear artist's version of events—what they're going to say about the story. "If you don't tell the reader that version of events, then when your story comes out, [the smear artists] put out information to make readers feel like you didn't tell them the full story. It's like being a defense attorney in a trial. If you don't address the arguments made by the other side, you lose credibility. You have to present fairly and prominently what their responses are, even if they won't [personally] give them."

Gerth says another strategy that character assassins use against journalists is to go to the sources in a story and try to get them to change their account—or find someone else to rebut them. Therefore, he says he makes sure his sources are on the record as much as possible, and that he takes immaculate story notes. "I'm seventy-one years old and . . . like three-dimensional chess or Go, when you deal with these people, I guess it keeps your brain sharp."

Did the decades-long smear of his work take a toll on his reputation?

"I think there are people out there who say, 'He's a reporter who wrote that Whitewater hoax story,' or something," says Gerth. "I can't say it bothers me. . . . I actually relish dealing with all these adversities. I'm still standing.

"I kinda like it," Gerth concludes. "Because I like the combat. I like a challenge."

Meantime, the Clintons have other fish to fry besides Jeff Gerth.

The Collusion

When it comes to placing narratives in the news, leaked Clinton campaign emails reveal that the practice of negotiating exclusives, timing, and percentages has become quite the trend. One example is found in March 2015, when Clinton is under fire for the discovery that she used private servers for classified government business as secretary of state, and that she destroyed thousands of emails that had been subpoenaed. Clinton aide Cheryl Mills emails colleagues the following optional scenarios to use the media to spin Hillary's email controversy:

Option A:
6:00 pm Monday: Publication of embargoed AP story on deletion (includes HRC statement and Q&A)
6:05 pm Monday: Release statement and Q&A
7:30 pm Monday: HRC makes statement on use of personal email and deletion at Gracie Mansion and (Does/Doesn't) take questions.

Option B:
1:30 pm Tuesday: HRC speech at UN
3:00 pm Tuesday: One-on-one sit down with TV. Pre-negotiate 50% of interview on emails, 50% of interview on Foundation/HRC record on women
Determine time to release statement and Q&A depending on air time of story
OR
3:00 pm Tuesday: Publication of embargoed AP story on deletion (includes HRC statement and Q&A)
3:05 pm Tuesday: Release statement and Q&A
4:00 pm Tuesday: Press conference in a private room at the UN

It's startling to read in black and white how confident the Clinton campaign seemed that it could puppeteer a range of favorable scenarios with news organizations, down to the percentage of an interview that should be devoted to positive questions versus the controversy at hand.

Also in March 2015, emails indicate the State Department and White House somehow made arrangements to shield Secretary of State John Kerry from questions about Hillary's emails in an appearance on CBS News' *Face the Nation*.

"Think we can get [the interview with Kerry by CBS] done so he is not asked about email," writes Obama aide Jennifer Palmieri to State Department spokesman Jen Psaki. Indeed, despite the fact that Kerry's appearance on *Face the Nation* happened two days after Clinton held her first press conference on the emails, CBS didn't ask a single question about the controversy! That's noteworthy since the first question most any neutral journalist would want to ask Kerry (as current secretary of state) would be about the email developments. However, when the email is exposed CBS News insists there was no agreement to limit questions.

With transactional journalism the order of the day, reporters willingly place themselves in the ridiculous position of clawing and competing to get invited into the inner circle so they can receive nothing more than planted political narratives. Emails show Eleanor Clift of the *Daily Beast* appears to feel left out when she discovers she's not invited to a private dinner for reporters given by Clinton campaign chair Podesta.

On April 10, 2015, Clift emails Podesta, "John, I completely understand why dinner at your home did not include someone like me, who's a known quantity to Clinton campaign veterans. But I wanted to make an appeal for an early opportunity to get myself and the Daily Beast Political editor, Jackie Kucinich, on your radar so I/we can write and report knowledgeably. There's a long campaign ahead, and I'd like to establish a line of communications. Is there an assistant I should go through? I look forward to working with you (and maybe getting some of that pasta and walnut sauce dish!!) All best, Eleanor."

Two days later, Clinton officially announces her candidacy amid her campaign's fresh panic over the impending release of the Peter Schweizer book *Clinton Cash: The Untold Story of How and Why Foreign Govern-*

ments and Businesses Helped Make Bill and Hillary Rich. The *New York Times* has exclusively reported some of Schweizer's advance material, and in emails revealed by WikiLeaks, *Hill* columnist Brent Budowsky appears to be looking out for the Clinton campaign. Budowsky emails in what can be viewed as a somewhat accusatory tone, asking the *Times* if it had a quid pro quo agreement with the *Clinton Cash* author.

"Exactly what is this exclusive agreement [between the *Times* and the *Clinton Cash* author]?" Budowsky asks the *Times.* The *Times* replies that it made no payment for the book material. Less than nineteen minutes later, Budowsky forwards his *Times* email exchange to Hillary campaign chair Podesta, as if a loyal soldier reporting back to the general.

Clinton adviser Jim Margolis goes on to email colleagues that it would be "good to get a copy" of *Clinton Cash* prior to its publication. (He's not talking about buying it on Amazon.com.) Podesta replies that obtaining a bootleg copy of *Clinton Cash* is a job for you-know-who: "Feels like what [David] Brock is good at."

And before long, Brock's Media Matters has conjured up an encyclopedic smear of Schweizer, urging the media to be "cautious" about his book because the author "has a disreputable history of reporting marked by errors and retractions, with numerous reporters excoriating him for facts that 'do not check out,' sources that 'do not exist,' and a basic failure to practice 'Journalism 101.'" Other internal campaign emails reveal the pro-Hillary camp constructing tweets to spread the smear, including: "If you can't keep track of Schweizer's fabrications, distortions in 'Clinton Cash' @MediaMatters can help." The tweet includes a link to a Media Matters blog attacking Schweizer.

More emails lay out the raw nature of closed-door negotiations with journalists during the ongoing frenzy over *Clinton Cash.* On May 2, 2015, the Clinton camp is furious that NBC has supposedly violated an agreement that dictated percentages regarding how the network's final story was supposed to have been written, in exchange for NBC being granted an interview with former president Clinton.

"Going in, NBC agreed to do 70 percent of the piece on work of the [Clinton] Foundation and 30 percent about the book," the Clinton campaign's Palmieri writes to other staff.

"Cynthia McFadden was the interviewer and didn't ask one question about work of the Foundation. Not one," Palmieri complains. "Absurdly, NBC is still promising Craig that they will stick by 70-30 agreement by using footage of the events and Cynthia describing the work of the Foundation."

Palmieri continues, "Not sure it will help, but I called Chuck Todd (as head of [NBC] political unit) to let him know how outrageous and ludicrous this was and that our side of the house is watching to see how NBC handles this."

In case you're unclear, that's a veiled threat to restrict NBC's future access—or worse.

"I think we have to make this public," Palmieri continues. "We are being hit by the press for not getting more attention for the good work of the Foundation, [we] take a network to Africa to see the work, give them an interview with the President [Clinton], and they do not ask ONE question about the work of the Foundation."

But if NBC didn't make good on its supposed agreement, it seems others were more than willing to help. The Clinton camp indicates it was able to enlist *New York* magazine to punish NBC with a negative article. Palmieri writes in an internal email, "Craig has gotten in touch with NY mag this am to do a story about how grossly the media has handled the story on book/foundation and make this experience with NBC part of that story."

Time and again, the internal emails make it crystal clear that political forces today have scandalous access to journalists, and feel they simply need only devise a propaganda plan and choose the reporter or news outlet to execute it. In July 2015, the Clinton campaign's Palmieri gets an advance briefing about a soon-to-be-published *New York Times* story, though it's unclear how she received the insider access.

"I got a briefing on the story, it's in a much better place," Palmieri writes in an email to Clinton and colleagues. "Takes the viewpoint that 20 years after WJC [Bill Clinton] declared 'the era of big government is over,' HRC [Hillary] is putting forward more liberal agenda that would expand government's role. It refers to HRC's 'policy ideas' as opposed to 'plans,' notes she hasn't rolled them out yet, and will do an economic speech on Monday. It says that if her ideas were enacted they would likely cost in the 'hundreds of billions of dollars,' does not put a number on it, which is good. There is a good bit in there about Bernie's plans too, and how he would represent a bigger expansion of government and questions whether HRC's agenda will be seen as progressive enough in comparison. It should post later tonight or tomorrow."

In August 2015, as the Clinton campaign is reeling over the latest revelations about Hillary's email usage, her aide Cheryl Mills lays out her "personal preferences" for getting their side of the story out in the press, in the most favorable way possible:

I rank them in order of my personal preference,
1) Monday interview w/ Andrea Mitchell [of MSNBC] in NH (w/ a Sunday prep).
2) Sunday interview with Andrea Mitchell (Saturday prep)
3) Monday avail in NH (w/ Sunday prep)

On September 4, 2015, MSNBC's Andrea Mitchell conducts an exclusive interview in which Clinton apologizes for her email "confusion."

Coincident with this coordination with journalists, Hillary Clinton's well-oiled smear machine is humming away against her Democratic opponents for the nomination—even as she claims to have no knowledge of it. She and her Democratic socialist opponent, Bernie Sanders, are supposed to be playing nice. They've agreed to refrain from attacking one another publicly. But David Brock's Correct The Record super PAC decides to violate the pact and go decidedly negative. It emails a reporter, highlighting the supposed "similarities" between Sanders and a controversial politician in the United Kingdom who — the email said—suggested the U.S. assassination of Islamic terrorist Osama bin Laden was a "tragedy." The email also likens Sanders to the widely reviled, late Venezuelan leader Hugo Chavez. When the email is made public, a Sanders spokesman issues a written response stating, "It is disappointing that Secretary Clinton's super PAC is spreading disinformation about Bernie. This is exactly the kind of politics that Bernie is trying to change." The smear may have proven to be a miscalculation on Brock's part: Sanders reportedly uses the attacks as ammunition to raise $1.2 million for his campaign.

Correct The Record also dispatches spies to watch and record other Clinton opponents on the campaign trail, hoping for trip-ups that it can lather into major-league smears. Word gets out on the street that Correct The Record plans to hit Vice President Joe Biden—hard—if he has the nerve to formally challenge Hillary for the Democratic nomination. It almost sounds like a threat.

"I have no knowledge of what they are doing," Clinton tells reporters when asked about Correct The Record's dubious assaults on her challengers. But, in fact, Hillary's campaign has given more than a quarter of a million dollars to Correct The Record, and they're coordinating directly in their efforts.

Sanders tells his supporters that Correct The Record's actions against him are "the kind of onslaught I expected to see from [Republican megadonors] the Koch brothers or Sheldon Adelson." But to Brock? It's business as usual. "Standard opposition research," he tells reporters. "There's no dirty work involved here. It's just putting out facts."

Hillary isn't Sanders's only obstacle. His most daunting opposition turns out to be the machine that powers the entire Democratic party: the Democratic National Committee (DNC). In August 2015, Sanders and fellow Democrat Martin O'Malley publicly proclaim that they believe DNC has "rigged" the primary debate system to Clinton's advantage. It appears they're correct when WikiLeaks later posts a treasure trove of DNC emails. Some of them suggest Clinton campaign officials coordinated with the DNC in structuring primary debates to Clinton's benefit. An email from April 2015 indicates the DNC had supported the Clinton camp's desire to limit the number of debates, and to keep them on a schedule that would make them less visible. According to emails, the Clintonites had even obtained and circulated among themselves an advance draft of a DNC press release on the matter.

In the fallout over the leaked emails, DNC chairwoman Debbie Wasserman-Schultz gets pushed out of her job on the eve of the Democratic National Convention. She's even booed out of chairing the convention itself, and forced to retreat in scandal.

Meanwhile, the liberal press finds its support divided between Bernie and Hillary and at each other's throats over dueling smears. *Mother Jones* is on Clinton's side and accuses Sanders of corrupting the thoughts of young millennials. "[Sanders is] the one who convinced [Millennials] that Clinton was in the pocket of Wall Street," writes Kevin Drum in a *Mother Jones* blog. "[Sanders is] the one who convinced them [Clinton] was a corporate shill." *Mother Jones* editor Clara Jeffery tweets that she herself has "never hated millennials more" because many weren't willing to vote for Clinton.

Salon, on the other hand, takes up the mantle for Sanders and attacks the *Mother Jones* writer Drum. "Well, shame on Sanders for telling the truth?" shoots back *Salon's* Daniel Denvir. "Drum doesn't like Sanders and thinks that Clinton has spent a 'literal lifetime' fighting for progressive values. Unfortunately for Drum, many young people disagree." In other articles, *Salon* criticizes the "toxicity of the 'Bernie is white and for whites only'" smear supposedly being driven by the Clinton camp.

As fall 2015 progresses, John Harwood of CNBC and the *New York Times* frequently emails privately with Clinton campaign officials, offering compliments and soliciting editorial input. (Harwood is the debate moderator who had famously confronted Trump with a question that sounded more like a snarky editorial remark: "Let's be honest. Is this a comic-book version of a presidential campaign?") In a September 2015 email, Harwood specifically asks Democratic Party officials to provide questions for his upcoming interview with Republican Jeb Bush. "What should I ask Jeb [Bush] . . . in Speakeasy interview tomorrow?" Harwood emails Clinton campaign chair Podesta.

In October 2015, the Clinton campaign apparently uses PBS's Judy Woodruff to "put the news out" that Hillary intends to reverse her support of the controversial Trans-Pacific Partnership (TPP) trade deal. To frame the coverage in a way most favorable to Clinton, the campaign arranges for Woodruff to break the "news" in an interview with Clinton, and then plans to release a coincident paper statement.

"I told PBS to hold till 345pm and that we would send the statement to our travelers after they put the news out (we should give them 15 minutes of breathing space)," writes the campaign's Palmieri in an internal email. "We can move up PBS' time if need be." Clearly, the Clinton camp believes it has enough sway with PBS to dictate timing of new releases.

A month later, on November 13, Clinton campaign press secretary

Brian Fallon indicates the campaign has successfully planted a negative story about Clinton critic Senator Charles Grassley with "friendly" journalist Maggie Haberman, formerly of *Politico* and now at the *New York Times*. "After hitting a wall with other outlets, NYT will do a story," Fallon emails to another Clinton ally. "Could pop this weekend." Three days later, Haberman publishes the article.

For his part, Donald Trump isn't enjoying the same friendly relationships with the mainstream press. But he has his own advantages.

The Wildcard

Wildcard is the name of a fictional superhero in Marvel comics. He was unpredictable because he didn't have just *one* superpower. He could copy the superhuman powers of anyone else. It was impossible to foresee what he might be able to do from one moment to the next. He became mighty among men.

Amid all the attacks, Trump proves as incalculable as Wildcard. A bully one moment, kindhearted the next. Brash and unapologetic. He's savvy yet reckless, reliable only in terms of his unpredictability. There's no way to accurately poll his popularity or place odds on his voter appeal. He throws the whole "establishment" into disarray. His strengths and vulnerabilities fuse together and manifest as an erratic character that strikes fear into the hearts of his enemies; they cannot eliminate him because they can't begin to understand him.

As soon as Trump announces his candidacy on June 16, 2015, virtually all experts, polls, and media label him an attention-seeking, narcissistic sideshow to be lampooned and parodied. Nine days after he puts his hat into the ring, the Spanish-language network Univision begins a particularly vicious vendetta against The Donald. Anchor Jorge Ramos launches into multiple diatribes against Trump, mischaracterizes Trump's criticism of illegal immigration as if it were an anti-immigrant position, and falsely claims that Trump was incorrect to say that some illegal immigrants are murderers and rapists. (According to the Obama administration's own statistics, Trump is correct. In 2013 and 2014 alone, U.S. Immigration and

Customs Enforcement set loose in the United States 66,565 illegal immigrant criminals, who had 166,877 convictions, including 11,301 rapes or other types of assaults and 395 homicides. By mid-2015, more than 2,000 of those released criminal illegal immigrants had been convicted of new crimes in the United States, including felonies and gang offenses.) Univision also cancels the planned airing of Trump's Miss USA pageant. And Univision's CEO is publicly critical of Trump.

The news media reports the Univision developments as if they are the death knell for the Republican candidate. What they don't report is the political interests behind Univision. Its owner is Saban Capital Group, run by a top Clinton donor, Haim Saban. Saban and his wife ultimately gave more than $10 million to the pro-Clinton super PAC Priorities USA Action.

Despite the public assault by Univision and many other pro-illegal-immigrant interests, Trump doesn't back off his get-tough talk. As he refuses to follow the normal Republican script of retreat and mea culpa, many voters view his approach as refreshing; one of strength and conviction. They see him taking on the establishment in every sense of the word: political parties and the media, too.

A big part of Trump's madcap act is his ability to land an unrepentant counterpunch. Senator John McCain becomes the first fellow Republican to directly attack Trump in July 2015, by referring to his ardent supporters as "crazies." Trump fires back in an appearance at the conservative Family Leadership Summit in Ames, Iowa. He calls McCain a "coward" who's masquerading as a Vietnam War hero. (McCain had spent five and a half years as a prisoner of war.)

The McCain skirmish marks the first major clash between Trump the candidate and the press. Much reporting on the spat takes liberties, veering from the facts, in order to make Trump look worse. In an article for my website, SharylAttkisson.com, I call into question a *Washington Post* article by Philip Rucker, which he begins by stating, "Republican presidential candidate Donald Trump slammed Sen. John McCain (R-Ariz.) . . . by saying *McCain was not a war hero because he was captured* by the North Vietnamese" (emphasis added). In fact, as I point out, Trump had stated the opposite: that McCain *is* a war hero because he was captured. Further, the *Post* had selectively edited out Trump saying, "He is a war hero," a sentence that would have contradicted the *Post*'s premise. Here's more of what I wrote about it on July 18, 2015:

> . . . *the Post is accurate in reporting that Trump initially said McCain is "not a war hero." But then, Trump immediately modified his statement saying—four times—that McCain is a war hero:*
> *"He is a war hero."*
> *"He's a war hero because he was captured."*
> *"He's a war hero, because he was captured."*
> *"I believe, perhaps, he's a war hero. But right now, he's said some very bad things about a lot of people."*

While the *Post* might have been able to justify reporting that it felt Trump had "implied" McCain was not a war hero because he was captured, or that the *Post* felt Trump was being sarcastic when he said McCain *is* a war hero because he was captured, it's simply untrue to state that Trump said McCain was *not* a war hero because he was captured.

This matter of wording may seem like an insignificant, technical distinction, but it's not. The *Post* has violated basic tenets of good journalism. Reporters may characterize comments and put them in context, but they're not entitled to alter actual quotes, even if they strongly dislike the person who uttered the words. To Trump's detractors, his actual remarks were bad enough in their own right; the idea that the press felt compelled to make them sound worse spoke volumes. It would set the tone for the next sixteen months.

Amid the Trump-McCain spat, the news media demand apologies . . . not from McCain for insulting Trump's supporters, but from Trump. They insist he drop out of the race. He's not fit to run. Instead, he doubles down. They can't believe he's not crumbling under the pressure.

Had he apologized then, he wouldn't have survived the summer.

Next, the press tries another tactic. They collectively become convinced that if they show viewers more of Trump, the national audience will drum him out of the race. So the media air what they see as his offensive remarks over and over again. They plaster the news with videos showing

Trump appearing at events and speaking to reporters. But they're stunned to discover the unthinkable: the more exposure they give to Trump in an effort to marginalize and ridicule him, the more some people like him. *And the news ratings go up!*

About this time, Trump is beginning to get pounded mercilessly in the media for saying "all Mexicans are rapists." *Except he never said that*. The widespread mischaracterization of his words is stunning from my viewpoint as a traditional journalist. One rare voice who calls out the press on this point is a Bernie Sanders supporter, University of Texas at Austin history professor Alberto Martinez. In an article for *Salon* in December 2015, Martinez writes a commentary titled "The media needs to stop telling this lie about Donald Trump. I'm a Sanders supporter—and value honesty. Trump's words on Mexicans have been misconstrued by all sides. This liberal, Puerto Rican professor says enough."

Martinez goes on to say that his students and coworkers repeatedly misquote Trump as having said "all Mexicans are rapists." He points out that Trump actually said something quite different. Referring specifically to *illegal* immigrants, Trump said, "They're rapists, and some, I assume, are good people."

"You might well dislike Trump's words. I did," notes Martinez. "But let's not make it worse. He did not say that all Mexicans are rapists. Yet that's what many commentators did. For example, *Politico* misquoted Trump by omitting his phrase about 'good people.' They said he was 'demonizing Mexicans as rapists.' They argued that Mexicans do not really commit more rapes in the U.S. than whites. But that's not what Trump claimed."

The professor then listed other news sources that he said misrepresented Trump's words in offensive ways:

New York Times: "Trump's claim that illegal Mexican immigrants are 'rapists.'"

Time: "Trump's comment that Mexican immigrants are 'rapists.'"

Associated Press: "Trump called Mexican immigrants rapists and criminals."

CBS News: "Trump defends calling Mexican immigrants 'rapists.'"

Los Angeles Times: "describing Mexican immigrants as 'rapists.'"

Fortune: "in a speech branding Mexican immigrants as criminals and rapists."

Hollywood Reporter: "he referred to Mexican immigrants as 'rapists.'"

Huffington Post: "He called Latino immigrants 'criminals' and 'rapists.'"

Washington Post: "He referred to Mexicans as 'rapists.'"

Martinez goes on to conclude, "Which is worse? Writers excerpted the phrase: 'they're rapists,' as if it were about all Mexican unauthorized immigrants, or worse, about all Mexican immigrants, or even worse, about all Mexicans. But that's not what he said. That's not what he meant. It was just a remark about some of the criminals crossing the border."

Professor Martinez and I are lone voices in the wilderness. The media would largely continue misconstruing Trump's words and position on this issue throughout the campaign and beyond.

With Friends Like This . . .

After he perseveres through the first three months of the campaign, defying all predictions, Trump faces stepped-up rhetoric from his GOP opponents. In September 2015, Republican operative Liz Mair publishes an opinion article in the *Daily Beast* titled "This Is How You Beat Donald Trump."

"There is no existing blueprint for how you kill off a candidate like this," Mair notes. She continues with advice such as taking the fight to the places where Trump's "low information" supporters get their information, focusing on his business record, and replicating his "brash, loudmouthed" tone.

Mair is a smear artist who runs a firm that says it "assembles and distributes opposition research, especially to online media, in advancing our clients' objectives (mostly corporate, trade association and charitable clients)." She's organized an anti-Trump group called Make America Awesome but won't disclose who her clients are.

Pretty soon, a more familiar name in the Republican smear game also jumps into the anti-Trump mix: political consultant Rick "Dr. Evil" Berman. Berman's nonprofit "Enterprise Freedom Action Committee 501" ends up paying his own for-profit PR firm $355,000 to launch a campaign against Trump using Google and Facebook ads. Will Tucker of the Center for Responsive Politics tells me that Berman may have met his match in Trump.

"Berman's strategy is shoot the messenger and attack the credibility of the messenger. . . . [He] might have met someone who is a worthy challenge," Tucker says.

We have no way of knowing who enlisted Berman to go after Trump. Under IRS rules governing his type of groups, Berman doesn't have to reveal his donors. And Tucker struck out when he tried to find out. He says a spokeswoman for Enterprise Freedom Action wouldn't tell him.

"There is no required disclosure of donors for the kind of groups that Berman uses to attack people's credibility," Tucker notes. But he says we might glean a hint in the fact that Trump's message threatens traditional sectors in the Republican establishment, including corporate and industry interests, with whom Berman worked before.

Before 2015 ends, the United Kingdom joins in the effort to try to crush Trump. A half-million people sign a petition to ban him from Britain. British prime minister David Cameron weighs in, calling the GOP candidate "stupid" and "wrong." Most people don't know it, and the news media doesn't report it, but there's a Clinton connection here, too. Cameron's campaign strategy adviser had been none other than former Obama adviser Jim Messina, who now heads the pro-Hillary super PAC Priorities USA.

For her part, Clinton inadvertently evokes a smear from days gone by. She publishes a tweet stating that sexual assault survivors must "be heard, believed and supported." The message raises the specter of the infamous "Nuts and Sluts" smears she allegedly helped direct against Bill Clinton's accusers in the 1990s. A few days later, at a campaign event in Nashua, New Hampshire, a reporter gingerly dips her toe into the unspeakable mud and confronts Hillary on the seemingly hypocritical position.

"You recently came out to say that all rape victims should be believed," says the woman.

Hillary senses what's coming. She's prepared. She nods a little, then reflexively pinches and wipes her nose with her left hand.

The woman continues. "But would you say that about Juanita Broaddrick, Kathleen Willey, and/or Paula Jones? Should we believe them as well?" she asks, referring to some of the women who claim Bill Clinton victimized them.

"Well, I would say that everybody should be believed at first *until they are disbelieved based on evidence,*" Hillary replies. She manages a big smile. She's delivered the key line without wincing. Applause from the audience! A few of them shout "Woo! Woo!"

Audience-Stacking

Clinton braves her own campaign smears but there are two big differences between hers and the ones hitting Trump and Sanders. First, most smears against Clinton simply don't take as firm a hold in the mainstream media, whose established priority is demonizing Trump. Second, Clinton's rapid-response machine is whip-quick at deflecting and spinning to minimize damage, and the news media generally laps up the suggested narrative on her behalf.

During a debate in October 2015, Democratic presidential candidate Lincoln Chafee questions Clinton's ethical compass as she faces the FBI probe of her email practices as secretary of state.

"We have to repair American credibility after we said that Saddam Hussein had weapons of mass destruction and he didn't," Chafee tells a Las Vegas audience, alluding to Hillary's low scores in the trust department. "I think we need somebody with the best and ethical standards as our next president. That's how I feel."

CNN moderator Anderson Cooper asks Clinton if she wants to respond. She replies: "No."

It's a bad moment for Clinton. Possibly a very bad moment. She's speechless in response to a criticism of her most vulnerable quality, made by a fellow Democrat. But then, something strange happens. Wild applause erupts from the audience! Not only are they unbothered by Clinton's response, but they seem to like it—no! They *love* it!

I've learned to trust my pangs of cognitive dissonance. I suspect the audience is stacked. This is a form of astroturf: a way to manipulate reality and shape perception of an event. The practice of audience-stacking deserves some discussion.

Debates have long been known to make or break a candidate. Consider Vice President Richard Nixon's sweaty, five o'clock–shadow performance against Senator John F. Kennedy (who won) in 1960. Or California governor Ronald Reagan's "Are you better off?" line in the 1980 debate against President Jimmy Carter (who lost his bid for reelection). Today's strategists know there are two things more crucial than simply having a good debate performance: 1) avoiding a fatal flaw and 2) being able to prompt the other guy to make a fatal flaw. But debates are a contests of uncertainty and spontaneity. How can the puppet masters game the system?

By stacking the audience.

It's not a new tactic. Abe Lincoln is said to have used just such a strategy to help win the Republican nomination at the 1860 convention, held in Chicago. Author Gordon Leidner wrote that Lincoln supporters "assigned two men with noted stentorian voices to lead the cheering. One of these men reportedly had a larynx powerful enough to allow his shout to be heard across Lake Michigan." When Lincoln's nomination was seconded, "the uproar was 'beyond description. . . . A thousand steam whistles, ten acres of hotel gongs, a tribe of Comanches might have mingled in the scene unnoticed.'"

I suspect Clinton's supporters had been guided not only to cheer her zingers—but also to fiercely applaud her flubs. Applauding her errors would distract from them and serve to confuse the audience at home. More important, it would lead the news media to report the desired narrative. Instead of exercising independent judgment and analysis, they would hear the applause and declare Clinton's blunder to be her winning moment.

That's exactly how it turns out. After the audience applauds Clinton's bad answer, the news media replays the clip as an example of how soundly she defeated her debate opponents. Accounts of her supposed victory are dutifully and gleefully circulated by the usual suspects in the press and soon saturate social media.

"Hillary Clinton had the perfect response," proclaims a post-debate *Slate* headline. The article, written by Christina Cauterucci, includes the clip and raves "Watch the wonderful exchange." Strikingly similar language touting Clinton's supposedly "perfect responses" to various challenges is used by occupydemocrats.com, fusion.net, *New Century Times,* mic.com, and *Elle,* to name a few.

Modern-day Republicans stack the audience, too, sometimes against each other. In the 2016 Republican presidential debates, the operative audience tactic is "jeers" rather than "cheers." During a debate prior to South Carolina's February primary, Trump gives answers that would seem to be popular among his ardent supporters. Yet the audience responds with loud boos. Once again, cognitive dissonance: Trump has the largest single block of supporters in the Republican field, yet he's generating the biggest audience disapproval at a Republican debate? As soon as the boo brigade breaks out, "news" of it is circulated on social media. Bloggers recount it mirthfully. Video clips are passed around. The news media has its assigned narrative.

"Trump Gets Booed!" "Trump Booed Over and Over," "Watch Trump Get Booed," shriek headlines from *USA Today* to *Time.* "Donald Trump Booed Loudly!" declares the *International Business Times.*

After the debate, the award for Most Erroneous Analysis has to go to *Fortune* reporter Dan Friedman. He facetiously declares the winner of the Republican debate to be Democrat Hillary Clinton (as if all of the Republicans proved to be losers). He also says, "Donald Trump's performance Saturday night may have improved his standing with Democrats, but it appeared poorly suited to Republicans in South Carolina and other upcoming primary states." But the actual outcome of the South Carolina primary is evidence that astroturf doesn't always work. It turns out Trump's supporters are more likely than others to disregard the popular media narratives. And so, contrary to Friedman's prediction, Trump wins South Carolina by double digits and takes home all the delegates. Nobody else comes close.

If journalists would open their minds and engage in independent thought rather than advancing spoon-fed narratives, they might sniff out more interesting stories—like the one about politicians stacking audiences. Instead it's Trump who ends up exposing the phenomenon. During the debate, he comments that the audience members jeering him are big

Republican National Committee (RNC) donors—special interests who want Jeb Bush to be the nominee, not him.

"The reason they're not loving me is I don't want their money," Trump says in response to audience taunts. "I don't want their money and I don't need their money and I'm the only one up here who can say that." Trump's analysis rings truer than that of the news media. In fact, this debate audience isn't a random mix of attendees off the street, as some viewers at home might believe. The RNC allocated tickets.

"Let me just tell you, we needed [debate] tickets," Trump continues to tell the debate audience. "[But] you can't get them. You know who has the tickets? . . . Donors, special interests, the people that are putting up the money."

RNC chairman Reince Priebus later denies accusations that he stacked the audience with anti-Trump donors. Here's his explanation as to who got tickets. First, he says, each of the six Republican candidates got one hundred audience seats.

"When you have 600 people in a room that are there as guests of the candidates, guess what? They are going to be pretty excited to either be for their candidate or against other candidates," Priebus insists, explaining the boos for Trump. "That's pretty natural, that's what happens. That's what this is and I think it's pretty normal."

The thing is, there were 2,000 seats in the venue. So who was in the 1,400 seats remaining after the RNC gave the candidates 600? According to the RNC, 300 spots went to CBS, Google, and the debate hall (so that's 300 more audience members likely against Trump). Then, the national Republican Party (also against Trump) gave out 367 tickets. Finally, the state Republican Party and locally elected officials (presumably anti-Trump) received 550. Now you see how the audience was stacked with a majority who opposed Trump and was prepared to shout boos to sway the audience at home.

There's more audience-stacking on the Democrats' side in July 2016 for the Democratic National Convention. The fix is necessary because the Democratic National Committee (DNC) fears that devoted Bernie Sanders supporters will disrupt Hillary Clinton's big speech as she accepts the nomination for president. The Sanders crowd has already booed down and forced out Debbie Wasserman-Schultz as DNC chair and head of the convention after WikiLeaks emails revealed the DNC was in the tank for Hillary all along, just like Sanders supporters suspected. The emails also revealed distasteful references by DNC officials regarding race and religion. So the DNC knows it needs to manage the giant convention audience to maintain control and order. How can it make sure Hillary isn't disrespected or humiliated on international TV?

Actors!

Sanders delegates begin posting Internet videos reporting that the DNC has hired actors at fifty dollars apiece to fill hundreds of seats at the convention and shut down Sanders supporters. They say the DNC has also installed noise-cancellation devices so their jeers won't be heard. It's a carefully constructed artificial reality. And little of this is reported by the mainstream news.

Chapter Eight

||||||||||||||||||||||

The Road to the Conventions

As 2016 begins, Sanders is drawing enthusiastic crowds and a surprising level of support among the very voters Clinton needs. But the road to the convention teaches Hillary's Democrat-socialist challenger how tough it can be on the receiving end of well-funded smears.

First, a rumor circulates that Sanders is scheming to cheat in the upcoming Iowa caucuses by busing in kids from out of state. Sanders blames Hillary's super PAC for the disinformation.

"Every one of you knows, you know it, that every day you're being flooded by all of this negative stuff from Secretary Clinton's super PAC," Sanders tells reporters. "I don't want my integrity and honesty being impugned. I have no idea who says this. This is a lie, an absolute lie. We will win or we'll lose, we'll do it honestly."

Meanwhile, Brock's work on behalf of Hillary continues to spark internal conflicts. After Brock is quoted in *Politico* predicting that Trump will win the Republican nomination, Neera Tanden of the pro-Clinton Center for American Progress emails Clinton campaign chair John Podesta, "David Brock is like a menace. I can think of no worse message for Hillary right now than she's preparing for the general [election]." She also refers to Brock as "a conspiracy theorist." The same month, Brock publicly issues a call for Sanders to release his medical records and immediately meets with pushback from other Clintonites. (Perhaps it's because, as we later learned, Hillary had her own health issues.) In any event, Podesta smacks down Brock in a public tweet telling him to "chill out." Tanden follows up by emailing Podesta, "Maybe [Brock] actually is a republican plant. Hard to think of anything more counter productive than demanding Bernie's medical records." Longtime Clinton ally Lanny Davis fires off his own email to Brock, copying Brock's fundraiser Mary Pat Bonner, begging: "For God's sake David stop—I believe this is very harmful to HRC [Hillary Clinton]. No one I know who supports HRC is anything other than repulsed and disgusted by your call for medical records release—I am talking about dozens of people all day today. Please please stop this—and apologize."

Brock would later tell *Politico,* "I tried to have a strategy with regards to Senator Sanders. . . . I got in trouble when I requested his medical records. I got in trouble with the campaign—the campaign was unhappy that I did that. I never knew if they were unhappy substantively, or they were just unhappy because they didn't control it. This was a very controlling culture."

Sanders gets back at Clinton by highlighting her ties to the wealthy banking industry. In February 2016, Sanders supporters and Republicans launch a multipronged push for Clinton to release transcripts of her paid Wall Street speeches. A conservative super PAC called Future45 fires off negative TV ads and a digital campaign against Clinton ahead of Super Tuesday. Future45 backers include hedge fund managers Paul Singer and Ken Griffin as well as TD Ameritrade founder Joe Ricketts (who's simultaneously funding opposition to Trump through Our Principles super PAC).

"Hillary Clinton gave speeches to the biggest banks on Wall Street after one of the worst financial crises in American history," says the narrator in one attack ad. "But Hillary won't tell us what she said to those banks. They paid her over one million dollars and are contributing millions more to elect her. . . . So before you promise your vote to Hillary, don't you deserve to know what she promised to them?"

Next, Clinton operatives lash out against Bernie through the nation's opinion-editorial pages. (Remember, I told you earlier that op-eds are prime astroturf real estate, often amounting to little-disguised efforts to advance political or corporate agendas. Sometimes the op-eds aren't even written by the person whose name is signed at the bottom.) Leaked campaign emails reveal the Clinton campaign asking former Obama Interior Department secretary Ken Salazar to sign an op-ed against Bernie—their idea, but written in Salazar's name.

"Secretary, We are looking to push back on Bernie's professed support for immigration. We would love your help on this," writes a Clinton campaign official in an email dated February 15, 2016, and titled "Pushback on Immigration."

Salazar expresses ready willingness. "[W]e can draft an oped that is supportive of Secretary Clinton's approach to immigration reform, and contrast her efforts to Bernie's. The piece can then be used in other States, besides Colorado—e.g., Nevada, Texas, Florida, etc."

Five days later, Salazar is quoted in a *Washington Post* news piece "warning Nevada Latinos to beware of Bernie Sanders." Also, Clinton surrogate Senator Claire McCaskill appears on MSNBC to label Sanders's message "extremist," likening it to that of Republicans Ron Paul and Pat Buchanan. (Clinton would later select Salazar to lead her transition team.)

In March 2016, Brock's continued anti-Sanders efforts come under scrutiny in the media. The *Daily Beast*'s Lloyd Grove files a story about Brock's takeover of a liberal website called *Blue Nation Review,* under the category Dirty Tricks, asking, "Is a propaganda arm of Hillary Clinton's presidential juggernaut masquerading as an independent news and opinion site?" Grove notes, "The Blue Nation Review seems to have evolved from a blog dedicated to creating 'a place where progressives can debate' to an attack dog for Hillary Clinton . . . [It] seems more a comfortable venue for negative Sanders stories that Brock wasn't successful in placing with mainstream news outlets like the *New York Times* and the *Washington Post.*"

Tad Devine, a top strategist for the Sanders campaign, tells the *Daily Beast* that *Blue Nation Review* is "the pond scum of American politics." "I'm sure they're going to do whatever it takes to throw mud at Bernie and discredit him and lie about him, and deceive people," Devine says. "And that's their business. That's what they do for a living." The article notes: "As with an increasing number of political whodunits during this election cycle, the fingerprints of Hillary hit man David Brock are all over the crime scene."

Eight months after its inception, *Blue Nation Review* claims it "helped shape the national conversation" and takes credit for many political propaganda initiatives, including being "the first to call Trump's full pivot to white nationalism," furthering the narrative that nothing short of the Ku Klux Klan has taken control of the Republican Party.

Brock manages many other misrepresentations and successful disguising of his interests. It's a publicity coup when the president of his Correct The Record super PAC, Brad Woodhouse, repeatedly appears in news segments with no mention of his Hillary campaign ties. In a live post-presidential-debate segment on Fox News in 2015, viewers aren't told Correct The Record is a political super PAC founded by Brock as "a strategic research and rapid response team designed to defend Hillary Clinton from baseless attacks." Woodhouse is presented as if he's a Democratic analyst with no particular horse in the race. On TV he declares that none of the GOP candidates were "all that effective" in their debate arguments against Hillary. When asked if she'll be the official nominee, he answers, "Absolutely!" He goes on to chide Democrats Bernie Sanders and Martin O'Malley for having the nerve to press for more debates with Clinton.

On March 29, 2016, Woodhouse is back on TV defending Clinton (again, without the disclosure that he's officially working on her behalf). A reporter asks him about the FBI investigation into Clinton's email controversy. *Nothing to it,* says Woodhouse. On the other hand, he's universally critical of Clinton's opponents, whether Sanders or the vast Republican field. On May 2, 2016, Woodhouse is on TV yet again, managing to take another swipe at Sanders. Woodhouse and Correct The Record are officially in Hillary's camp. They'll always push the Clinton agenda. It's the house specialty. But the public gets the false impression that Correct The Record is simply a fact-checking authority.

In April 2016, after a debate performance that's widely viewed as disastrous for Hillary, Correct The Record is at the ready to declare the opposite: "Good Night for Hillary, Bad Night for Bernie."

"The reviews are in," declares Correct The Record. "Last night was a strong performance for Hillary Clinton, while Bernie Sanders reiterated his out-of-touch positions on gun violence, continued to tell the Southern half of the country their votes aren't as important, and said President Obama should withdraw his Supreme Court nominee if he's elected president."

Soon, Correct The Record becomes parent to a new astroturf project called Barrier Breakers. It pledges to spend $1 million to "push back against" anyone attacking Hillary on social media. In a press release issued in spring of 2016, the group says it's already "addressed more than 5,000 people that have personally attacked Hillary Clinton on Twitter." The impact is seen online as Correct The Record operatives bully Sanders supporters on Twitter, Reddit, and Facebook. The effort is designed to look like grass roots. But outraged Internet users quickly figure out it's an organized, paid campaign.

"This explains why my inbox turned to cancer on Tuesday," writes one user who had criticized Clinton on the social media site Reddit. "Been a member of reddit for almost 4 years and never experienced anything like it. In fact, in all my years on the internet I've never experienced anything like it. . . . It was a pure bombardment on my account, it went on for hours." Another Reddit user advises, "The best tactic to use against 'professionals' is to simply downvote and move on. The more you argue with them, the more likely people will read the astroturfer's posts."

A digital consulting firm executive weighs in on the orchestrated social media pushback from Camp Hillary, remarking that it's "meant to appear to be coming organically from people and their social media networks in a groundswell of activism, when in fact it is highly paid and highly tactical."

Bernie also continues to take hits from the pro-Hillary-minded DNC. Leaked emails show the DNC conspired to attack him over his religion or lack thereof. In a May 2016 email, the DNC's chief financial officer suggests they "get someone to ask" Sanders about his religious views. "It might make no difference, but for KY [Kentucky] and WVA [West Virginia] can we get someone to ask his belief," writes the DNC's Brad Marshall. "Does he believe in a God. He had skated on saying he has a Jewish heritage. I think I read he is an atheist. This could make several points [*sic*] difference with my peeps. My Southern Baptist peeps would draw a big difference between a Jew and an atheist."

Sanders is said to be furious at all of the smear efforts lodged against him by fellow Democrats. "Nobody has apologized," he tells NBC in an interview after one DNC email leak. "But this does not come as a surprise to me or my supporters. There is no doubt that the DNC was on Secretary Clinton's campaign from day one."

Democratic operatives are also busy keeping Donald Trump embroiled in demonstrations on the road. His popularity is growing—though you'd never know it from watching the news—but he's increasingly battling unruly protesters inside and outside his large rallies. They block roads, pelt his supporters with eggs, kick and beat them, tear at their hair, beat on their cars, rip up their signs, and call them names. Rarely, a Trump supporter gets violent with the demonstrators. Almost exclusively, the news media faults Trump for the violence wherever it occurs. In March 2016, aggressive protesters swamp the venue of his planned rally at the University of Illinois at Chicago. To those experienced in the art of the smear, it immediately smacks of an organized astroturf effort disguised as a spontaneous, grassroots movement. One giveaway: the presence of Bill Ayers, a controversial acquaintance of President Obama's and cofounder of the communist Weather Underground revolutionary group, which conducted numerous violent attacks in the United States during the Vietnam War. Ayers was linked to the Weather Underground bombings of the U.S. Capitol, the Pentagon, and New York City Police Department headquarters in the 1960s and 1970s. Though declared a "terrorist" by the FBI, Ayers was later hired as a distinguished professor at the University of Illinois. Now retired from the university in 2016, he can't resist showing up at his alma mater to protest Trump's appearance. There's a dangerous vibe at the protests. Demonstrators appear to be trying to incite violence. They become so disruptive, Trump cancels the rally. It's a huge victory for the organized opposition. It's the first and only time Trump will succumb to obstruction at one of his speeches. Ayers can't help but take partial credit on TV for getting the Chicago rally scrubbed.

"I've never seen anything this big at the University of Illinois at Chicago," Ayers tells a news crew. "It's huge. And it's galvanized Latino students, black students, Muslim students, and white students. And everybody feels like, look, this is a university, we don't need, you know, this kind of organized hatred to be spilling into our center."

The George Soros–funded MoveOn.org also steps up to take credit following the Chicago success story. "We've been ramping up our efforts for months," writes MoveOn in an email to supporters, "from the 'We Are Better Than This' ad we helped organize in *The New York Times* in December, to our collective advocacy for refugees under attack from the GOP, to the support we provided students in Chicago last night by printing signs and a banner and recruiting MoveOn.org members to join their peaceful protest. . . . We'll support MoveOn.org members to call out and nonviolently protest Trump's, bigoted, misogynistic, xenophobic, and violent behavior and show the world that America rejects Trump's hate."

Later, a Democrat operative captured on undercover video by the conservative "Project Veritas" describes how party officials had trained and organized agents to attend Trump rallies and then bait Trump supporters into lashing out, knowing the media would smear Trump when it happened.

Establishment: In Denial

The nation's first primary is the Iowa caucuses, held on February 1, 2016. Less than two weeks before the contest, on January 21, *Real Clear Politics* shows Trump with a polling average in the state of 29 percent. It's an enviable number considering there are seventeen Republicans in the race sharing a piece of the pie. But Trump is about to suffer under the power and weight of negative ads. The Republican anti-Trump super PAC Our Principles drops $1 million on four anti-Trump television commercials, buys radio spots, and fires off 350,000 pieces of direct mail to try to change the minds of possible Trump supporters. One day before the caucuses, Our Principles places more ads in local newspapers. By the day of the vote, Trump has lost five percentage points. He walks away with 24 percent, nudged out of first place by Senator Ted Cruz, who takes home the win with 27 percent. Our Principles claims credit for knocking Trump down to number two.

Three days after Trump's second-place finish in Iowa, I'm on my way from Washington, D.C., to Sarasota, Florida, to moderate a town hall debate between Jim Messina, head of the pro-Hillary Priorities USA, and

Republican Karl Rove, the strategist behind the conservative super PAC American Crossroads (then a presumed backer of Jeb Bush).

Messina and Rove are iconic establishment figures and two of the biggest names in the smear game. They're one another's yin and yang, their respective party's institutional experts in the billion-dollar political data industry. They've perfected the game of buying, selling, and analyzing stats to their advantage, and of garnering big donations, spending money on attacks, and persuading voters—or so they thought—and they've both set their apparatus into motion against Trump. It's worth briefly examining what their apparatus entails.

During our town hall debate, Messina and Rove brag that political operatives like themselves have collected dozens of pieces of data on most every voter—including you. They say that the information is gathered from websites you visit, your public records, your credit card purchases, innocent online surveys that you take, TV boxes inside your house, and your grocery store purchases as recorded by your super saver cards. Data gurus use the information to project, sell, and target. Utilizing mysterious metrics developed by bright young minds and computer algorithms, they crunch information about who in your household watches what programs on which televisions, what pets you own, what kinds of cars you drive. And from all of that, they extrapolate how you feel about social issues, who you might vote for, and how to persuade you. All of their research in 2016 leads them to laugh off Trump's candidacy. At least, that's what they want the public to believe as they advance their respective anti-Trump narratives. Messina, who ran Barack Obama's successful 2012 campaign, tells reporters prior to our event that he would love nothing more than for Trump to be Hillary's opponent. And he gives Trump a grade of "D minus" for his campaign to date.

"I think there's a difference between having a rally and running a campaign, and I think he's having rallies," Messina adds. "I think he's running a pathetic campaign and the fact that no one can tell—Karl and I have run the last two winning campaigns—we can't tell you who's in charge of his campaign. Because the answer is: He is."

More than once, Messina quips that he *prays* that Trump will be the Republican nominee. "I'm pretty religious and I wake up every morning and drop to my knees and say please, God, give me Donald Trump," Messina says, as the audience laughs. "But God doesn't like me that much."

For his part, Rove is equally dismissive of Trump. In an article in the *Wall Street Journal,* he predicts that if Trump were to win the Republican nomination, "the GOP will lose the White House and the Senate, and its majority in the House will fall dramatically." In the end, Trump wins the White House, Republicans retain their Senate majority, and they do not dramatically lose House seats. *Wrong, wrong, and wrong.*

Several months after the Sarasota town hall, when Trump does garner the Republican nomination, Messina is still singing his same tune. He happily tweets: "Proof there is a God: I prayed every night for a year for Trump to win R primary. SHE EXISTS, and she made him win! Tx God."

Be careful what you wish for.

They don't know it yet, but Trump will render Messina's and Rove's entrenched systems functionally worthless in the blink of an eye. The secretly gathered information, the well-honed political connections, the smears, the cozy Washington, D.C., alliances, the revolving door, the back-scratching, the favors bought and earned, the whole darn establishment.

On February 20, 2016, shortly after Rove and Messina predict Trump's demise at their town hall, Trump brings home a big victory in South Carolina's primary, besting Cruz by ten points. This causes mass hysteria among the Republican establishment, particularly at the conservative Our Principles, which fires off a desperate-sounding memo to fellow GOP interests.

"It's time for Republicans to come together and share a roadmap on how to prevent Donald Trump from hijacking our great Party," writes Our Principles executive director Katie Packer, a former Mitt Romney staffer. "Through extensive research, we've learned how to do just that." The memo continues with a point-by-point list of ways to stop the Trump train. "It's time for all efforts aimed at exposing Donald Trump to follow the same strategy. If all of us join forces in a concerted effort to expose his record and his rhetoric, it is possible to stop him."

Our Principles also starts up a website, TrumpQuestions.com, to disparage Trump's positions on key conservative issues. A subtitle in a red banner reads: "How Much Do You Really Know About Donald Trump?"

Another candidate might collapse under the pressure from both left and right. Instead, Trump goes on the offensive against a major donor to Our Principles: Chicago Cubs co-owner Marlene Ricketts.

"I hear the Rickets [*sic*] family, who own the Chicago Cubs, are secretly spending $'s against me," tweets Trump. "They better be careful, they have a lot to hide!"

Five days later, GOP smear operator Liz Mair of Make America Awesome takes to social media to, literally, "shop" dirt on Trump.

"Guys, FWIW, we have a ton of opposition research info on Trump's business record. Have tried to shop it, many reporters too scared to use," she tweets on February 25, 2016. "If you're interested, email me. Understand, I have to give it to whoever I think will make the biggest splash with it."

Within minutes, some in the quasi-news media take the bait. At least three supply their email addresses in rapid response and ask Mair to send the oppo research. Later Mair takes credit for providing damaging material used against Trump in a primary debate. Perhaps it's the culture of self-centered social media, selfies, and self-absorption that makes it impossible for some smear artists to resist grabbing credit for a hatchet job.

"Very pleased to see several of the attacks we've used vs Trump, and which data shows work on his voters, were invoked tonight," Mair tweets after the debate. "All we wanted."

A group called Bask Digital Media is behind yet another Republican attack against Trump. One of its clients is the super PAC Conservative Solutions, or "CS Pac" for short, which is backing Republican senator Marco Rubio of Florida for president at the time. The group has already targeted presidential candidate and New Jersey governor Chris Christie in New Hampshire and gone on to bash Trump with negative ads in Florida, Snapchat messages in Virginia declaring him to be a "Con Artist," and websites named "trumpknowsnothing.com" and "trumpwontfoolus .com." Before Florida's March 15, 2016 primary, outside groups spend about $8.7 million on anti-Trump TV ads. Trump reportedly spends a paltry $2.4 million—yet ends up trouncing the competition in the Sunshine State. After that, Rubio closes the curtain on his presidential bid and Bask Digital's anti-Trump websites disappear as quickly as they arose. Bask takes a bow for its work on behalf of Rubio, tweeting, "Marco is an honorable and inspiring leader. We are proud to have worked with @*cspac* in support of @*marcorubio*?."

Utah is a different story for Trump after Mair's Make America Awesome conjures up a classic smear. Just ahead of the March 22 primary in the Mormon-thick state, Make America Awesome aims below the belt, publicizing a risqué, seminude photo of Trump's wife—a former model—from an old *GQ* magazine shoot, posing on a bearskin rug. The new caption reads, "Meet Melania Trump. Your next first lady. Or, you could just support Ted Cruz on Tuesday." It sparks an instant rumpus between Trump and Cruz. Trump tweets out a threatening counterpunch: "Lyin' Ted Cruz just used a picture of Melania from a G.Q. shoot in his ad. Be careful, Lyin' Ted, or I will spill the beans on your wife!"

Make America Awesome also inundates Mormon women with anti-Trump ads on Facebook and Instagram. Its website promotes anti-Trump talking points and interactive "Dear Don" e-cards that sport cartoonish Trump photos with insults that Trump haters can send to their friends (or Trump himself):

> *"Dear Donald, my financial adviser said to say no to guys with four bankruptcies. Sorry."*
>
> And:
>
> *"I only date candidates who have the balls to debate."*

Cruz blows away Trump in Utah, taking close to 70 percent of the vote. He denies having anything to do with Make America Awesome—or the bearskin rug caper. But there does seem to be some connection. At least one news report notes that Make America Awesome and the campaign of Republican Carly Fiorina, soon to be named Cruz's running mate, used the same Alexandria, Virginia, address. In mid-April, I search through official Federal Election Commission filings and find Make America Awesome paperwork that discloses it backs Cruz.

In terms of money, Mair's Make America Awesome is small potatoes.

All told, a check of election records shows, it only spent about $35,000 during campaign 2016. But the group brags that it got a lot of bang for the buck. It tells reporters that its low-budget strategies, radio ad buys, and social media amplification enabled it to "punch well above [its] weight."

Mair didn't respond to my multiple requests for an interview. But she couldn't resist blowing her own horn in an April 2016 interview published in the *Huffington Post*:

> [A] lot of what we do is actually collating and distributing (without our fingerprints attached—a somewhat common and highly effective political campaign practice) opposition research. Some, if not most, of the stories that have legitimately caused Donald Trump the biggest problems in recent weeks and months have been initiated by our group, which is not big or well-funded, but has a lot of staunch grassroots supporters.

Mair gets back in the mix a bit later in the election cycle when news is recirculated from 1992 where, critics say, Trump defended convicted rapist, boxer Mike Tyson. (Trump had said in interviews that "to a large extent" he thought his friend Tyson had been "railroaded" and that "what happened to him" was a "travesty.") After the controversy resurfaces in 2016, Mair jumps in on Twitter with another credit grab and an "I told you so."

"Dear media: Make America Awesome pitched many of you the Mike Tyson clip back in, like, February. Many of you ignored us; others rejected it," she tweets.

A week after his Utah defeat, Trump provides more grist for the media mill during a town hall meeting in Green Bay, Wisconsin, led by MSNBC's Chris Matthews. Trump states that women who get abortions should be punished.

Matthews: Do you believe in punishment for abortion, yes or no as a principle?
Trump: The answer is that there has to be some form of punishment.
Matthews: For the woman.
Trump: Yeah, there has to be some form.

The comment draws immediate condemnation from pro-choice advocates and elicits a quick revision from the campaign, which issues a statement saying Trump *meant* that if abortion were outlawed, doctors who perform abortions should be punished.

Amid the fallout, I have my second interview with Trump for my *Full Measure* program, this time in Wisconsin. (My requests for interviews with Clinton continue to be declined.) Behind the scenes, the Trump campaign seems rattled and on edge. On camera, I ask him for more clarity on his abortion position.

"A lot of people said that my answer was a beautiful answer," Trump insists. "You have no idea how many people. Now, I'm thinking in terms of the torment and punishment that women will give themselves. They give themselves tremendous punishment."

Trump then deflects by attacking Chris Matthews. Honing his strategy of making the media part of his message.

"The question was asked by, you know, a guy with not good ratings, in all fairness," Trump tells me. "I've actually always liked Chris, but he has lousy ratings. I did the show as sort of a favor to him. I didn't know it was going to be such a crazy thing, what happened. But it wasn't a very important show. Hasn't been. Won't be. But he asked me a question and he asked me hypothetically. He said hypothetically, if this should happen. And he mentioned the word illegal."

I'm not the only one still probing on the abortion question. Nearly every major news outlet publishes multiple stories. The *Guardian* declares it to be the "biggest crisis of [Trump's] campaign." But the more I see Trump attacked from all sides, the more I continue to hear from a diverse group of ordinary folk who are still planning to vote for him. They think the media is biased and out of touch.

It's against this backdrop that I make an appearance on Bret Baier's *Fox Special Report* on April 1, 2016. In the "Candidate Casino" feature, I'm the first guest analyst—perhaps the only one—to predict a solid win for Trump.

"Regardless of how [the] Wisconsin [primary] turns out, all my money's on Trump," I say.

"Wow, a black chip!" remarks Baier. "We rarely see black chips here at this table. It's good to have you. You are a high roller!"

"And this is not a personal vote. It's an anticipation of what I think the voters might do," I tell the other panelists.

Cruz wins the April 5 Wisconsin primary and the media universally declares Trump to be in "Full Meltdown Mode." Little do they know.

Meanwhile, David Brock is now busy out west in California advancing the familiar narrative that Hillary Clinton *wants* to face off against Trump as the Republican pick. At an April 2016 meeting of the Soros-supported Democracy Alliance in Santa Monica, Brock says he has enough dirt to "knock Trump Tower down to the sub-basement." He tells the donors that Trump "was not properly vetted by his rivals or the press." His smear groups have held back damaging information, Brock says, that will be unleashed if Trump faces Clinton in the general election. The entire Brock event is reported in *Politico*. Where did *Politico* get this inside info? Why, from Brock's super PAC American Bridge. More inside-the-Beltway reporting planted by insiders to be read by insiders.

"American Bridge is building a database of all the regular people— from unpaid vendors to harassed tenants to defrauded students at Trump University—who got screwed over for one reason only," Brock tells the liberal megadonors in Santa Monica, according to *Politico*. "We sat on it all so as not to help the candidates who might have been stronger general election candidates."

Then again, they're not *really* sitting on it . . . it's just been leaked to *Politico*. When messengers toss the ball in one direction, I tend to look in the other to see what we're missing. Does Brock secretly know that a match up against Trump would be Clinton's worst nightmare?

By early May, the conservative Our Principles super PAC has shelled out an incredible sum to try to turn voters against Trump: more than $17 million. Yet on mid-Atlantic Super Tuesday, Trump sweeps five states: Connecticut, Delaware, Maryland, Pennsylvania, and Rhode Island. Trump's circus act is turning out to be not that of a clown, but an acrobat. Or maybe death-defying funambulist.

With no powerful super PAC yet making surreptitious smears on his behalf, the media and the public watch as Trump conducts much of his own dirty work right out in the open. When Univision cuts ties with Trump's Miss America and Miss Universe pageants—Trump sues. When women accuse Trump of sexual aggression—Trump evokes Bill Clinton's history of bad behavior. When the *New York Times* prints excerpts from Trump's old, stolen tax returns—Trump says Hillary is the criminal for destroying thirty-three thousand emails after they were subpoenaed. When a super PAC supporting Cruz smears Trump's wife, Melania— Trump fires up his Twitter account, threatening to bring Cruz's wife into the fight, and hits the reputation of Cruz's father.

"I mean . . . what was [Cruz's father] doing with Lee Harvey Oswald shortly before the death? Before the shooting [of President John F. Kennedy]?" Trump asks rhetorically in a May 3, 2016, phone interview on Fox News. He's referring to a tabloid-published photograph that purportedly depicts Cruz's father associating with John F. Kennedy's assassin. "It's horrible!" remarks Trump.

Later that day, Trump demolishes Cruz in the Indiana primary, where Cruz had been favored just a few weeks before. The New York billionaire is on a winning streak that will cement his nomination. Each time analysts, pundits, and reporters are proven wrong about Trump's fate, they launch new projections that prove equally as misguided—as the Republican field whittles down from 17 candidates to 10, and 6 and 3, all the way to the GOP nomination.

Meanwhile, Across Town . . .

As Donald Trump pulls ahead in the Republican field, Hillary Clinton's main super PAC gets down to serious business. Priorities USA Action jumps in with negative ads. One of them, titled "Speak," shows women mouthing some of Trump's derogatory comments about women. The commercial draws criticism from PolitiFact, which finds the ad wrongly implies Trump had used the F-word when he'd actually only mouthed it or said it "very softly, if at all," and, in any case, says PolitiFact, Trump wasn't referring to women in the first place. Priorities USA plans to spend an incredible $6 million over three weeks showing that commercial and a companion ad in the swing states of Florida, Nevada, Ohio, and Virginia.

With the rhetoric heating up, so does the shocking transactional journalism between the press and the Clinton campaign. More emails become public from the hacks into the email systems of the Democratic National Committee and Clinton campaign chairman Podesta. It's fair to ask, *Would hacks of emails written by the Republican National Committee and Donald Trump campaign officials reveal similarly scandalous material?* There's little doubt that embarrassing content would likely be found within GOP private exchanges, too. One can speculate that such exchanges might show Trump officials coordinating with right-leaning blogs and websites to plant stories and gain positive coverage. However, based on my experience, it's difficult to imagine such emails would show Trump officials as able to call the shots and dictate terms of news coverage at supposedly neutral, mainstream outlets as extensively as Democrats managed to do.

In a February 2016 internal campaign email, Clinton press secretary Nick Merrill describes a friendly relationship between CNN producer Dan Merica and Clinton. "They are basically courting each other at this point," Merrill quips.

The following month, emails reveal CNN and ABC contributor Donna Brazile, then vice chair at the Democratic National Committee, feeding the Clinton campaign an advance question prior to a CNN primary debate.

"One of the questions directed to HRC [Hillary Rodham Clinton] tomorrow is from a woman with a rash," Brazile writes to the campaign on March 5, 2016. "Her family has lead poison and she will ask what, if anything, will Hillary do as president to help the ppl of Flint [Michigan]." At the debate the next day, a woman fitting the description Brazile gave asks a similar question.

A week later, emails indicate Brazile is at it again: she obtains and feeds an advance CNN town hall question to the Clinton campaign. The subject line of the email on March 12, 2016, reads, "From time to time I get the questions in advance." Brazile then passes along the text of a lengthy question about the death penalty, commenting, "Here's one that worries me about HRC." The next day, an audience member asks the question in CNN's town hall with Clinton and Sanders.

When emails revealing the apparent collusion become public in fall of 2016, both CNN and Brazile claim she couldn't have possibly gotten her hands on advance material. However, *Politico* obtains an internal CNN email from one of its moderators reflecting the very death penalty question Brazile passed along to the campaign prior to the town hall— identical in wording, spacing, and capitalization. CNN points the finger of blame for the leak at its town hall partner, TV One cable network, and severs its ties with Brazile.

Why political operatives like Brazile are invited so integrally into the fold at news organizations in the first place is part of a crucial transformation that's taken place in the news business. Largely as a result of efforts like those of Media Matters—its media training of pundits, its outreach to journalists, and its paid efforts to train and hire "reporters" who write for and go on to work in the press—partisan operators have quite literally infiltrated newsrooms in a significant way. They're included in planning and discussions. Invited in as guests. Hired on as paid analysts, anchors, and reporters. Political operatives are becoming journalists and vice versa. Newsrooms are, in some respects, becoming political operations and vice versa. This helps explain why shocking displays of bias, and even the reporting of blatantly false information, are often allowed to go unpunished. Sometimes they're even rewarded.

As the campaign marches forward, news reporters engage in increasingly brazen editorial attacks against Trump. On March 29, 2016, at a CNN town hall, reporter Anderson Cooper asks Trump about a squabble he's having with fellow Republican Ted Cruz. When Trump responds, quite correctly, that Cruz had lashed out first, Cooper responds, "With all due respect, sir, that is the argument of a five-year-old." Cooper's remark is covered, as if news, by the likes of *Salon, Gawker, Variety, Media Matters,* and *U.S. News & World Report.* "Anderson Cooper Shuts Down Donald Trump," declares *Salon.*

It seems Donna Brazile isn't the only direct nexus between CNN and the Clinton campaign. April 2016 emails indicate the Democratic National Committee is plugged in when it comes to CNN's interviews with Republican candidates. On April 25, a DNC official circulates an email titled "Trump Questions for CNN." The official tells colleagues, "[CNN anchor] Wolf Blitzer is interviewing Trump on Tues ahead of his foreign policy address on Wed. Please send me thoughts by 10:30 AM tomorrow." On April 28, there's another DNC internal email, titled "Cruz on CNN." This time a DNC official emails party colleagues that "CNN is looking for questions. Please send some topical/interesting ones. Maybe a couple on [Republican candidate Carly] Fiorina. Someone please take point and send them all together by 3pm. Thank you!"

During the same time period, Dana Milbank of the *Washington Post* apparently turns to the DNC to obtain opposition research on Trump. In an April 21, 2016, email, a DNC official writes colleagues, "research request: top 10 worst Trump quotes? Milbank doing a Passover-themed 10 plagues of Trump. Off top of my head, I'm thinking: · Punish women · Mexicans as rapists · Ban Muslims · Shoot someone in middle of 5th ave · Rough up BLM protestor · Anchor baby · Do a lot worse than waterboarding · Blood coming out of her wherever · Spill beans on ted's wife · Talked about penis on stage at debate[.] Any other big things I'm missing? And can you pull bullets for these?" The resulting Milbank article, titled "The Ten Plagues of Trump," cites eight of the DNC suggestions.

Politico's chief investigative reporter, Ken Vogel, gets caught in a compromising position on April 30, 2016, when he emails one of his soon-to-be-published stories to DNC communications official Mark Paustenbach.

"[P]er agreement . . . any thoughts appreciated," Vogel writes.

Paustenbach then passes along Vogel's draft to the DNC's head of communications, Luis Miranda.

"Vogel gave me his story ahead of time/before it goes to his editors as long as I didn't share it," Paustenbach writes.

News flash: Paustenbach is in the act of "sharing it."

Paustenbach continues: "Let me know if you see anything that's missing and I'll push back."

Vogel would later defend the act of sending prepublication material to the DNC as a sort of fact-checking exercise. Let me clarify: this goes way beyond checking facts, in my view. Normal accepted practices may include reading back specific quotes to a source for accuracy or verifying a particular fact. But sharing an advance copy of an entire story about a campaign controversy with one of the interested parties is strictly verboten in honest journalism.

At least it used to be.

Perhaps the most shocking admission by a transactional journalist comes in an email on April 30, 2015. Chief *Politico* political correspondent Glenn Thrush sends an advance draft of part of an article to the Clinton campaign's Podesta for approval.

"Please don't share or tell anyone I did this," Thrush writes. "Because I have become a hack I will send u the whole section that pertains to u. . . . Tell me if I fucked up anything."

Podesta signs off and the article is published.

The same month, Thrush sends eight paragraphs from another as-yet-unpublished article to the Clinton campaign's Palmieri with the title "please read asap . . . don't share." Palmieri immediately shares, forwarding to colleagues and writing, "Glenn Thrush is doing a story about how well launch went and some part of it will be about me—which I hate. He did me the courtesy of sending what he is going to say about me. Seems fine."

(On December 12, 2016, the *New York Times* announces it has hired "I-have-become-a-hack" Thrush, referring to him as a "stellar addition" and "premier political journalist." Thrush joins Maggie "friendly-journalist" Haberman and Peter Baker, husband of *Politico* editor Susan Glasser, who will be on the *Times* team assigned to cover the Trump White House fairly and impartially. A *Huffington Post* article about the announcement refers to Haberman as a "former *Politico* star" and omits mention of the high-profile controversies over the reporters' partisan ties.)

These are some of the connections that Donald Trump must face and fight as he and Hillary Clinton move toward Election Day as their parties' respective nominees.

Chapter Nine

||||||||||||||||||||||||

General Election

Amazingly, on May 4, 2016, Donald Trump becomes the presumptive Republican nominee: Last Man Standing on the GOP side. He's defied predictions and sidestepped the media hatchet jobs. At the same time, an uncanny phenomenon that's begun to take shape over the past ten months begins to solidify. The media are no longer just tools of the smear artists; they've become formidable smear artists in their own right.

As the hard reality of a Trump nomination sets in with compunctious Republicans, the conservative Our Principles super PAC announces it will give up actively opposing Trump. For the first time, Trump gets a shot at meaningful financial support from a brand-new super PAC called Great America, led by longtime GOP political consultant Ed Rollins. Rollins was national campaign director for Ronald Reagan in 1984, winning 49 of 50 states.

Great America begins by plunking down $5 million to buy pro-Trump TV ads. Almost immediately the group clashes with another Trump backer, Roger Stone, and *his* preferred super PAC: Committee for American Sovereignty, which was said to be started by Trump business interests. Rollins was on record in the past calling Stone "a little rat." The super PAC feud between them is personal.

Stone is a well-known tour de force on the smear circuit. The story goes that he was just nineteen years old in the 1970s when he executed his first political dirty trick. A supporter of Richard Nixon for president, young Stone reportedly came up with an idea in 1972 to make a campaign contribution to Nixon challenger Pete McCloskey under the fake identity of a socialist. Stone then mailed the donation receipt to a newspaper as supposed proof that McCloskey was affiliated with the radical, socialist left.

Over the next four decades, Stone cornered the dirty tricks market. In 2008, he started an anti–Hillary Clinton 527 political group named Citizens United Not Timid. It was more for his own entertainment than for any meaningful tactical purpose: Stone told the *New Yorker* he named the group so he could refer to it by its acronym. (Figure it out.)

"I thought it up in a bar," Stone says. "I was having fun!"

In April 2016, Rollins's Great America and Stone's Committee for American Sovereignty begin a fierce competition for the blessing of the Trump campaign. "[Stone's Committee for American Sovereignty] is really going to go after Hillary," an insider tells me. Whichever super PAC wins a candidate's tacit approval gets the bulk of contributions from donors. But there's division in the ranks on Team Trump. His convention manager, hedge fund manager Paul Manafort, sides with Stone, while Trump campaign manager Corey Lewandowski favors Rollins.

"Plenty of money people are waiting to write checks [to help Trump]," says an operative. "But they don't know which super PAC to write it to." The lack of clarity muddles Trump's fundraising efforts. "Hillary is very organized. Bush was, too," remarks the operative. "There was no confusion over which PACs the candidates approved of and appreciated. But with Trump, it's not clear, hindering the traditional organization effort. Trump still hates super PACs. He hates them all. But he realizes one is necessary."

"Could Trump win without the help of a super PAC?" I ask.

"We don't know anything," the operative replies. "There's nothing traditional about his campaign so far. Anyone who tells you they know is out of their mind."

The super PAC rivalry plays out until June 20, 2016, when Lewandowski is fired from the Trump train and Great America ends up with the edge. But two months later, Manafort also leaves the Trump campaign amid turmoil and controversy, a casualty of his alleged business dealings with Russian interests in Ukraine. (Trump's supposed ties with Russia would later emerge as the big-league focus in a future smear.)

Before the election is over, Great America will have spent over $25 million "broadcasting more than 17,500 TV spots and 250,000 radio ads." By its own account, it also "secured over 250,000 contributors, built a file of millions of active, newly engaged Trump supporters, placed over 5 million phone calls, and sent over 2.5 million pieces of mail." In contrast, the Committee for American Sovereignty reports spending only $64,000 to help Trump.

On the heels of Trump sewing up the GOP nomination, transactional journalism shifts into overdrive. Emails posted on WikiLeaks have already shown the DNC to be both accommodating and controlling in its dealings with favored left-leaning reporters. But not all members of the press are in good standing with the party apparatus—and leaked emails demonstrate that, too. On May 13, 2016, a Fox News freelancer named Fred Lucas writes a politely worded email asking the DNC to comment on "Donald Trump's attacks against Secretary Clinton as an 'enabler' of President Clinton's alleged misconduct with women." Rather than provide a comment to the apparently despised Fox, DNC spokesman Luis Miranda forwards the email to his colleague Mark Paustenbach with the comment, "Is there a Fuck You emoji?" DNC press assistant Rachel Palermo chimes in with "hahahahahahahaha." Paustenbach adds, "We're not responding at all."

When the reporter follows up, Paustenbach writes Miranda, "The asshole from fox emailed us again. . . . I did some research and there's still no 'fuck you' emoji, unfortunately."

DNC officials respond quite differently to CNN political commentator Maria Cardona. On May 18, 2016, Cardona sends them a draft of her CNN opinion piece that smears Bernie Sanders, blaming him for party discord, and urges him to prevent embarrassing disunity at the upcoming Democratic National Convention in Philadelphia. In other words: get on board with Hillary.

"Subject: URGENT—DRAFT CNN OPED ON NV . . . I want to make sure it is not to [sic] heavy handed. Please let me know asap!

Thanks!!" writes Cardona to DNC officials. That's followed by an email exchange in which the officials suggest edits to Cardona's story.

"Is this better?" Cardona asks in a subsequent email, seeking approval after revising a paragraph accordingly.

Cardona is an admitted Hillary supporter and a superdelegate for Democrats. She also works at a campaign public relations group connected to a pro-Hillary super PAC. It's bad enough, in my view, that news organizations routinely allow themselves to be used to publish propaganda written by political operatives. But for Cardona to work directly behind the scenes with the DNC on an opinion piece to be published by CNN crosses a serious ethical line, in my opinion.

In other emails, DNC officials indicate they also have a symbiotic relationship with Greg Sargent of the *Washington Post*. On May 20, 2016, they're formulating a plan to spin some negative news about Hillary.

"[W]e need to see if we can place a story FIRST rather than just dropping a press release to make sure the first story out of the gate is as helpful as possible," writes the DNC's Miranda to his colleagues. "Placing a story" is more effective than issuing a press release because ordinary people are more likely to view it as legitimate news. More important, in today's environment, getting a "news story" published virtually ensures other "reporters" will copy the item and pass it along. The audacity of it is that the DNC apparently knows it won't have to search far and wide to find a reporter willing to act upon its request. It's just a matter of choosing one from the pack.

"I think the best reporter to give the news to ahead of time is Greg Sargent at the *Washington Post*," suggests the DNC's Paustenbach. "But, the specific reporter is not as important as getting it to an outlet before the news breaks so we can help control the narrative on the front end. Otherwise this may likely get spun in a not-so-helpful way. We should also get Rep. [Elijah] Cummings on the phone with that reporter."

Miranda makes a hard push to use the *Post*'s Sargent, in particular.

"[C]an we please consider giving Sargent the first bite to get a good first story out there? Can I have him call you? We had been working him for weeks in general on writing up something positive, we think he'd play ball," writes Miranda.

What's the "news" item about which the DNC so desperately wants to "control the narrative"? We can guess by looking at the story Sargent published in the *Post* the same day: it's a story providing helpful spin for Clinton on a new poll that found 28 percent of Sanders supporters would not vote for Hillary.

"[The poll] sounds worrisome [for Hillary]," Sargent writes. "But it turns out that things may have been worse in 2008, as the [presidential] primary battle between Hillary Clinton and Barack Obama wound down."

Sargent goes on to cite a 2008 poll that found even more Clinton voters at the time said they'd vote for Republican John McCain if Obama beat Hillary in the Democratic primary. Sargent is delivering the message to readers that the new poll isn't as bad for Clinton as it looks. *Obama had worse marks in 2008 and still got elected. Now Clinton can, too!* If this is indeed the story peddled to Sargent by the DNC, it's a propaganda coup. All under the guise of reporting the news.

The First Big Hit Piece

Ten days after Trump locks up the nomination, his enemies, including the media, are deeply steeped in their operations against him. On May 14, 2016, the *New York Times* publishes a blockbuster article titled "Crossing the Line: How Donald Trump Behaved with Women in Private." It's accompanied by the dramatic subtitle "Interviews reveal unwelcome advances, a shrewd reliance on ambition, and unsettling workplace conduct over decades."

Even by the *Times'* increasingly loose standards, it's a blatant hit piece. It begins with a former Trump girlfriend recounting a pool party in 1990 at Trump's Mar-a-Lago beach club in Palm Beach, Florida. Trump sounds like the worst kind of predator.

> *Donald J. Trump had barely met Rowanne Brewer Lane when he asked her to change out of her clothes. . . . "He suddenly took me by the hand, and he started to show me around the mansion. He asked me if I had a swimsuit with me. I said no . . . I hadn't intended to swim.*

He took me into a room and opened drawers and asked me to put on a swimsuit. . . . He brought me out to the pool [in front of a crowd] and said, 'That is a stunning Trump girl, isn't it?'

Next, the authors of the *Times* article, Michael Barbaro and Megan Twohey, insert their own personal commentary without labeling it as their opinion: "This is the public treatment of some women by Mr. Trump, the presumptive Republican nominee for president: degrading, impersonal, performed." The story is widely picked up and published by other national media.

There's just one problem.

As soon as the article is published, Brewer Lane goes public and insists she never found Trump's behavior to be any of the negative things the reporters said it was. In fact, she claims that she was stunned to read the *Times*' version of her story, and she challenges both its accuracy and the reporters' motivations. Brewer Lane says that Trump "never made me feel like I was being demeaned in any way, he never offended me in any way." In fact, she'd gone on to date Trump after the incident in question. In other words, the example the *Times* used to establish the thesis of Trump's "unwelcome advances" turned out not to be an unwelcome advance at all, according to the would-be victim. In an interview with Fox News on May 16, 2016, Brewer Lane publicly shames the *Times* and sets the record straight with her account of events.

"The *New York Times* told us several times that they would make sure my story that I was telling came across, they promised several times that they would do it accurately, they told me several times and my manager several times that it would not be a hit piece and that my story would come across the way that I was telling it and honestly and it absolutely was not," she tells Fox. "They did take quotes from what I said and they put a negative connotation on it. They spun it to where it appeared negative. I did not have a negative experience with Donald Trump."

Faced with their lead subject discrediting their reporting, the *Times* reporters stand by their story. But Trump's supporters, and even some critics, are disturbed by the disconnect between the article and what Brewer Lane is saying afterward.

A *New York Times* story like this—even though allegedly untrue—would take down a weaker candidate. But Trump once again proves to be the anti-smear Wildcard. The article backfires and serves to punctuate his theme of media bias.

For other journalists looking for material in their self-described mission to destroy Trump, the Democratic National Committee offers much fodder. A leak of a 237-page DNC dossier in June 2016 provides a hint as to the vast political efforts mounted against the Republican nominee. Titled "Donald Trump Report," it formally outlines Trump's flip-flops and incendiary remarks so they can be exploited in the media. It also reveals the "Top Narratives" the DNC has apparently developed to use against him: "Trump Has No Core, Divisive and Offensive Campaign, Bad Businessman, Dangerous & Irresponsible Policies, Misogynist in Chief, Out of Touch and Personal Life."

Summer of Media Discontent

As summer is drawing near, the days are growing longer, and a new frontier appears on the horizon in the smear game. It's one that's been brewing beneath the surface throughout the campaign and will continue to have an impact long after the votes are cast. Fake news.

July 2016 brings one of the first major incidents of fake news of the campaign, before the term becomes a household word. A website calling itself *WTOE 5 News* reports that Pope Francis has taken an unprecedented step and endorsed Donald Trump for president. It's not true. But word of the fake Trump endorsement gets circulated nearly a million times on Facebook. (In 2015, another fake site reported that the pope endorsed Bernie Sanders, but that story didn't pick up as much traction.) The viral success of the Trump story is duly noted by those seeking to make money off the clicks that such stories garner from unsuspecting readers. But it also captures the attention of smear merchants who will increasingly turn to fake news in the coming weeks to further their narratives.

Trump keeps going like the Energizer Bunny, rising from pronounced states of death, confounding all projections. And the press is suffering a severe case of the summer doldrums. They try a succession of new themes to snuff him out. No longer are they merely the middlemen or willing tools of political operatives. They're functioning as an opposition party.

After Trump's July 21 speech to accept the GOP nomination at the Republican convention, Hillary campaign chair Podesta releases a public statement that declares, "Tonight, Donald Trump painted a dark picture of an America in decline." A directive has been implicitly issued to the press and pundits to portray Trump's vision as "dark." The media is off and running.

> Joe Scarborough of MSNBC: "It was a *dark* speech."
> Former Republican National Committee chairman Michael Steele: "dystopian and *dark*."
> NBC News: "Donald Trump Takes America on a Journey to the *Dark* Side."
> *New York Times:* "His Tone *Dark*, Donald Trump Takes GOP Mantle," and "a *dark* vision of America."
> *Politico:* "a *darkening* America."
> CNN: "Was Donald Trump's speech too *dark*?"
> David Gregory on CNN: "*dark* vision for America."

Two facts are particularly noteworthy. First, a striking number of ordinary people I interact with, many of them Trump supporters, described Trump's speech in positive terms. Yet news personalities and pundits in the media almost universally described the same speech in negative terms. Second, an uncanny number of Trump critics chose to use the very word Podesta had suggested—*dark*—rather than other descriptions, such as *bleak, grim, hopeless, gloomy, pessimistic, depressing,* or *negative.* The media's strikingly similar analyses raise important questions. Are they meeting and conspiring in an organized sense? Are they unaware that they're being shaped and used as propaganda tools?

I argue there are elements of both in play. Through sources at various national news outlets, I'm aware of internal meetings being called by news management to discuss the necessity of aggressively covering Trump in a way that tilts strongly negative, with a fervor never before applied to other candidates. I also know that, in some instances, news organizations are co-ordinating with one another, and with Democrat operatives, on elements of their coverage. I'm aware there's a serious case of groupthink among many journalists that tends to put them all onto the same general editorial page. And I realize there's been a soft infiltration of news organizations by political operatives.

So rather than offering truly original analysis, or representing differing views, the media pursues a propaganda campaign to smear the politician they see as their mortal enemy.

All of this evokes the dicta of successful historic propagandists described earlier. From Alinsky's *Rules for Radicals:*

- "Ridicule is man's most potent weapon."
- "Keep the pressure on. Never let up."
- "development of operations that will keep a constant pressure on the opposition."
- "Pick the target, freeze it, personalize it, and polarize it."
- "Not every item of news should be published. Rather must those who control news policies endeavor to make every item of news serve a certain purpose."
- "Propaganda must facilitate the displacement of aggression by specifying the targets for hatred."

And from Hitler's propagandist Goebbels:

"A lie told once remains a lie but a lie told a thousand times becomes the truth."

Mainstream news reporting is heavily negative on Trump through July, but it becomes positively over-the-top tyrannical in August. The *New York Post* breaks the first major exclusive after the GOP convention. The headlines state, "Melania Trump Like You've Never Seen Her Before," "Menage a Trump," and "Melania Trump's Girl on Girl Photos from Racy Shoot Revealed." While you might think Mrs. Trump's racy modeling shots in a French magazine from nineteen years ago aren't terribly consequential, *au contraire*! They constitute a Watergate-level scandal as far as the media is concerned. Important questions must be explored. On August 2, 2016,

AP further advances the deep investigations into Trump's Slovenia-born wife by raising the possibility that, decades ago, she had (gasp!) worked on a modeling job in the United States while on a visa that didn't yet entitle her to work. The allegation is said to be based on unverified documents "found recently in storage" and "provided to the Associated Press" by unnamed figures. Many news outlets pick up the "big" story.

"Did Donald Trump marry an undocumented worker?" asks the *Daily News* in an article on August 4, 2016, referring to the AP report. *Politico* copycats with "Gaps in Melania Trump's immigration story raise questions." The *Los Angeles Times,* Britain's *Daily Mail,* CBS News, *Mediaite,* the *Washington Post,* and *USA Today* publish their own versions. While they eagerly forward the unsubstantiated speculation about Melania, they reserve all of their journalistic skepticism for explanations that may be favorable to Melania. When her former agent steps forward to say that he personally secured the proper visa for her back in the late 1990s, *Daily News* reports that as nothing more than a "claim" and adds, in a suspicious tone, that he "offered no documentation."

Once Melania has been thoroughly smeared, a Trump lawyer, who happens to be a Hillary supporter, steps forward and publicly certifies that Melania had been on a legitimate visa when she worked in the United States, and that the press had gotten the dates of the photo shoot wrong. A photographer involved in the job confirms it. *USA Today,* the *Post,* and *Politico* issue brief corrections and clarifications that don't receive the same prominent news coverage as the original articles. But to James West at left-leaning *Mother Jones,* the exoneration of Melania is cause for even greater suspicion. He writes, "Melania Trump's Photographer Just Made Her Immigration Story Even More Confusing: There are so many lies, what are we to believe or not believe?" The media's false reporting is lost amid a sea of purposefully generated confusion intended to deflect blame and leave voters not knowing what to believe.

Media critic Howard Kurtz is one of the few noting the decidedly unjournalistic tone of the sordid saga. "Where are the corrections from everyone else who ran with this story?" he asks on his Fox News program, *Media Buzz.*

Over the course of just two days during the Melania smears, August 2 and August 3, the press also seeks to create an impression of the Trump campaign in irreparable chaos and disarray. There's no way for him to come back, they declare. He may as well write his own obituary. *Never mind, they're writing it for him.*

"Donald Trump is out of time," concludes the *Daily Beast*'s Goldie Taylor. "There may be three months to go until Election Day. But the race between Donald Trump and Hillary Clinton is all but over." "Is Donald Trump Testing His Exit Strategy?" asks the *Chicago Tribune*'s Clarence Page. The *Washington Post*'s Eugene Robinson posits, "Is Donald Trump Just Plain Crazy?" *Forbes* states: "As Trump's Campaign Flounders, Hillary Clinton Dominates The National Ad War." The *New York Times* touts Clinton's fundraising advantage: "Hillary Clinton's Campaign Raised $63 million in July, Its Best Mark." They're all busily crafting their own artificial reality, hoping to convince voters that it's the real world: The Trump campaign is in utter collapse. He can't possibly win.

The *New York Times* also breaks the big "news" that Clinton is so far ahead, and so confident, she's already measuring the drapes at the White House. "Hillary Clinton Campaign Takes First Steps in Presidential Transition." The narrative is picked up by everyone from local news to the *Sydney Morning Herald* in Australia. *USA Today* publishes a one-sided piece promoting Clinton's supposed "legions of female donors." No acknowledgment is provided of Trump's favorable fundraising trends, such as his high percentage of small donors (possibly reflective of grassroots popularity among ordinary Americans), or his number-one donor "industry" being "retirees" (versus Clinton's, which is Wall Street interests). NPR makes it sound as though Trump should just throw in the towel and put everyone out of their misery: "Can This Campaign Be Saved? GOP Scrambles to 'Reset' Trump." The *Washington Post*'s Chris Cillizza declares, "Trump's campaign in full blown panic/collapse mode" in an article titled "Why Donald Trump's Campaign Is Like a Speeding Car with Its Parts Falling Off." (Cillizza's past offerings include "Donald Trump's Dark Twisted Fantasy in 30 Seconds" and a bold but incorrect prediction that Ted Cruz would be the GOP nominee.) The *Atlantic* asks, "Is the Trump Campaign Collapsing?" featuring a large photo of Trump, captured in an unflattering pose that makes him appear to have his hand at his own throat. "The Donald Trump campaign is unraveling," declares

Atlantic writer David Graham. *Esquire* claims: "A Mutiny Is Brewing on Trump's Nuclear Submarine: The captain has lost his mind, and they're scrambling below deck."

Much as "dark" was the order of the day in July, we can identify several discrete smear narratives adopted by the media in August:

Implosion. *Vanity Fair* claims "MASS DEFECTIONS EXPECTED AS DONALD TRUMP'S CAMPAIGN IMPLODES." *Raw Story* writes of "Trump's latest implosion." *New Statesman* asks, "Is Donald Trump finally imploding?" Politicsusa.com says "Donald Trump Continues to Implode Before Our Eyes." *New York* magazine's Jonathan Chait predicts "Donald Trump's campaign might actually implode," and remarks it's "sad for the Trump staffers, who have worked so hard to give an unstable demagogue control of the executive branch."

Criticism from Obama. President Obama's predictable proclamations against Trump are treated as if they're major, breaking news. On August 2, 2016, *Politico* reports that Obama "ridicules Republicans for sticking with Trump." The *New York Times* reads, "Obama Says Republicans Should Withdraw Support for Trump." And CNN quotes Obama as saying "Trump 'unfit' for presidency."

Crying baby. When Trump teases about a crying baby at a rally, it's reported as if it's big news, and as if he's serious. "Donald Trump Jousts with a Crying Baby at His Rally," blares the *New York Times* on August 2, 2016. NPR's headline reads, "Trump: 'Get That Baby Out of Here.'" *Politico:* "Trump at rally: 'Get the baby out of here.'" And *Slate* writes, "Watch Donald Trump Kick an Actual Baby Out of His Rally." No matter that the baby's mother, a Trump supporter, tells reporters the obvious: that she took Trump's comments as good-natured humor.

Pence divide: The usual suspects try to stoke a supposed divide between Trump and his running mate, Mike Pence. "Mike Pence Should Get Donald Trump to Withdraw," writes the *New York Times.* "Where Donald Trump and Mike Pence Don't Agree" is the topic of an in-depth story by CBS News.

Meltdown: *Time* weighs in with a cover showing a cartoon depiction of Trump as a featureless mouth, melting away like a hot wax statue with a one-word caption: "Meltdown." The cover is in turn covered by other media, as if it's news. "Donald Trump melts on the cover of *Time* Magazine," declares *Advertising Age*. The *Washington Post* writes, "Donald Trump should hate this *Time* magazine cover, but he'll probably hang it in his office." (*Time* will later follow with another cover showing Trump entirely melted away, implying—again—that he's finished off as a candidate.)

Dangerous: Much as the Clinton camp pointed the media toward the "dark" narrative in July, they're able to plant a "dangerous" narrative in August. On August 16, 2016, Clinton tweets: "It's not just that Trump doesn't know what he's talking about when it comes to national security. His words are dangerous, and they hurt us." Dana Milbank of the *Washington Post* is banging the same drum. He writes an opinion article titled "The Singular Danger of Trump."

White racist: The collective David Brock propaganda groups begin a theme and meme of Trump and his supporters as "white nationalists." Brock's *Blue Nation Review* pummels Trump in six days with smear articles titled "Trump Shakes Up Staff, Embraces White Nationalism," "Trump's Purity Test for Immigrants Is More Evidence of His White Nationalist Plans," "Trump Is Seeking a White Nationalist Awakening NOT the White House," "NEW VIDEO: Trump Is Now Leading a White Nationalist 'Awakening,'" "Is Trump's New 'America First' App Designed to Connect White Nationalists?," and "Trump Delivers Anti-Black Rant: 'You're Living in Poverty, Your Schools Are No Good.'"

There's no question Trump is making his share of incendiary remarks—as do many politicians in countless circumstances—but uniquely, in this instance, the press gives itself perpetual permission to step away from its reporting role and take him on in an intensely personal and biased sense. The story line of Trump's campaign being in dire straits saturates the Web, social media, and TV news without regard to the fact that these news sources have been proven entirely wrong in their predictions over and over.

When very real discord occurs in the Trump campaign, it provides that grain of truth that feeds the media frenzy. The *New York Times* reports allegations that Trump adviser Paul Manafort once consulted for Ukraine's pro-Russia ruling party. It becomes a campaign issue, with Democrats saying it's a serious conflict for Trump advisers to be linked to Russia while President Vladimir Putin is behaving aggressively and disregarding human rights. The *Times* quotes sources who say Manafort's name was found in a secret ledger indicating he'd gotten $12.7 million in cash payouts from Russian interests. Manafort dismisses the reports as "silly" and "nonsensical." He adds that he's never performed work for the governments of Ukraine or Russia, and never received an "off-the-books cash payment." In a statement, he does acknowledge he's "done work on overseas campaigns," including in Ukraine, prior to its 2014 parliamentary elections. "All of the political payments directed to me were for my entire political team: campaign staff (local and international), polling and research, election integrity and television advertising," says Manafort. It continues to fascinate me that top U.S. political operatives are being hired around the world to affect elections in foreign countries—at the same time the smear happens to be going global.

In another example of journalistic double standards at work, there's no similar outrage over word that the Clinton Foundation reportedly received $8.6 million from a Ukrainian-based foundation from 2009 to 2013. Some would consider that a serious conflict of interest because the foundation took the money while Hillary was secretary of state and in a position to influence policy during the buildup to the Ukrainian crisis, when war broke out between the post-revolutionary Ukrainian government and pro-Russian fighters. But the media finds this foreign connection far less interesting than most any negative news about Trump, whether real or manufactured.

While many in the media seem to give Clinton the benefit of the doubt at every turn, they continue to interpret and portray Trump's comments in the most damaging light possible, dismissing explanations that fight their narrative. For example, at an August 2016 rally, Trump tells the crowd that any of Clinton's future U.S. Supreme Court picks as president would likely dial back constitutional gun rights.

"Hillary essentially wants to abolish the Second Amendment," Trump says. "By the way, and if she gets to pick her judges, nothing you can do, folks. Although the Second Amendment people, maybe there is. I don't know."

When Trump says the "Second Amendment people" might be able to do something about Hillary's judicial picks, I infer that to mean the powerful gun lobby—many Democrats among them—could influence who Clinton chooses, or which Supreme Court nominee she could get approved by the Senate. But to the news media and Trump's other opponents, he has just issued a call to murder Clinton! The super PAC Democratic Coalition Against Trump reports Trump's remark to the FBI as a threat of violence. The press goes wild. Among them is former CBS News anchor Dan Rather. In a Facebook rant on August 9, 2016, Rather hangs up the façade of objective journalist and writes in part:

> *No trying-to-be objective and fair journalist, no citizen who cares about the country and its future can ignore what Donald Trump said today. When he suggested that "The Second Amendment People" can stop Hillary Clinton he crossed a line with dangerous potential. By any objective analysis, this is a new low and unprecedented in the history of American presidential politics. This is no longer about policy, civility, decency or even temperament. This is a direct threat of violence against a political rival. It is not just against the norms of American politics, it raises a serious question of whether it is against the law. . . . To anyone who still pretends this is a normal election of Republican against Democrat, history is watching. And I suspect its verdict will be harsh. . . . This cannot be treated as just another outrageous moment in the campaign. We will see whether major newscasts explain how grave and unprecedented this is and whether the headlines in tomorrow's newspapers do it justice. We will soon know whether anyone who has publicly supported Trump explains how they can continue to do. . . .*

Rather ends by encouraging other journalists to cast aside their professional neutrality and become political advocates to try to defeat Trump.

"The institution of ht epress [*sic*] and how it'sviewed [*sic*] and what it can do is more important than any single election," writes Rather on Facebook.

It turns out the rest of the press doesn't need Rather's prompting. The typical reporting on Trump is so biased that Fox's Kurtz remarks, "In the last ten days it is almost like the press put out a mob hit on Donald Trump. . . . A lot of journalists . . . feel that Trump is so dangerous . . . that they feel that it is almost their patriotic duty to 'take him down.'" Kurtz further notes, "Once you adopt the view that this guy has to be stopped for the good of the country, then you have shed any pretense of objectivity."

The *Columbia Journalism Review* (*CJR*) also analyzes the remarkable trend, noting that "modern-day journalists are . . . pushing explicitly against Donald Trump." *CJR* appears to lend sympathy to the bias by likening it to the treatment famed CBS journalist Edward R. Murrow gave to the infamous senator Joseph McCarthy and his 1954 congressional hearings to root out anti-American activities inside the government.

"We . . . are witnessing a change from existing practice of steadfast detachment, and the context in which journalists are reacting is not unlike that of Murrow," writes *CJR*. "The candidate's comments fall outside acceptable societal norms, and critical journalists are not alone in speaking up."

In September, David Brock's Citizens for Responsibility and Ethics in Washington (CREW) files an IRS complaint against Trump and his charitable foundation. It's yet another astroturf move against the GOP nominee. The partisan complaint is widely reported as if news, without the context that CREW has become a tool in Media Matters' smear toolbox. Many articles refer to CREW as if it's a neutral group, calling it an "ethics group" or "Washington nonprofit." The *Hill* simply calls it "a watchdog group."

As summer draws to a close, Clinton creates her own smearable moment. Speaking at a New York City fundraiser of gay supporters on September 9, 2016, with Barbra Streisand as the headliner, Clinton flings the worst kinds of insults at Trump supporters:

> *You know, to just be grossly generalistic, you could put half of Trump's supporters into what I call the basket of deplorables. Right? The racist, sexist, homophobic, xenophobic, Islamaphobic—you name it . . .*

He tweets and retweets their offensive hateful mean-spirited rhetoric.
Now, some of those folks—they are irredeemable, but thankfully they
are not America.

The audience chuckles. But many Americans don't find the remarks funny at all. Republicans seize the opportunity. They borrow a page from the Media Matters playbook and quickly circulate the relevant excerpt of Clinton's speech. "Wow, Hillary Clinton was SO INSULTING to my supporters, millions of amazing, hard working people," Trump tweets. "I think it will cost her at the polls!" Before long, social media kicks into action and #BasketofDeplorables begins trending on Twitter.

Some liberal media outlets attempt to defend Clinton, positioning her remarks next to offensive things Trump has said. But it's a net loss for Clinton. For once, her faux pas is critically reported in mainstream outlets, including CNN, *New York Times,* CBS, and NBC. Even NPR advises, "Memo to candidates: Stop generalizing and psychoanalyzing your opponents' supporters. It never works out well for you."

The following day, Clinton issues a statement that reads, in part, "Last night I was 'grossly generalistic,' and that's never a good idea. I regret saying 'half'—that was wrong."

Two days later, Clinton will suffer the largest setback to date in her campaign.

Hillary's Health and More Smears

Aside from the fundraisers, Hillary has been lying low, making few public appearances, forsaking press conferences, and having several very public, uncontrollable coughing fits. Trump adviser Rudy Giuliani raises questions about the health of the Democrats' nominee and implies the mainstream press isn't giving the matter due coverage. In a TV interview, he suggests that Americans go online and conduct a search for "Hillary Clinton illness." He knows that such searches will turn up Internet videos raising questions about Clinton's physical state. As legions of curious observers burn up the Internet with searches, the news media comes to Clinton's defense. They're on message with the conspiracy theory narrative.

"Google should fix this," tweets Farhad Manjoo of the *New York Times,* implying that the Internet search engine should somehow prevent people from seeing certain stories and videos about Hillary. "It shouldn't give quarter to conspiracy theorists." Ironically, Manjoo is advocating that Google commit a conspiracy to stop people from researching Clinton's ill health, which he calls a conspiracy theory. Left-wing apparatus *Vox* chimes in with an article titled "The Bonkers *Conspiracy Theory* about Hillary Clinton's Health" (emphasis added). Media Matters accuses a news network reporting on the issue of "mainstreaming *conspiracy theories* about Hillary Clinton's health." *Vice* picks up the theme, writing, "How *conspiracy theories* about Hillary Clinton's health went mainstream." CNN publishes an article "Debunking *conspiracy theories*" about Clinton's health. CNN media critic Brian Stelter instructs the media: "Do Not Give Oxygen to '*Conspiracy Theories*' that Hillary Clinton Is 'Secretly Ill.' " *HuffPost* writes, "Let's call the *conspiracy theories* about Clinton's health what they are. . . ." *ThinkProgress* writes, "Trump campaign embraces *conspiracy theory*. . . ." From MSNBC: "Trump, allies push *conspiracy theory* about Clinton's health." NPR: "Trump adds fuel to *conspiracy theory* about Clinton's health." You get the idea. Everybody's on the same page, using tried-and-true astroturf language to smear anyone asking questions about Clinton's medical condition. We later discovered that Clinton was, indeed, secretly ill at the time. Yet these reporters declared definitively, as a matter of fact, that she was not.

Questions about Clinton's health, whether grounded or far-fetched, had little to do with supposed conspiracies. But applying the "conspiracy theory" moniker was intended to convince the public to tune out the discussion, in much the same way as other common astroturf terms, such as *debunked, bonkers, tin-foil hat, shoddy, discredited, quack, phony, bogus, denier,* and *crank,* to name a few.

Less than a month after the widespread misreporting, Clinton suffers a medical episode that forces her to leave a 9/11 remembrance ceremony in New York City. A bystander posts video online showing aides supporting Clinton as she is hustled away from news cameras and helped to her van. She briefly slumps, then collapses before being dragged into the vehicle. After a strange period of radio silence, the Clinton camp finally announces that a doctor had secretly diagnosed Hillary with pneumonia two days before, and that she'd become dehydrated at the 9/11 ceremony. All along, it turns out there had been valid questions about Hillary's health but—until her public collapse—the media had assisted in controversializing those questions as conspiracy theories. Yet I don't remember hearing many mea culpas, corrections, or apologies from the reporters and writers who had falsely claimed they somehow knew Hillary had no health issues. Instead they went ever more confidently onward with their incorrect declarations and prognostications.

In subsequent days, Bill Clinton reveals something surprising in an interview with CBS News: for years Hillary has "frequently" struggled with inexplicable medical episodes. Bill quickly corrects "frequently" to "rarely" in the interview but, when pressed, he won't say how many times.

> **Bill Clinton (live on *CBS This Morning*)**: [*I*]*t's a mystery to me and all of her doctors, because frequently—well not frequently, rarely— but on more than one occasion, over the last many, many years, the same sort of thing happened to her when she got severely dehydrated.*

In a sub-scandal, the *CBS Evening News with Scott Pelley* would later edit out the mention of "frequently" from Bill Clinton's remarks, making it seem like Hillary's mystery episodes were less regular.

> **Bill Clinton (edited replay on CBS *Evening News*)**: [*I*]*t's a mystery to me and all of her doctors. Rarely—but on more than one occasion, over the last many, many years, the same sort of thing happened to her when she got severely dehydrated.*

When asked about the edit, the network explained it was made purely to save time.

Bill's possible gaffe aside, now that there's a grain of truth to the ill-Hillary narrative, her enemies take full advantage. Her pneumonia and fainting episode become fodder to escalate into a full-blown smear. Websites suggest she's using a "body double." Social media and blogs circulate "proof positive" of the body double—side-by-side photos. One picture shows "the real" Clinton several months before the 9/11 incident. The other shows the "obvious body double" emerging from daughter Chelsea's apartment after the collapse. She's clearly using an imposter to hide the precarious state of her health, say the smear artists. On-the-spot expert analysis is offered by armchair tweeters. "Hillary's INDEX finger is longer than her RING finger. This ISNT [*sic*] Hillary," declares one, with the conviction of a detective who's performed a painstaking forensic examination. "Too young, too thin," tweets another, indicating that Hillary's "body double" isn't an identical match. When asked his opinion about it in a television interview, Roger Stone replies, "Look I think anything is possible when it comes to duplicity and the Clintons."

In late September, after the first Hillary-Donald debate, Democrat Howard Dean lobs a grenade of his own, questioning Trump's fitness. A medical doctor, Dean tweets that the sniffing sounds Trump made at the debate podium could be due to cocaine use. (Trump has always said he neither drinks, smokes, nor uses drugs.)

"Notice Trump sniffing all the time," Dean tweets. "Coke user?"

Even to some Democrats, that crosses a line. Later, a reporter asks Dean if he really thinks Trump is on drugs.

"So, look, do I think at seventy years old he has a cocaine habit? Probably not," Dean concedes. "But, you know, it's something that—I think it would be interesting to ask him and see if he ever had a problem with that."

The media jabs Trump again after three bombs detonate in the New York City area. Islamic terrorists are ultimately found responsible. As the events are sorted out, Trump casually refers to one explosion as being caused by a "bomb," before the FBI officially uses that terminology. The press goes berserk, accusing Trump of making unfounded, reckless, and bigoted conclusions. After all, the media has grown accustomed to waiting for the government to tell them what they can and can't report, and what words may be used. It took the Obama administration days to use the word *terrorism* after the San Bernardino, California, Islamic extremist attacks in December 2015, which killed fourteen and injured twenty-two. During those days, most journalists wouldn't even utter the words "suspected terrorism," though that was a perfectly reasonable interim deduction, based on the early evidence. Now, after the September 2016 New York–area explosions, the media is scandalized that Trump would dare utter the B-word ("bomb") without the government stamp of approval. But the real scandal is another case of selective editing by the media: they edited out remarks made by Hillary Clinton, who had also referred to the attack as a bombing—just like Trump.

The week of the New York attacks, I get my third interview with Trump for my *Full Measure* program. (Clinton still says no to my interview requests.) I address the media's treatment of him, and his disdain for the media.

> **Me:** Do you see yourself [as president] banning reporters from certain events and things like that?
>
> **Trump:** No, I don't see that, but a lot of people have done it, and a lot of people, a lot of different businesses have done it. The press has been very, very dishonest. I mean, even recently when I said yesterday, the bombing, and she said, the bombing, and they criticized my use of the word *bombing*, but not hers and they cut it out. . . . So, the relationship with the press is—it's not a question of good, all I want is honesty. And if there's something wrong or something bad, I can handle that, but when you do something great, and they try to make it as negative as possible, constantly, it's really not a fair situation. . . . You see outside, you see the kind of crowds we have. [The press] never show the size of the crowd, ever. The only time they show it is, is a little bit of protest someplace within the crowd, then all of a sudden they show, and then people say, wow, what a big crowd that is.

By now many news outlets have openly acknowledged their bias against Trump. They get on board with the Clinton campaign, which is urging them to conduct live "fact-checks" of Trump's statements. Many of the "facts" are "checked" in a light most unfavorable to Trump. Somehow Clinton escapes similar scrutiny. *Politico* editor Susan Glasser later tells me the publication assigned a team of reporters to "fact-check every word out of Donald Trump's mouth" for an entire week of the campaign. They concluded "Donald Trump uttered a lie, or an exaggeration, a falsehood once every five minutes." I ask Glasser what they found when fact-checking Clinton. Glasser tells me they didn't have the resources to fact-check Hillary, too.

The media imply their drastic behavior is justified because Trump is a Hitler in the making. Nothing short of American Democracy is at stake! No longer is there any real pretense of neutrality. Major publications pursue overtly political agendas. For the first time in its thirty-four-year history, *USA Today* announces a stark departure from its practice of not weighing in on the presidential race.

"The editorial board is taking a position on the race," announces *USA Today* editorial page editor Bill Sternberg on September 29, 2016. "Specifically, we are urging voters not to support Donald Trump."

That's how dangerous Trump is, the newspaper is saying. *Anybody but Trump.*

New York Times editor Dean Baquet also acknowledges there's a new and different tone to the newspaper's coverage when it comes to candidate Trump. "[W]e now say stuff. We fact-check him. We write it more powerfully that it's false." The *New York Post* observes that the *Times'* proclamation in essence gave the green light for *Times* reporters to openly skew their coverage thereafter. "[T]he floodgates opened," reports the *Post,* "and virtually every [*Times*] so-called news article reflected a clear bias against Trump and in favor of Clinton. Stories, photos, headlines, placement in the paper—all the tools were used to pick a president, the facts be damned." In many ways, this election marks the death of "the traditional news" as we once knew it.

Against that backdrop, it's hard *not* to suspect there's collusion at play in the September debate when NBC moderator Lester Holt chooses not to press Clinton on her potentially illegal destruction of government emails that were under subpoena. Yet Holt *does* buttonhole Trump on his failure to release his tax returns.

Lester Holt: Mr. Trump, we're talking about the burden that Americans have to pay, yet you have not released your tax returns. . . . Don't Americans have a right to know if there are any conflicts of interest?

Trump: I don't mind releasing. I'm under a routine audit, and it will be released, and as soon as the audit is finished, it will be released.

Holt doesn't let it go there. He repeats his question. He follows up on Trump's answer again. Then Clinton weighs in on the subject. And it's almost as if—she *knows* something.

"Maybe he doesn't want the American people, all of you watching tonight, to know that he's paid nothing in federal taxes," says Clinton.

Trump practically confirms Clinton's speculation when he leans into the microphone and retorts, "That makes me smart."

The following day, the *New York Times* punctuates the point. "For someone as wealthy as Mr. Trump to pay no federal income taxes would be remarkable, and it was a startling twist," remarks the *Times*. The newspaper pushes the topic for several more days, speculating about Trump's taxes, until it emerges with a giant exclusive report: it obtains and publishes Trump's partial tax records from more than twenty years ago. The *Times*' analysis of Trump's 1995 documents is given front-page treatment as a national scandal (though a careful read reveals the *Times* determined there appears to be nothing illegal about Trump's tax avoidance).

But what's most telling in this scenario is a follow-up article in which the *Times* reveals that it had received Trump's tax records anonymously in the mail on September 23: three days before the debate in which the press made Trump's tax records a central question. Was there behind-the-scenes coordination—smear operators working with reporters to "tee up" the Trump tax story at the debate and in the immediate aftermath? In its coverage the *Times* declared, "Mr. Trump's refusal to make his tax returns public—breaking with decades of tradition in presidential contests—has emerged as a central issue in the campaign." Indeed, it emerged as a central issue precisely because the *Times* helped make it one. (Much later, MSNBC would obtain several pages from Trump's 2005 income tax return showing—to the cable news channel's chagrin—he actually paid $35 million in income taxes that year, at a rate well above that recently paid by Bernie Sanders, Mitt Romney, and Barack Obama. Yet there would be no corrections or apologies from the media for their mistaken pronouncements and implications.)

At the same time, the news media and establishment are also turning to polls to try to squash Trump. Polls that show him ahead? They're reported as "outliers" that are not to be believed. In fact, according to the media and pundits, such polls should be exorcised from any averages and bullied out of existence. Polls showing Trump trailing? Well, the bigger Clinton's lead, the more credible the poll! In fact, two weeks before the election, when an ABC News poll finds Clinton is an improbable 12 percentage points ahead, the results aren't dismissed as an outlier, but are widely reported without question, as if an accurate reflection of national sentiment.

ABC News posts the headline "Clinton Vaults to a Double-Digit Lead, Boosted by Broad Disapproval of Trump." *Politico* reports the same news featuring a smiling photo of Clinton. "Hillary Clinton has opened up a 12-point advantage over Donald Trump following their final debate last week and has reached the critical 50-percent mark, according to a new poll released Sunday," reads the article.

Meantime, I'm suffering a severe case of cognitive dissonance. The polls showing Clinton wildly ahead don't match with what I see and hear in the real world as I travel the country, watch Trump's rallies and Clinton's speeches, and listen to friends and strangers of all stripes. So I begin examining the poll methodologies. I discover a lot that the media isn't reporting. In Campaign 2016, it turns out polls are just another form of astroturf, with selectively chosen respondents, and selectively reported results, designed to give the impression there's overwhelming and universal opposition to Trump—when there isn't.

For example, on August 10, Bloomberg reports "Clinton up 6 on Trump in Two Way Race." But looking at the actual Bloomberg poll, I find that Clinton's lead over Trump has shrunk in the past five months from 18 points to within the margin of error. It's a remarkably positive sign for the Trump campaign.

No news outlets report this.

Furthermore, Bloomberg's article cherry-picks poll results that look best for Clinton: figures that add in "leaners." What are leaners? Respondents who were first asked who they'd vote for, then answered that they didn't plan to vote or didn't know who they'd vote for, and *then* were pressed to pick a candidate they were leaning toward anyway. This is how Bloomberg got to the 6-point spread cited in its headline. That's double the actual spread found in the poll of just 3 percentage points (not counting these "leaners"). I also find buried in the Bloomberg poll the fact that Trump has improved his standing in eight categories when it comes to being associated with positive phrases, while Clinton is down in seven categories. Again, that's not reported in the news.

This isn't to suggest that reporting on the Bloomberg poll or any other should have favored Trump. Ideally such reporting should reflect general positives and negatives for each candidate, if they exist, and include relevant trends for context and perspective.

As the months go on, I continue to pore through various polls, passing up the headlines and searching through the methodology disclosures. I learn that many polls are lopsided in terms of whom they interviewed— significantly more Democrats than Republicans. I contact individual pollsters. I ask: Do they really think 25 percent more Democrats are going to vote on election day (since they interviewed 25 percent more Democrats for their poll)? They tell me they're doing their best to prognosticate yet admit, in response to my questions, that they don't have a way to model for a wild card like Trump. They're using demographics from a six-year-old census and turnout models from 2012. Who knows what Trump's turnout will actually be? Yet these polls are promoted without question by a rabidly anti-Trump media. It's more evidence that the news is reporting through its own selective filter.

The Mothers of All Smears

It's October 2016. Both Clinton and Trump are about to be challenged by the final smears of the campaign, more daunting than any that predate them. For Trump it's the *Access Hollywood* audiotape, Russia ties, and his charitable foundation. For Clinton it's her charitable foundation, WikiLeaks, and Pizzagate—all of which will prompt a postelection push to label and silence "fake news."

On October 7, the *Washington Post* is first to publish an audiotape recording of Trump speaking privately with Billy Bush of *Access Hollywood* eleven years before. Off camera, but still wearing a microphone, Trump describes in lewd terms how much he loves women, and boasts of grabbing them in a private place. "When you're a star, they let you do it," Trump is overheard saying. His enemies hope this revelation delivers the deathblow.

Over the course of the next week, incessant reporting about the audiotape leads newscasts, dominates social media, and commands the political landscape. Trump's words are described as "lewd, misogynistic and predatory." Some critics even equate them to the crime of rape and insist that he be prosecuted for assault (much as they insisted Trump was inciting murder with his earlier comments on how gun rights advocates might influence Hillary's judicial selections as president).

Certainly the *Access Hollywood* tape merits coverage. But the disproportionate attention it's given, to the exclusion of nearly every other world news event, is extraordinary by any neutral measure. Polls, if you can believe them, begin to show that the tape and news coverage are eating into Trump's support in the crucial final weeks of the campaign. Watching from the outside, I again sense the press is out of step with much of the public. As distasteful as the tape is, many of Trump's supporters are sticking by him. They view the publicity onslaught as more proof that the news media is putting its thumb on the scale, trying to shape what citizens think and how they vote.

Several days after release of the Trump tape, I go to the drive-through at a fast-food restaurant I frequent in northern Virginia. The manager is foreign-born and fascinated by U.S. presidential politics. Every time he's seen me at the drive-through window in the past six months, he asks, "Who's going to be president?"

"Trump," I always reply.

On this occasion, he pauses before asking the usual question. He quizzically lifts one eyebrow.

"Who's going to be president?" he asks.

"Trump," I say.

"But the tape," he remarks, as if he expected a different answer. "They keep playing it over and over and over." He points to the TV monitor mounted behind the counter inside. "Every time you turn on the news."

"I know," I say. "But that's the news media. I think there are a lot of people out in the public who care about different things. Not the tape." I think for a moment. "Do *you* care about the tape?" I ask.

"No, I don't care." He shrugs. "But they keep playing the tape over and over."

It turns out the tape is just the opening act. After the press whips up national outrage, a parade of women come forward accusing Trump of aggressive and unwanted advances in the distant past. A few years ago the news media would have treated such serious and salacious accusations with marked circumspectness. I was in the CBS News newsroom in the late 1990s when Bill Clinton's accusers started going public. I witnessed a great deal of journalistic deliberation over which accusations we should air and how to report them. Each case was considered individually. I believe, in the end, we decided *not* to report more cases than we reported. Not that we didn't believe the women, but because the charges were extremely damaging, and we didn't have enough information on a short turnaround to judge whether the alleged victims could reasonably be telling the truth. But today, it's different. Each breathless allegation against Trump is printed, published, and aired with lightning speed.

Even after the colossal success Trump's opponents have enjoyed with the *Access Hollywood* audiotape and the subsequent accusations from women, they know they can't rest on their laurels. They follow with a narrative that attempts to convince voters the election is already over. Hillary *will* be the next president. The media dutifully obliges.

"Trump's path to an electoral college victory isn't narrow. It's nonexistent," declares Stu Rothenberg in the *Washington Post*. In the October 18, 2016, article, which is labeled neither opinion, commentary, nor analysis, he writes, "Now, with early voting already underway and only three weeks left until Election Day, the writing is on the wall. Clinton is headed for solid popular-vote and electoral-vote victories that are larger than Obama's were over Romney."

A week later, a *Washington Post* article by Philip Bump sustains the theme. The headline: "There is no possible way Donald Trump's team actually believes this is their path to 270." He goes on to ridicule the Trump campaign's Kellyanne Conway for her analysis of the electoral map showing that Trump *can* win. Bump calls it a "joke" and presents his own alternate map where, naturally, the only conceivable outcome is a Clinton victory. (Conway turned out to be correct; Bump was egregiously in error. However, as of this writing, I can't find record of any such acknowledgment by the *Post,* which appears to continue to view Bump as a credible writer with such offerings as "The Web of Relationships between Team Trump and Russia.")

The press also revives discussion of Trump in terms of a "meltdown." After making that the theme of its August cover, *Time* now sports a new cover article promising to take us "Inside Donald Trump's Total Meltdown." MSNBC adds that it's "Watching Donald Trump reach the 'total meltdown' stage." And *Mother Jones* insists, "Trump Meltdown Continues Apace."

For her part, Clinton is fending off the drip, drip, drip from WikiLeaks releases of those damaging internal emails. Some of them imply the Clintons and their charitable foundation have possibly engaged in serious pay-for-play deals. Even Hillary's daughter, Chelsea, expressed worry in the emails and called for an independent audit. The audit concluded some donors believed they were giving money to the Clinton Foundation for a "quid pro quo"—in return for some favor or action. They reveal Clinton's own campaign officials think she exercises poor judgment and surrounds herself with questionable characters (they specifically refer to David Brock). And they expose the embarrassing extent to which Clinton's public statements and excuses are developed by political committee using PR firms, pollsters, and donors. A subsequent leak of the transcripts of Clinton's Wall Street speeches shows she admitted to apparent duplicity: taking "a private position and a [different] public position" on various issues.

At first, most of the national press ignores these revelations. But conservatives circulate them widely on social media, right-wing websites, and Fox News. Soon some of the more scandalous items are covered, if reluctantly so, by national news outlets. For example, one story that makes mainstream news from the WikiLeaks documents is how Bill Clinton received a generous and possibly inappropriate $1 million "birthday gift" from the country of Qatar to the Clinton Foundation when Hillary was secretary of state. To complicate matters further for the Clintons, their foundation failed to notify the State Department of Bill's gift, even though Hillary had signed an ethics agreement promising to alert State ethics officials of such donations. The Clintons deny such notification was required in this instance.

Even as Hillary's scandals finally begin to permeate the news, she continues to benefit largely from a sympathetic and supportive press. According to my sourcing, the *New York Times* has obtained blockbuster information about the Clinton Foundation: that the FBI has been intensely probing the charity. But the newspaper has decided to sit on it. Among other things, the *Times* is said to know that multiple FBI field offices are involved in the Clinton Foundation probe, including New York, Washington, D.C., Los Angeles, and Little Rock. But a decision has been made at the newspaper not to report this information, which could damage Clinton prior to the election, according to my sourcing.

In contrast, there's no such plan at the *New York Times* to protect Donald Trump. The *Times* reports on assorted scandals about his charity. The Trump Foundation is relatively small: it took in about one-half million dollars in 2013, compared to the Clinton Foundation's $150 million the same year. That makes the global Clinton Foundation roughly three hundred times larger than Trump Foundation in terms of finances, not to mention the fact that Clinton's charity is run by an ex-president and a former secretary of state who were dealing with sensitive foreign countries seeking favor on policy and financial issues. Yet while the *Times* sits on news of the FBI investigation into the Clinton charity, it finds it much more newsworthy that Trump's charity paid $20,000 for a portrait of Trump. And the *Times* jumps on the news when New York State attorney general Eric Schneiderman, a Clinton supporter, opens an aptly timed investigation into the Trump Foundation. In other words, the *Times* goes after Trump on relatively small issues while staying mum on the more serious FBI investigation into the Clinton Foundation.

Unofficial GOP operative Roger Stone is back in the picture in the campaign's final weeks, stoking rumors about impending WikiLeaks material that will supposedly be worse for Clinton than what we've already seen. He's lurking in the background working on behalf of Trump—though, he says, not officially on the campaign.

"[L]ook, I'm a brand name when it comes to dirty tricks. [Trump] called me a henchman, and I don't really object to that, but henchmen get paid, and I have been paid nothing by Trump," Stone tells *GQ*.

Stone pumps up the as-yet-unseen WikiLeaks material by saying he's heard that it's "potentially politically devastating" and "indictable." When Clinton supporters, including former CIA chief Mike Morell, respond by suggesting that Stone and Trump have Russian connections, and that Russia is behind the WikiLeaks leak of Clinton emails, a source tells me Stone and his associates are shaken.

"I do not and have never worked for any Russian interest—public or private. I have no Russian clients," Stone says in an interview with the website Infowars. "I have not received a penny from any Russian interest. I do not now and have never worked for Russian Intelligence. Any claim to the contrary is demonstrably false. This is the New McCarthyism." He goes on to say that he fears for his life if Clinton becomes president.

"I have no intention of ending the fight to expose their epic corruption, ruthlessness and lies," he says. "Therefore, if in the near future you hear that I was depressed and took my life, got hit by a truck crossing the street, or killed in a freak hunting accident, you will know that I was murdered and that Hillary Clinton is the chief perp."

While the WikiLeaks releases serve to smear Hillary, and Hillary and the media smear Trump, the fake news phenomenon rears its head again in a major way. On October 12, 2016, anonymously posted Internet videos begin claiming that a video of Bill Clinton will soon surface and "plunge the presidential race into chaos." The rumor never crosses over into the news, and even most of the famously partisan websites avoid the subject sensing a ruse. But millions of people learn about it online. "SHOCK-ING VIDEO on the horizon," claims one version of the video, viewed 2.6 million times. "Anonymous says there is video of Bill Clinton raping a 13 year-old girl on Jeffrey Epstein's 'Orgy Island.'" No video ever surfaces.

Another salacious and insidious rumor about Hillary Clinton circulates at the end of October and bleeds on past the election: Pizzagate. It's a rumor that Democrats, including Clinton campaign chair Podesta, are involved in a child trafficking sex ring headquartered at a Washington, D.C., pizza parlor (that happens to be run by David Brock's ex-boyfriend). The talk is based in part on emails posted by WikiLeaks in which Podesta makes various references to pizza. Accusers say words in the emails are code for pedophilia terms and activities. For example, say theorists, "cheese pizza" refers to "child porn." Some analysts try to track down the origins of the rumor. They trace it to foreigners who are supposedly manufacturing and spreading the gossip to attract Web traffic and make money from people who click on their websites. Meantime, the pizza restaurant at the center of the Pizzagate rumor is bombarded by accusations and threats.

In an interview, the restaurant's owner calls Pizzagate "an insanely complicated, made-up, fictional lie-based story" and "a coordinated political attack." As with the phantom Bill Clinton tape, the mainstream news avoids covering Pizzagate. There's no evidence that any of the allegations are founded. It only becomes news shortly after the election when a disturbed man apparently motivated by Internet reports bursts into the pizza shop and fires shots, looking for evidence of child victims but finding none. The media covers that story for the purpose of debunking Pizzagate rumors. A poll later finds a majority of both Clinton and Trump supporters didn't take the rumors seriously, if they heard them at all.

The single most damaging smear to Clinton originates the last Friday in October 2016. FBI director James Comey shocks the nation with what indeed may be the most startling move ever made by a federal law enforcement body so close to a national election. He notifies leaders of several congressional committees that the FBI is reviewing new evidence in Hillary's use of private email servers as secretary of state.

"In connection with an unrelated case," Comey writes to Congress, "the FBI has learned of the existence of emails that appear to be pertinent to this investigation."

The "unrelated case" is that of former congressman Anthony Weiner. He's just come under FBI investigation for allegedly texting sexual messages to an underage girl. Weiner happens to be the husband of top Clinton aide Huma Abedin, and as it turns out, some of Abedin's work emails have been discovered on a computer confiscated from Weiner as part of the investigation. Some of those emails were to and from Hillary.

You can't make this stuff up.

The Comey announcement is a bombshell. That day, Trump begins a rally by saying he has a "very critical, breaking news announcement." Many in the audience have already heard. They cheer.

"I have great respect for the fact that the FBI and the Department of Justice are now willing to have the courage to right the horrible mistake that they made," Trump says, referring to Comey's initial decision in July to not recommend charges against Clinton. "This was a grave miscarriage of justice that the American people fully understood, and . . . everybody's hope is that it is about to be corrected," Trump tells supporters.

Clinton's enemies shift into overdrive, calling for her to withdraw from the campaign and evoking images of a future Clinton administration that would be under constant FBI investigation. *What happens if a sitting president gets indicted? Can she pardon herself? Surely she'd be impeached. Will there be a constitutional crisis?* The questions become a constant theme at Trump's capacity-crowd rallies in the final days of the heated campaign. Memes begin circulating on social media. Hillary is depicted peering through prison bars in a black-and-white-striped uniform or an orange jumpsuit. The hashtag #HillaryforPrison begins trending on Twitter.

As you might guess, the FBI news also begets countersmears. Clinton's supporters demand that Comey resign. *He's not to be trusted. He's trying to affect the election. He's in the tank for Trump.*

More news breaks as November opens. Word of the FBI probe into the Clinton Foundation finally leaks out. It's not reported by the *New York Times,* which has long known of the investigation but stayed mum, according to my information. Instead it's other national publications that break the news. Fox reports an indictment is "likely." (It's not.) The *Hill* picks up that incorrect story.

The drama doesn't end there.

On November 5 a shocking story appears on what turns out to be a fake news website: the *Denver Guardian.* It claims that an FBI agent involved in the Hillary Clinton investigation has murdered his wife and committed suicide.

"Investigators believe FBI agent, Michael Brown, 45, shot and killed his 33-year old wife, Susan Brown, late Friday night before setting the couple's home on fire and then turning the gun on himself," reads the faux article, which racked up at least 567,000 shares on social media.

Finally, in what has to be the weirdest twist of all, the FBI's Comey reemerges two days before the election with another letter to Congress. This time he announces that analysis of the new Anthony Weiner email evidence is complete, and there will be no charges against Clinton.

"Based on our review, we have not changed our conclusions that we expressed in July with respect to Secretary Clinton," Comey writes on November 6, 2016. That ignites more outrage and smears, this time from Republicans. *Somebody must have gotten to Comey. How could his agents have reviewed all the new evidence so quickly? How could there be no charges against Clinton?*

Comey has got to be the first FBI director alternately smeared and praised by both Democrats and Republicans inside of two weeks.

Besides the primary smears of the candidates, there are ancillary smears in their orbits. Right before the election, when the polling website *FiveThirtyEight,* run by the statistician Nate Silver, doesn't have Trump lagging as far behind Clinton as his detractors would like, websites like *Huffington Post* attack the messenger. They smear Silver and accuse him of gaming the system. "Silver is changing the results of polls to fit where he thinks the polls truly are, rather than simply entering the poll numbers into his model and crunching them," writes the *Huffington Post*'s Ryan Grim. Silver appears rattled by the attacks and defends his methodology in a Twitterstorm that ends with, "When you go low, I go high 80% of the time, and knee you in the balls the other 20% of the time."

Come election night, it's pundits and some in the news media who melt down as they come to realize all the smears they've efforted were for naught. As Trump wins Florida and other key states, news outlets report it as if it were a Greek tragedy. Not only does Trump win, but Republicans also end up holding on to a majority in the Senate. And although double-digit gains by Democrats were widely predicted for the House of Representatives, they pick up only six seats; the GOP retains a strong majority, 241–194. In the NBC News newsroom in New York, some producers bury their heads on desks and sob as the results become clear. Friends of mine in the media post expressions of denial and hatred on social media, speaking of the "horrors" coming to the White House under a President Trump, a dangerous "white supremacist" "Nazi" "fascist" who will be responsible for ending our republic.

In the end, countless polls and analysts proved to be embarrassingly wrong in Campaign 2016. The missteps, smears, and biases will go down in history (depending on who's writing the book). Many insisted Trump had "no electoral path to victory." Going into election night, the *Washington Post*/ABC News poll had Clinton winning by 4 percent. *Slate* came up with what it called "~100 Percent Accurate Electoral Forecast Averagifier," which concluded Clinton had an 81 percent chance of victory. *FiveThirtyEight* had Clinton winning Florida, Pennsylvania, Michigan (by more than 4 points), North Carolina, and Wisconsin (by more than 5 points). But Trump took each state. On election night, the *Detroit Free Press* rushed to call Michigan for Clinton. It was a mighty mistake. Trump won the state by more than ten thousand votes.

So in the battle of the smears, the Wildcard comes out on top. In fact, I think Trump was elected partly *because* of the smears. He was put into office by supporters steeled by criticism from Clinton, who had called them "the basket of deplorables . . . Racist, sexist, homophobic, xenophobic, Islamophobic, you name it." Seeing themselves mischaracterized in the news media, Trump's supporters learned to view the media's criticism of Trump with skepticism. With dislike for and distrust of the media so widespread, perhaps the most effective thing the press could have done to thwart Trump would have been to embrace him. But they just couldn't see it.

The election results spark consternation and panic within the establishment of both major parties and the media. Democratic operatives find themselves in a particularly thorny position. Liberal donors had shelled out more than $700 million to try to put Clinton in the Oval Office, far outpacing Trump's spending. They had their vast network and much of the mainstream media on their side. They even got assistance from Trump's Republican opponents. *How could they have lost?* The Clinton campaign and its smear machine, including David Brock, cannot absorb the blame or else they'll be finished off in big-money politics. They must figure out new, more effective ways to stay relevant and influence public opinion. As such, they will quickly initiate new strategies that involve pointing the finger at Russia, FBI director Comey, and the U.S. electoral system. And they'll step up the rhetoric over fake news, defining what it is and who's guilty of committing it. They'll put the supposed threat of fake news into the daily news headlines, portraying it as more insidious than most any other threat—be it China's saber-rattling, Islamic extremist terrorism, Iran's expansion in the Mideast, or North Korea's program to develop an intercontinental ballistic nuclear-armed missile capable of reaching the United States. Fake news, they will tell us, is an existential threat to America.

Chapter Ten

Brave New World of #FakeNews (and Chilling Efforts to Censor It)

After a campaign riddled with smears from start to finish, many believed the election would bring a welcome respite from the whole sordid mess. That the media diet would return to normal, tamer fare. But it turns out Campaign 2016 was just the appetizer.

In the aftermath of Donald Trump's shocking victory, forces on the left and right desperately seek to process what just happened and how. After all, the most powerful and well-funded propagandists in politics—liberals, conservatives, and the media—have been soundly defeated. Made into fools. Schooled by a political amateur. Now they're on a new mission. They must deconstruct what went wrong. Find new relevance. Win back their power.

It's in this context that the term *fake news* emerges at the forefront of nearly every postelection political and news discussion. Until now, many successful smears relied heavily on a grain of truth. A kernel of fact that could be mined from the past, manipulated, exaggerated, or spun into something larger and more destructive. But in the fake news business, all a smear artist needs are a good story, a Facebook account, and a website that looks something like an actual new source. Transactional journalism and its reliance on the services of the traditional news media are no longer mandatory. Fictitious stories and falsehoods can quickly go viral through social media and in obscure corners of the Internet. Without the real-news middleman.

This is the context for the new battleground in the smear wars. But before the soldiers and generals have even girded their loins and donned their armor, they've already begun fighting to control the definition of what, exactly, constitutes fake news. Much like the smear itself, its definition depends on where you sit.

It's not as if there's a supreme dictionary authority that gets to decide how to define fake news for everyone (though some are trying). From its inception, it's clear that liberals, who are first to heavily promote the phrase "fake news," mean to reference conservative misinformation and right-wing websites. And there's certainly plenty of that. Agence France-Presse declares matter-of-factly that it's the right wing that's guilty of fake news, and that Obama has been plagued by eight years of "false scandals over his place of birth that have forced him to play media-critic-in-chief." Some liberals also blame demonstrably false narratives—reports that she was seriously ill, about to be indicted by the FBI, and using a body double—for Hillary Clinton's defeat.

But Trump and conservatives counterpunch by quickly applying their own idea of fake news as committed by the mainstream media and left-wing websites. Plenty of that, too, including reports of Trump's supposed links to Russia president Vladimir Putin and white supremacists.

Suffice to say those accused of producing or being fake news tend to define it in terms that exclude themselves and point to the other guys. To complicate matters, we have to consider the possibility that double agents are generating fake news about themselves to justify the movement to crack down on supposedly fake news. There's already evidence of such twisted plots. Shortly before and after the election, the Southern Poverty Law Center reported an uptick in hate-related crimes. There were dozens of shocking news accounts of pro-Trump racist and Islamophobic violence. In New York City, there was news of an eighteen-year-old Muslim-American woman mercilessly harassed by Trump supporters who tried to steal her hijab veil on the subway. There were news reports about

Trump supporters spray-painting "Trump Rules" and "Black Bitch" on an African-American woman's car, and "Trump" next to a Nazi swastika on a storefront window. There were news reports about a black church in Mississippi burned and spray-painted with the words "Vote Trump." Many in the press blamed and harangued Trump for these incidents. *Won't you condemn what your supporters are doing?* The left-wing propaganda site *Daily Kos* published an actual headline that read, "Trump Empowers White Supremacists to Kill as a Matter of Policy, then Remains Silent About It." Trump responds to the media outcry against him by publicly imploring those committing hateful acts to "stop it."

But many of the hate crimes are soon revealed as fake news staged by Trump opponents to look as though they'd been committed by his supporters. The Muslim-American "victim" in the subway was ultimately arrested for making up the account, according to New York City police. An African-American man was eventually arrested in the case of the spray-painted "racist" messages in Philadelphia. Another black man was arrested and charged with defacing and setting fire to the Mississippi church. He was a member of the congregation! When these arrests are made, the press doesn't blame or harangue Clinton or Obama. Nor does it ask them to apologize for the violent acts and false accusations, as they've done to Trump. Nor does the press offer its own apologies for its initial rush to unequivocally blame Trump supporters for the crimes, despite lack of evidence.

Liberals and conservatives declare war on one another in the media over fake news. Conservative websites and social media explode with outrage, asking, How can the *New York Times* credibly report on fake news after the fallout over its own front-page exposé about Trump's mistreatment of women during the campaign? (The "victims" in the article later defended Trump and said the newspaper took their words out of context.) Conservatives ask, Where's the outrage over the media's mantra that Trump had "no electoral path to victory," and other false narratives designed to defeat him? What about the major newspaper that falsely reported on election night that Trump had lost Michigan?

On January 20, 2017, *Time* magazine seems to inadvertently prove the point when one of its reporters, Zeke Miller, erroneously reports that incoming president Trump has removed a bust statue of Martin Luther King from the Oval Office. The incendiary claim is born of a bias that used to be verboten in responsible journalism: Miller later explained that he looked around, didn't see the bust, and then, without verifying his suspicions, tweeted out the false information that the bust was gone. He also reported the "story" to the entire national press "pool," meaning it was widely circulated. When the White House responds by quickly posting a photo on social media showing the bust was still very much in the Oval Office, it's revealed that Miller hasn't followed the most basic tenets every college journalism student is taught: check your facts. Not long ago, such an amateur error would have excluded the offending reporter from work at any reputable publication. But in today's environment, it's considered a routine part of business. There's no evidence that Miller's publisher took any punitive actions against him and, as of this writing, he was still listed as working for *Time*.

When conservatives present gross examples like this as evidence of fake news, a new party line develops among liberals. Liberal commentators defend the acts of fake news, arguing that "honest mistakes" are far less serious than people *knowingly* generating fake news online (like conservatives). I could easily argue the opposite: mistakes at "real" news organizations are more harmful, because more readers are likely to believe them than off-brand online sites. Regardless, both sides continue to define fake news in a way that lends sympathy to their interests.

Although fake news may appear to many Americans to have emerged quite suddenly, it's been taking root for years. It's the logical evolution of a phenomenon that's been shaped, stretched, and fertilized with money and ingenuity.

The Roots of Fake News

John H. Johnson, author of *Everydata: The Misinformation Hidden in the Little Data You Consume Every Day,* divides fake news into five categories: 1) news that's entirely false; 2) news that's slanted and biased; 3) pure propaganda; 4) stories that misinterpret or misuse data; and 5) imprecise and sloppy reporting.

Under these definitions, fake news has been embedded in our culture for decades. Long before the Internet, newspaper magnates hyped stories for circulation or in secret partnership with the government. As noted in the *Asia-Pacific Journal,* Joseph Pulitzer, of the *New York World* and *St. Louis Post-Dispatch,* and William Randolph Hearst, of the *New York Journal* and *San Francisco Examiner,* competed for readers in the late 1890s with "exposés, stunts, comics, sports coverage, women's features, and exciting accounts of foreign conflicts. They believed that war, especially the way they reported it, sold papers." Some critics accused the papers of doing the bidding of President William McKinley to shape popular perceptions and pump up sentiment for a U.S. declaration of war against Spain.

In the midtwentieth century, the supermarket rags gave populist appeal to blatantly fake news, with front-page images of aliens abducting and impregnated unsuspecting (usually large-breasted) earthling women. The *National Enquirer* published its first issue as a sensational tabloid in 1953. *Weekly World News* sported headlines like "Garden of Eden Found. U.S. Grows Trees from Seeds." From the *Globe:* "Bush on Cocaine in the White House." The tabloids are the "clickbait" of the pre-Internet era, and they developed a devoted following. Presumably most readers believed none of what they read in the rags; certainly a few believed all of it. And every once in a great while, the tabloids broke true news. In 1987, the *Enquirer* alone had the moxie to put a tail on Democratic presidential candidate Gary Hart. It unearthed his affair with model Donna Rice, complete with a photo of Rice sitting on Hart's lap aboard his yacht, *Monkey Business.* Hart promptly withdrew from the race. Over the years, slandered celebrities gripe about the tabloids, and some sue, but nobody speaks seriously of "curating" them, removing them from store shelves, or censoring them from public view.

In the 1990s, news organizations exploit the new technology of email, blogs, and websites to vastly expand their audiences, and viewers increasingly turn to online sources for entertainment and information. The new millennium brings a social media revolution, most notably the advent of Facebook, Twitter, and YouTube. As we've seen, they provided the means by which smears can be accomplished with unprecedented speed, breadth, and deadly precision. A rumor that would have circulated among a relative few can now develop a global following. Technological tricks are used to alter images and create new, false realities to fool the most discriminating eye. On December 14, 2012, a shooter barges into Sandy Hook Elementary School in Newtown, Connecticut, and murders twenty children and six school employees. Multiple blogs, videos, and social media sites quickly begin circulating conspiracy theories, insisting the whole event was staged by actors in a hoax drummed up by the government. According to the theorists, the supposedly dead children have since shown up as a group, disguised but very much alive and well, at White House events and football halftime shows.

When false information like this crosses over from the shadowy corners of the Internet to be believed by large swaths of readers, it's officially "fake news" (although it wasn't called that until recently). Sometimes fake news is picked up and reported seriously in the domain of once-respected straight news outlets. How? The news organizations may be guilty of not checking facts carefully enough. They could be in a rush to beat the competition. Or they might be advancing an agenda. Long before 2016 one finds countless, blatant examples of damaging misinformation making its way to the mainstream through reckless or malicious disregard for truth.

In 1996 a news media frenzy wrongly links security guard Richard Jewell to the bombing of Centennial Olympic Park in Atlanta. In truth, Jewell was a hero, spotting an unattended backpack and moving people away from it before the bomb inside exploded.

Also in 1996, I was able to call out a shocking incident of government-generated fake news. It happened after I broke the story on the *CBS Evening News* that Chinese spies had obtained design plans to our most advanced nuclear warhead, called the W-88. I knew from the best sources that U.S. officials, try as they might, had not been able to identify a suspect in the case. But as soon as my story ignited a global scandal, the government offered up the name of the supposed spy: Taiwan-born scientist Wen Ho Lee, who worked at the U.S. Los Alamos National Laboratory. Government officials "leaked" Lee's name to national news media, including me—as the reporter who'd broken the original story. Other reporters widely reported that Lee was the likely spy. I took a more circumspect approach because my inside sources were firm on the point that Lee wasn't really a credible suspect. They told me that the Clinton administration had been embarrassed by the theft and needed to make it seem as if the culprit had been caught. The FBI claimed Lee failed a lie detector test, and that they had their man. But it wasn't true. I was later able to exclusively report that the FBI lied about Lee's polygraph, which he'd actually passed with flying colors.

In the end, Lee was never charged with spying, and he sued the federal government for unlawfully leaking his name to news organizations. Ultimately the government and several news organizations paid Lee a settlement: the *Washington Post* for reporting by Walter Pincus, the *New York Times* for reporting by James Risen, the *Los Angeles Times* for reporting by Bob Drogin, the Associated Press for reporting by Josef Hebert, and ABC for reporting by Pierre Thomas. The news outlets said their reporters did nothing wrong but that they agreed to pay a settlement so they wouldn't have to disclose the names of the government sources who'd leaked Lee's name. The big takeaway for me was the realization that our own government could be guilty of fingering a fake suspect and generating a fake story about him—and get it all widely reported in the news. The government isn't beyond telling big lies.

There's fake news again on September 11, 2001. Reporting in the confusion after the terrorist attacks, CBS News' Jim Stewart erroneously reports that the doomed, hijacked Flight 93 went down "in the vicinity of [presidential retreat] Camp David." But it crashed nowhere near there. An honest mistake based on bad information or a hastily drawn conclusion.

Three years later, in 2004, CBS News anchor Dan Rather gets caught in a major case of fake news, using forged documents for a *60 Minutes II* report disparaging President George W. Bush's Vietnam-era military service. Prior to the segment's airing, a CBS manager had shown me the documents, not realizing they were forgeries, and telling me I might be assigned to do a big follow-up story for the *Evening News*. I immediately flagged the material as suspicious. I saw that the 1973-dated documents were clearly computer-generated rather than typed with a 1970s-era typewriter. Other red flags: they were purportedly signed by a now-deceased lieutenant colonel, and the format and language in them deviated from military documents I'd reviewed in the past. I refused to touch the story. Ultimately the documents were exposed as fakes. Dan Rather and several producers lost their jobs over the controversy.

I'm inadvertently wrapped up in another fake news story in 2008, when presidential candidate Hillary Clinton is repeatedly quoted uncritically in the press describing how she bravely dodged sniper fire on a trip to war-torn Bosnia as first lady twelve years before. She is apparently attempting to distinguish herself as more battle-ready than her opponent, Barack Obama. However, I had accompanied Clinton on that trip to Bosnia as a reporter in 1996. There had been no sniper fire. The events described by Clinton were wholly fabricated. On March 24, 2008, I prove it by showing the archive video from the Bosnia trip in a story for the CBS *Evening News*. After the newscast, Clinton apologizes and explains she repeatedly misremembered the events because she had been "overtired." The thing is, there were many other reporters on that Bosnia trip who knew that Clinton's story was fake—but stayed silent. *Why?*

On April 23, 2013, the Associated Press reports breaking news on its Twitter account: "Two Explosions in the White House and Barack Obama Is Injured." That leads to instantaneous panic and a major Wall Street reaction. Within minutes, the S&P 500 stock index loses more than $136 billion. It turns out it was all a hoax. AP's Twitter account had been hacked.

One of the most far-reaching and insidious fake news stories in recent times surrounds the police shooting death of suspect of Michael Brown, an African-American man, in Ferguson, Missouri, on August 9, 2014. The media widely reports bogus witness accounts of Brown getting shot while supposedly holding up his hands in surrender. The reportedly unjustified nature of the shooting sparks violent riots, stokes the Black Lives Matter movement, and creates a new protest gesture known as "Hands Up, Don't Shoot." It's followed by a rash of black men ambushing and murdering police officers around the nation. But in 2015, the U.S. Department of Justice (DOJ), led by Attorney General Eric Holder, reverses its initial claims and exonerates the white Ferguson police officer who'd shot Michael Brown. The DOJ determines the witnesses who claimed Brown's hands were raised when he was shot weren't telling the truth. But due to the original, widespread misreporting of the fake news, serious misconceptions about Brown's death persist to this day. Also in 2015, there's more fake news during riots in Baltimore. People tweet and retweet photographs purporting to show looted and destroyed storefronts. It turns out some of the images had been recycled from entirely unrelated events. For example, one photo posted as if it were showing a trashed KFC restaurant in Baltimore was actually a picture from a bombed-out restaurant in Pakistan.

In November 2014 there's fake news with major repercussions. *Rolling Stone*'s Sabrina Rubin Erdely reports on a sensational case of a fraternity gang rape that turns out to be not only questionable, but so unsubstantiated that the publication later retracts the article, and a jury finds Erdely guilty of malice in a defamation lawsuit.

On December 7, 2016, there's another fake use of a photo in a major news event. NBC's *Today* is reporting on the mistrial of a North Charleston, South Carolina, police officer who shot a black suspect. As the news show host tells viewers that Charleston's mayor is appealing for calm, the network shows a still photo of an angry mob of demonstrators. It makes it appear as though the city is on the verge of riots! But it turns out the provocative photograph wasn't taken after the mistrial, and the scene isn't anywhere near Charleston. It is a picture of people protesting after an unrelated incident in Baltimore in 2015. Viewers notice NBC's error and take to social media.

"Wow, @TODAYshow. Hire some fact checkers. Pretty lame to share Baltimore 2015 photo in today's story about Charleston mistrial," tweets one viewer. "What's up with this Today Show?" asks another. "Why use a picture of Baltimore when reporting on a Charleston situation? Poor reporting!?" A week earlier, NBC was among the news organizations that also misreported the police officer's trial had ended in mistrial—a week before the judge actually declared a mistrial.

Amid incidents like these arousing widespread mistrust of the news, NBC News anchor Brian Williams admits that a war story he's told for twelve years . . . is fake. He has claimed he was in a helicopter in 2003 that was hit by enemy fire over Iraq. But it turns out no missile ever hit his chopper. *Stars and Stripes* reveals the fabrication in 2015 based on accounts of soldiers who were there. NBC removes Williams from the anchor chair and he apologizes for telling the tale. For skeptical viewers, it's irrefutable proof of willful dishonesty at the highest levels in the media. *If NBC's top newsman would make up such stories, how can we rely on the news to be true?* After a suspension, Williams is reinstated in the anchor chair at

MSNBC—where he later criticizes the Trump team for spreading fake news.

There are other practices that some define as fake news. One of them is the common misapplication of *anti-immigrant* to Trump and his policies. In using the term, partisans and many reporters conflate legal immigrants with illegal immigrants, as if they're one and the same. To me, it's kind of like saying a burglar is the same thing as an invited visitor to your home. It's simply untrue. Whether one likes Trump or not, I find it difficult to logically make the case that Trump is anti-immigrant. He has repeatedly stated that he's pro-immigration; he married two immigrants (his current wife and an ex-wife) and therefore has children who are the children of immigrants. There's similar common misuse of other terms against Trump. His enemies try to portray him as anti-Semitic despite that fact that his daughter is a converted Orthodox Jew, and that—as president—Trump immediately cultivated a friendlier relationship with Israeli prime minister Benjamin Netanyahu than the previous administration ever had. Lastly, Trump's temporary immigration moratorium is mistakenly described far and wide as a "Muslim ban," despite the fact that most of the world's Muslims are unaffected, the countries it applied to were first identified under the Obama administration, and, most important, millions of Muslims are still very much welcome and living in the United States. If there were a Muslim ban then logic dictates that it would—well, ban Muslims. A few years back, responsible news reporters wouldn't give themselves license to use pejorative and challenged terms to describe a politician's positions (without attributing them as opinion), especially if the politician himself disputed the descriptions. But under today's loosening definition of what's acceptable in the news, most anything goes.

"Russia, Russia, Russia!"

Coincident with Trump's election is a concerted effort by Democrats and many in the media to convince the public that Russian president Vladimir Putin himself successfully intervened to put Trump in office, that Russia somehow "hacked" the U.S. elections, and that Trump and his consorts have long been conspiring with Russia to do unknown illegal things. The Democrats' leader in the Senate, Harry Reid, raised the specter during the campaign. In a letter to the FBI in August 2016, Reid complained that the Russians may try to "falsify official election results." In September, Hillary Clinton joined the chorus, telling reporters, "I'm really concerned about the credible reports about Russian government interference in our elections." But when Trump raised the idea that the election could be "rigged" in some way, Democrats ridiculed him and claimed he was "whining." At a White House news conference, President Obama said, "no serious person out there who [*sic*] would suggest somehow that you could even rig America's elections . . . I'd invite Mr. Trump to stop whining and go try to make his case to get votes." Obama also said Trump's suggestion of a "rigged election" was unheard-of. "I have never seen in my lifetime or in modern political history any presidential candidate trying to discredit the elections and the election process before votes have even taken place," said Obama in the October 2016 news conference. "It's unprecedented." (Except that Hillary Clinton had already done so first.) The media heralds Obama's remarks. Left-leaning *Politico* and NPR quote the president and tell Trump to "Stop whining." The liberal website *Slate* headlines its article "Watch Barack Obama's Masterful Donald Trump 'Rigging' Takedown."

In the wake of the election, allegations of Russian interference reach a fever pitch. Many in the news media treat it as a proven fact rather than an allegation or theory, although the public evidence is lacking. "Obama Strikes Back at Russia for Election Hacking," reads a *New York Times* headline, jumping on the propaganda train. "How Russia 'Hacked' Us in 2016," reads *Forbes*.

The final week of December 2016, the FBI and the U.S. Department of Homeland Security release a joint thirteen-page report describing "Russian Malicious Cyber Activity." It makes the case that two hacking groups believed tied to the Russian government were involved in hacking into the Democratic National Committee system during the campaign, providing thousands of emails through WikiLeaks. WikiLeaks founder Julian Assange strongly denies that the leak came from Russia, stating,

"Our source is not the Russian government . . . we didn't get it from a state." Former British ambassador Craig Murray backs up Assange's version: "I know who leaked them. I've met the person who leaked them, and they are certainly not Russian and it's an insider. It's a leak, not a hack; the two are different things." The differing claims don't stop the online media from declaring one side to be correct and the other to be lying. Left-wing *Vox* describes WikiLeaks unequivocally as "the source through which Russia released the hacked emails to the public," as if there were no dispute over the facts.

For my part, I decide to look past the media reports to see if I can separate fact from fake by looking at the existing evidence. First, let me be clear: Do I think it's possible Russia tried to influence the outcome of our elections? Absolutely. In fact, I consider it quite likely. Not because of the unsubstantiated conclusions in the press, but because intelligence officials I trust tell me that Russia and other nations have attempted to influence our elections for decades, the same way we've often dabbled in influencing foreign elections. My sources also tell me that, historically, they consider China to be a more egregious offender. If you've watched politics long enough, you may remember the scandal broken by the *Washington Post* in 1996. The *Post* reported evidence of China directing contributions to the DNC during the presidential campaign between Bill Clinton and Republican Bob Dole—a violation of U.S. law. Over time, Taiwan-born Maria Hsia, a fundraiser for Clinton's vice president, Al Gore, was convicted of illegal campaign fundraising; Taiwan-born Charlie Trie was convicted of improperly attempting to give large donations to the Clintons' legal defense fund; Taiwan-born Johnny Chung was convicted of violating election law after making large donations to the DNC (which were later returned); and Chinese-born John Huang—a DNC fundraiser and Commerce Department official in the Clinton administration—was convicted of campaign finance fraud.

Still, it's quite a leap for the news media to accept the notion that Russia actually got Trump elected, at least based on the public evidence at the time. First, the persistent claims that the "election was hacked" is a misnomer. There were no standing allegations by U.S. officials that the Russians (or anyone else) "hacked" into our elections system or altered vote counts. Even assuming the Russians were proven to be behind the "hacking" of DNC emails, it would be hard to show that it somehow "affected the election" or "helped Donald Trump win." For example, one would have to prove that a certain number of people in key states who voted for Trump were convinced to do so based solely on the email leaks (or that people who ultimately didn't vote for Clinton had been convinced by the emails). It would seem difficult to devise a scientific poll that could figure that out. Further, one would have to believe the emails somehow managed to be successful in only providing Trump an edge in the electoral vote but not the popular vote (which Clinton won). And finally, one would have to believe the emails somehow selectively swayed voters in key swing states, but not voters in states where Clinton won. In covering the news, journalists aren't supposed to report suppositions as unattributed facts, even if they consider them likely to be true. But rules that used to be standard-bearers of journalism are cast aside as the Russian drumbeat continues in the media, unabated.

On November 25, 2016, a *Washington Post* headline reads, "Russian Propaganda Effort Helped Spread 'Fake News' during Election, Experts Say." The article, by Craig Timberg, goes on to cite research from a new, mysterious website called PropOrNot (as in "propaganda or not"), which describes itself as a resource for "assembling tools and information to help identify and neutralize Russian propaganda." PropOrNot claims millions of Americans have been deceived in a massive Russian "misinformation campaign," and lists supposed Russian disinformation outlets, including many that were notably critical of Hillary Clinton, such as WikiLeaks, Infowars, and the *Drudge Report*. The article becomes the most widely read story on the *Post* website, and a top-circulated article on social media.

But the next day, the *Post* is inundated with criticism. The *Intercept* accuses the newspaper of promoting a "blacklist" based on the "claims of a new, shadowy organization that smears dozens of U.S. news sites that are critical of U.S. foreign policy as being 'routine peddlers of Russian propaganda.'" PropOrNot's agenda, say critics, appears to be to spur formal McCarthy-like government inquiries of entities accused of being Russian agents because they supported "policies like Brexit, and the breakup of the EU and Eurozone." The credibility of the *Post* article and PropOrNot quickly crumble. The *Intercept* says it "contacted PropOrNot and asked numerous questions about its team, but received only this reply: 'We're getting a lot of requests for comment and can get back to you today =) [smiley face emoticon] . . . We're over 30 people, organized into teams, and we cannot confirm or deny anyone's involvement.'" Numerous organizations listed as being "allied" with PropOrNot on its website tell the *Intercept* they never heard of it before the *Post* story. The *Post* ends up publishing an embarrassing editor's note. It reads, in part:

> *A number of those [websites on PropOrNot's Russia propaganda list] have objected to being included on PropOrNot's list, and some of the sites, as well as others not on the list, have publicly challenged the group's methodology and conclusions. The* Post, *which did not name any of the sites, does not itself vouch for the validity of PropOrNot's findings regarding any individual media outlet, nor did the article purport to do so. Since publication of The* Post's *story, PropOrNot has removed some sites from its list.*

In other words, as it claimed to draw attention to fake news, the *Post* may very well have gotten duped by, or been party to, fake news. Of the kerfuffle, the *New Yorker* writes, "the prospect of legitimate dissenting voices being labelled fake news or Russian propaganda by mysterious groups of ex-government employees, with the help of a national newspaper, is even scarier" than the prospect of Russian hacks.

The alleged Russia connection to Trump is further stoked by controversial reporting in January 2017 by CNN and *BuzzFeed* about unsubstantiated allegations against Trump in a "dossier" that was unverified and contained known errors. The incendiary documents claim Russia has been "cultivating, supporting and assisting" Trump for years. They also claim the Russians have documented weird sexual acts by Trump, and report that his lawyer, Michael Cohen, secretly met with Russian officials in Prague in the Czech Republic. Cohen disputes the claim, saying he's never been to the Czech Republic in his life and certainly didn't meet Russian officials there. He even offers up his passport to prove it. It turns out the dossier had been compiled for an opposition research firm called Fusion

GPS. One insider tells *Daily Caller* that the head of Fusion GPS is a notorious "professional smear campaigner." The dossier had been shopped to countless news organizations over a period of months. It was, perhaps, a significant feat that smear artists were able to get the oppo research product so widely covered in the media.

With the Russia narrative taking a firm grip on America in the news media, journalists and pundits begin to routinely refer to Russian interference in the election, and Trump's Russia connections, as if proven. The DNC issues daily email blasts and "War Room" updates ferreting out and attacking any and all Trump administration contacts with Russians. In February 2017, Obama intel officials leak to the press that they had eavesdropped on a pre-inauguration phone call between Trump's national security adviser, Lieutenant General Michael Flynn, and Russian ambassador Sergey Kislyak. After the call becomes public, Flynn backs off his earlier claim that he hadn't discussed current U.S. sanctions against Russia with Kislyak. He's subsequently forced out of the Trump administration because he had misled Vice President Mike Pence on that point. Next, Democrats go after Trump attorney general Jeff Sessions after it's learned he had two meetings with Ambassador Kislyak during the course of the campaign but didn't acknowledge them when asked at his Senate nomination hearings. (Sessions later says it was an oversight and recused himself from any investigation into Russian influence in U.S. elections.)

Flynn and Sessions should have disclosed all of their contacts with Russian officials. But once again, I find it a leap to conclude they were involved in illegal or improper conspiracies with Russia. Contact with Russia hardly equates to collusion. I remember President Obama's infamous "hot-mic" moment in 2012 in which he was overheard familiarly telling Russian president Dmitri Medvedev that he'd have "more flexibility" to negotiate with then–prime minister Putin after the election. I happen to know from firsthand sources that in the first six months of the 2016 election year, Obama secretary of state John Kerry communicated with Russian foreign minister Sergey Lavrov more frequently than their counterparts had ever done in recent memory. (They had thirty-seven phone calls and four meetings, I'm told. A large part of the discussions involved the United States and Russia possibly coordinating on military action in Syria, according to my sources.) Yet frequent contacts and coordination are not proof that Russia was in the tank for Democrats, or vice versa. Nor were the many meetings held between the Russian ambassador and leading Democrats, including Representative Nancy Pelosi and Senator Charles Schumer.

If Trump's collusion with Russia is independently proven with evidence, it will be a news story like no other, and worthy of unprecedented reporting efforts. Until and unless that time comes, any allegations should be treated as such and attributed to their various sources. But that's not how it seems to work in the brave new world of fake news. Today, if enough pundits, operatives, and media parrot the same narrative, it becomes incorporated into the fabric of the news as an accepted fact.

On March 5, 2017, Obama's former director of national intelligence, James Clapper, seems to blow the lid off all the news reports to date that concluded the Trump campaign had a proven role in fixing the election. In an interview on NBC's *Meet the Press,* host Chuck Todd asks Clapper if there is evidence of the Trump campaign colluding with Russia. "Not to my knowledge," replied Clapper. He adds that he saw "no evidence of such collusion" while he was in the Obama administration.

The Heyday of Fake News

If fake news (by other names) has always been around, why does it suddenly become the stuff of daily headlines toward the end of the 2016 campaign? The trail is fascinating and most enlightening. I trace the public ignition of the movement to September 13, 2016, and a group called First Draft, which announced a "partner network" to tackle "malicious hoaxes and fake news reports" that "are published in increasingly convincing and sophisticated ways." The group's goal seems to be to separate wheat from chaff. To prevent unproven conspiracy talk like Pizzagate from showing up in ordinary Internet searches or trending on popular social media sites. To relegate today's version of the alien baby story to a special Internet oblivion.

But you and I know that little happens by accident . . . ideas put before us are usually put there for a reason. When determining possible motivation behind any movement, it's helpful to know who's funding it. I learn that First Draft was founded in the United Kingdom in 2015 with primary backing from Google. The executive chairman of Google's parent company, Alphabet, is Hillary backer Eric Schmidt. Alphabet was Hillary's second-largest campaign contributor. According to internal campaign emails, Google offered up use of its jet to Clinton during her campaign. Schmidt and his team were tasked with helping build Clinton's campaign website. He also submitted "notes" to the campaign regarding his desire to help get Hillary elected, and outlining recommendations as to how she should organize her campaign. Therefore, is it unreasonable to think that Google's First Draft venture, which started up at the beginning of the 2016 election cycle and became the first to dive into the anti–"fake news" narrative, is driven by those seeking to advance Clinton and related political interests?

First Draft describes itself on its website as "a non-profit working on solutions to the challenges associated with trust & truth in the digital age." Its partners include Facebook, Twitter, YouTube, the *New York Times,* the *Washington Post, BuzzFeed,* and CNN, primarily left-leaning entities. I search for First Draft's tax filings, which nonprofits are required to publicly disclose, but I can't find them. When I contact the group, a spokesman tells me that First Draft hasn't actually obtained nonprofit status yet—but expects to receive it soon.

Exactly one month after First Draft announces its initiative, President Obama advances the cause with a pitch at the White House Frontiers Conference, held at Carnegie Mellon University in Pittsburgh. He blames a "wild, wild, west" media environment for destroying rational discourse online. "We are going to have to rebuild within this wild, wild west of information flow some sort of curating function that people agree to," declares the president. His use of the bully pulpit to focus attention on the subject is part of what I see as a calculated agenda. There's been no grassroots demand from the public. At the time, ordinary Americans aren't screaming for self-appointed curators to apply their version of ultimate "truth" on the rest of us. This is the invention of special interests. From that point forward, the topic of fake news dominates headlines on a daily basis. It's quite suddenly portrayed as a top challenge facing American democracy today.

In November 2016, President Obama continues the hard sell against fake news. "If we are not serious about facts and what's true and what's not . . . we can't discriminate between serious arguments and propaganda, then we have problems," he remarks. "If everything seems to be the same, no distinctions are made, then we won't know what to protect. We won't know what to fight for." The declaration smacks of irony. For example, it wasn't long ago that Mr. Obama himself promised—and the media uncritically reported—"if you like your health care plan, you can keep it." PolitiFact called it the Lie of the Year.

It's no surprise to me when David Brock's name next turns up prominently in the anti–fake news movement. He's jumping aboard the train. Or just maybe—he's conducting it. On December 5, 2016, *Huffington Post* publishes an opinion piece from him that seems to blame conservative fake news for Hillary Clinton's presidential defeat. Brock writes that fake news is "an existential threat to our democracy" and adds, "for the first time in our history, we have a minister of disinformation, [Trump adviser] Steve Bannon, who commanded a vast proto-fascist media empire, operating from a plum perch in the West Wing."

The next day, Brock holds a conference call detailing his plan to remake his flagship Media Matters into an effort that pivots from being a Fox antagonist into an arbiter of "alt-right" and fake news outlets (all conservative, of course). Brock says he'll work to pressure Facebook and Google to better filter out fake news. "[T]he first order of business is for some of these companies to adopt some standards and clean their own house," he says. Brock later criticizes the devastating, unsubstantiated rumors about his ex-boyfriend's pizza parlor, which was wrapped up in the Pizzagate fake news scandal. I find it an uncanny coincidence that there's a Brock connection to Pizzagate, which has become the poster child for "fake news," just as Brock happens to emerge to lead the anti–fake news movement.

Regardless, we now have the answer to the question of how Brock intends to reinvent himself after failing, twice, to get Hillary elected president. Counting just two of his super PACs, he's collected and spent more than $50 million in donor money in the four years from 2012 to 2016. How does he plan to recover from the high-cost failures, restore his image, find new relevance, and keep donor money rolling in? Apparently through creating and leading an aggressive campaign against his idea of (conservative) "fake news."

Brock's announcement is understandably viewed with skepticism by many who know him. "The ultimate huckster has announced he's going to lead the fight against fake news," quips one observer I know who has followed Brock's antics for years. A conservative blogger writes, "Virtually everything that David Brock does would qualify as 'fake news' under any objective criteria," pointing to Brock's efforts to use paid trolls to "gaslight" Bernie Sanders supporters and others who criticized Clinton on social media.

A day after Brock's conference call, he resigns from Citizens for Responsibility and Ethics in Washington (CREW), which, during his brief tenure, was transformed from watchdog into a highly partisan campaign tool to attack Republicans. "Due to my stepped up political activities in the American Bridge opposition research super PAC, I decided to step off CREW's board to ensure its public reputation for non-partisanship," Brock says in a statement.

The next day, the intensely political nature of the growing movement is underscored when Hillary personally jumps aboard the anti–fake news train. On December 8, 2016, she speaks to reporters after visits with members of Congress. She claims she's appalled by "the epidemic of malicious fake news and false propaganda that flooded social media over the past year." Again, there's irony, since Clinton herself has a long-standing relationship with fake news. She'd falsely blamed a YouTube video for the September 11, 2012, Benghazi terrorist attacks while acknowledging in private emails that Islamic extremists were to blame. She'd falsely said she dodged sniper fire in Bosnia. And she'd falsely claimed she never handled classified information on her private email servers—the FBI found 2,093 classified emails, including some that were top secret; 193 were formally classified at the time they were sent.

In her appearance at the Capitol, Clinton tells reporters, "It is now clear that so-called fake news can have real world consequences." She's referring to the arrest of a gunman who fired shots at the pizza restaurant named in Pizzagate. The suspect was apparently motivated by online fake news reports. "Lives are at risk, lives of ordinary people just trying to go about their days to do their jobs, contribute to their communities," Clinton continues. "It's a danger that must be addressed and addressed quickly. . . . It's imperative that leaders in both the private and public sector step up to protect our democracy and innocent lives." Clinton's terminology, particularly her dark description of "danger," evokes one of Brock's earlier smear campaigns. In 2010, he'd argued that the rhetoric of Fox News personality Glenn Beck endangered lives and democracy. "Fox has allowed Glenn Beck's show to become an out of control vehicle for the potential incitement of domestic terrorism," Brock wrote at the time, in a joint press release with donor George Soros. "No American should be quiet about these developments—the degradation of our media and the reckless endangerment of innocent lives."

The news coverage given to Brock's fake news focus provides fresh evidence of how he's truly set himself apart in the smear industry. As a political operative, he seems able to pick up the phone or send an email and get his message covered in outlets ranging from *Politico* to the *New York Times*. There are no other liberals or conservative counterparts in the smear game who seem to hold similar sway in the mainstream press.

Further complicating the questions of who is working to establish fake news as a cause célèbre and why—are the ticklish entanglements among the government officials, news outlets, nonprofits, and Internet corporations pushing the effort: Can these entities that have such vested political and financial interests really become trusted curators of news?

We've already established that Google is no political bystander. Before its connections to the Hillary campaign, it advised Obama and its representatives were invited to more than 420 closed-door meetings in the Obama White House. The government is hardly an impartial actor in the curating equation, either. Consider the May 2016 *New York Times* article quoting top Obama adviser Ben Rhodes seeming to brag about manipulating a young, inexperienced press corps. "The average reporter we talk to is 27 years old, and their only reporting experience consists of being around political campaigns," says Rhodes. "They literally know nothing."

The article also describes a "soft Orwellian vibe" produced as "Rhodes has become adept at ventriloquizing many people at once." A Rhodes assistant divulges some strategic secrets, telling the *Times,* "We have our compadres, I will reach out to a couple [of Washington reporters and columnists], and you know I wouldn't want to name them. . . ." He goes on to say he uses the reporters to plant positive spin on negative narratives, "and the next thing I know, lots of these guys are in the dot-com publishing space, and have huge Twitter followings, and they'll be putting this message out on their own."

Days after Brock and Clinton announce they're going after fake news, Facebook cracks. The social media site announces new steps to curb the spread of fake news. CBS News reports it's the result of "months of public pressure." As far as I can tell, the "months of public pressure" came not from the public at large, but from special interests executing an orchestrated campaign. Indeed, Brock would later tell donors that his Media Matters group was largely responsible for forcing Facebook's hand.

Facebook's new plan includes collaborating with Poynter Institute's PolitiFact, ABC News, FactCheck.org, the Associated Press, and Snopes. If you've read this far, you already know the possible perils of this idea from a neutrality standpoint: it relies on some of the very organizations that have gotten caught in compromising situations, engaged in transactional journalism, or reported biased and incorrect news themselves.

According to Facebook, each fact-checking entity will be "given access to a tool . . . to evaluate stories that may be inaccurate." If the chosen fact-checkers agree a story is misleading, it will get a "disputed" label and link to an article explaining why it's supposedly false. In a test run, disputed articles generate a pop-up warning that reads, "Disputed by 3rd parties. Before you share this story you might want to know that independent fact checkers disputed its accuracy." Facebook's "independent" fact-checkers could be ABC, which has been accused of shelving or skewing negative stories about its corporate parent, the Walt Disney Company; misreported that there was a possible link between the conservative Tea Party and the killer in a mass shooting in Aurora, Colorado, in 2012; and routinely allowed television host George Stephanopoulos to conduct political interviews in Campaign 2016 without disclosing his status as a Clinton Foundation donor and former top aide to President Clinton.

"We believe in giving people a voice and that we cannot become arbiters of truth ourselves, so we're approaching this problem carefully," says Facebook vice president Adam Mosseri. "We've focused our efforts on the worst of the worst."

In March 2017, the Google-funded nonprofit First Draft announces "A Field Guide to Fake News," which includes a category described as "anti-liberal" fake news sites, but none that are "anti-conservative." Apparently, under the definition used by First Draft and its partners, there aren't any left-leaning bad actors that are worthy of mention.

So, here's a timeline of the anti–fake news movement:

September 13, 2016: First Draft announces anti–fake news project.

October 13, 2016: President Obama announces need to curate online information.

November 17, 2016: President Obama condemns fake news as a threat to democracy.

December 4, 2016: Gunman fires shots at fake news Pizzagate restaurant owned by David Brock's ex-boyfriend.

December 5, 2016: David Brock op-ed calls fake news "an existential threat to our democracy."

December 6, 2016: Brock announces plan to turn Media Matters into fake news monitor.

December 7, 2016: Brock resigns from CREW to focus more on anti–fake news effort.

December 8, 2016: Hillary Clinton says fake news is putting "lives at risk."

December 15, 2016: Facebook and Snopes announce initiatives to curb fake news.

January 2017: Brock tells donors that Media Matters helped force Facebook's hand.

Brock, Clinton, and Obama may be correct about the dangers of fake news and propaganda. But I'm not the only one who thinks the sudden movement to curate news, itself, smacks of a rollout of a propaganda campaign. Investigative reporter Glenn Greenwald of the *Intercept* writes on December 9, 2016, "The most important fact to realize about this new term: those who most loudly denounce Fake News are typically those most aggressively disseminating it." A top national investigative journalist tells me, "The subset of news that is fake is very tiny and inconsequential. . . . The folks so upset about 'fake news' are really upset about news they don't like."

Of course, just because liberal partisans may have cooked up the anti–fake news movement doesn't mean there aren't conservative actors truly guilty of committing fake news. In March 2017, a fake news prototype called the *Conservative Daily Post* is outed. It had published popular, pro-Trump propaganda during the election under the name and likeness of former beauty queen Laura Hunter, who had hundreds of thousands of Facebook followers. A biography on the site described Hunter as "a well-known blogger and political activist known for her constant stream on Facebook" and claimed she had "been in the reporting and journalism world for almost two decades." It added that Hunter "is single and enjoys living with her dog in Eastern Tennessee." According to the *Washington Post,* Hunter's name was used to churn out mostly untrue anti-Clinton posts "at a dizzying clip, sometimes twice an hour—bogus stories about the FBI's investigation into Hillary Clinton's email server, or Bill Clinton's involvement in an illicit sex ring."

It turns out there *is* a real Laura Hunter—but she didn't write any of the stories attributed to her. According to the *Post,* an imposter used Hunter's name and photo. After the real Laura Hunter discovered what was happening, she sued the alleged perpetrators, claiming they turned her into "a spokesperson for a radical right-wing website that peddles fake news." Hunter's attorney added that her personal views are diametrically opposed to those expressed on the conservative fake news site.

For its part, once in office, the Trump team develops its own loose relationship with facts when it comes to the news. In justifying President Trump's executive order imposing a travel moratorium on seven Muslim-majority nations, his spokesman, Kellyanne Conway, appears on MSNBC and refers to radicalized Muslims being responsible for the "Bowling

Green massacre" in the United States. There was no such massacre. The Internet and television news light up with outrage and cries of "fake news." (Conway later explains that she meant to say "Bowling Green terrorists," referencing two foreigners from Iraq being indicted on terrorism charges in Bowling Green, Kentucky.)

Spotting Fake News

So how can busy people sort through the morass of fake news, efforts that threaten to censor information, and attempts to shape public opinion? Unfortunately, there's no foolproof method. Author John H. Johnson of *Everydata* has several suggestions. First, he says, consider the historical accuracy of the media outlets you follow. Second, think carefully about the credentials of those being quoted—are they real experts or simply self-proclaimed experts whose opinions are passed around among online news outlets? Third, he advises, "When you see a story and you're not sure if it's true, Google the headline and add the word 'false.' If the story isn't true, you're likely to get links from Snopes.com and other fact-checking sites explaining why it's wrong."

I take issue with the last piece of advice since I wouldn't trust Snopes as an unbiased fact-checker as far as I could toss a boulder. The idea of making truth police out of parties with political and corporate interests seems doomed at the start. Johnson agrees, to a point.

"I think we have to be careful about relying on others to take responsibility for our own decision making and consumption of news," he says. He implies that it's fine to use Snopes to detect blatantly untrue news. "Some things are verifiably false—'Pope Francis endorses Donald Trump' or 'Celebrity X died' when in fact they are still alive and well," says Johnson. But he concedes "other types of biases or falsities are more difficult to detect. Bias, misuse of statistics, or reporting incomplete information fall into that category."

In the end, Johnson concludes the general public should not be seeking a central arbiter of what is true or not. "I think the more important issue is that consumers know to check things—who is authoring the story, what are the underlying affiliations, what are the sources, are they verifiable. Also, I think if consumers can look at news stories and discern if there is even an attempt at balance—are two sides of a story being told? Is a headline sensational?"

In a telephone call, I raise similar questions with Jenni Sargent, managing director of First Draft, where the anti–fake news movement largely began in 2016. She also acknowledges difficulties in the task of divining ultimate truth.

"I've never heard one [social media or news organization] as wanting to have role of curator or arbiter," Sargent says. "They're definitely conscious of their responsibility of their algorithm [that selects trending topics] and how it surfaces. Currently, the more popular content is misinformation and false stories. But nuance comes with that. It would never be appropriate for any news organization to position themselves in the role of what's true and not. These are common challenges everywhere."

The Wild Card Factor

If Democrats believe they can create and own an anti–fake news campaign and use it to crush Trump, they once again sorely miscalculate. Trump begins flagging incidents of what he views to be fake news in the mainstream media. To an outsider, it almost looks like toddlers slinging peas at one another: as fast as reporters manage to call out Trump for supposedly committing fake news, he hits them back with his own examples of their supposed false reports. Pretty soon, Trump has effectively co-opted the phrase. At a news conference on January 11, 2017, CNN reporter Jim Acosta tries to ask a question and persists when Trump doesn't call on him. "You are fake news," Trump declares, pointing a finger at Acosta.

"It's all fake news. It's all fake news," Trump tells reporters at a February 16, 2017, news conference. A week later, at the Conservative Political Action Conference, he tells the cheering audience, "I want you all to know that we are fighting the fake news. It's fake, phony, fake."

The wild card.

Epilogue: The Smear Gone Global

IIIIIIIIIIIIIIIIIIIIIIIIIIIIIIIIIIIIIIIIIIIIIIIIIIIIIIIIIIIIIIIIIIIIIIIIIIIIIIIIIIIIIIII

Just as the smear has found preeminence in the United States, it's also become a global phenomenon.

"Everything in my life went to hell, thanks to the trolls," foreign journalist Jessikka Aro tells the *New York Times*. Aro found herself the target of the online Russian "trolls" after she began investigating, well, the use of online Russian trolls in a propaganda campaign, particularly in her home country of Finland. Her ordeal started when she uncovered a secretive Russian "troll factory" in St. Petersburg where astroturfers used the Internet—Twitter, Facebook, YouTube, and blogs—to sway opinion and create confusion to further political goals.

Each Russian troll, Aro discovered, was responsible for posting hundreds of online comments a day under different pseudonyms, in much the same way as government, PR firms, and operatives do here in the United States. She also unearthed use of propagandist decoys called "bikini trolls." Bikini trolls use photos of beautiful women as their fake identities so that they stand out on social media. As soon as Aro started exposing the troll tricks in her news reports, she says she became the target of an "extensive, international disinformation campaign." It became, says Aro, a textbook example of a Russian information/psychological operation.

Aro says character assassins embarked upon a brutal campaign that used virtually every modern tool of the smear. They fabricated scenarios about her from whole cloth, conducted opposition research into her personal life, and perverted grains of truth into an elaborate, fictitious narrative about her. They used the Internet and social media. They sought to harass her and confuse her would-be audience. As part of the harassment, she says she even received an ominous phone call with the sound of a pistol firing on the other end, and she received a text message supposedly from her father—who had died twenty years ago.

It's a nightmare.

"Pro-Kremlin propagandists . . . spread lies on fake news sites about me 'persecuting Russians living in Finland and putting together an illegal database of Putin's supporters,'" Aro tells the *Times*. "Facebook and Twitter trolls (and actual people following their example) questioned my investigations and mental health, and started conducting their own 'investigations' into my social media postings and other information about me." Aro also found herself parodied in a Russian-language music video posted on YouTube. Some of the lyrics, when translated into English are:

> *Oh Jessikka Aro haunted by the Russian Trolls, who cannot catch you,*
> *oh Jessikka. As if the Grand Troll Putin himself noticed you, otherwise*
> *you chose the Bond girl role in vain.*

The video features a woman in a blond wig wearing an American superhero costume (as if Jessikka), with toy trolls bouncing around her. Then, the song sings:

> *Dunno who invented the Troll-stories, but I twigged this as my mis-*
> *sion. I am the Victim of the Troll Army of the Great East, they chase*
> *me nonstop, breathing down my neck.*

This propaganda tactic has a familiar ring. They're lampooning Aro to make her seem ridiculous so the public doesn't take her work seriously. The music video also implies she has overinflated her own importance in believing the Kremlin would target someone so insignificant. *Ridicule is man's most potent weapon.*

The trolls also published Aro's personal contact information alongside their disinformation about her. Soon, her phone and email fill with angry messages. Her stalkers dig deeply into her background. They discover that twelve years before, she'd been fined for drug use. So they take that small grain of truth from long ago and manufacture new, scandalous stories that contain "libelous fantasies," she says, about her "selling drugs, having written my articles under the influence of illegal substances, being a 'NATO information expert drug dealer' and suffering from mental illness. The stories were published on fake sites that incite racism and on several anonymous far-right and conspiracy-theory sites," Aro tells the *Times*.

Aro continued her investigations despite the incessant attacks. When I reached out to her for this book, she told me she'd recently started an online crowd-source campaign to finance an investigative book project about the "information warfare waged by Russian President Vladimir Putin's regime." Last time I checked, she'd received more than $30,000 from online contributors.

Speaking of Russia, just about the time I was learning about Aro's travails, I happened to be headed to Russia myself. On June 4, 2016, I boarded an Air France flight bound for Moscow. I'd been invited by state-run Russia media to attend an international conference on journalism and freedom of information in, of all places, the former Soviet Union, convened by, of all entities, the Kremlin. I call it my oxymoronic trip: traveling to Russia to explore freedom of the press. At the time of my visit, Russia ranked an abysmal 180 out of 199 countries for press freedom, after Iraq, Sudan, and the Congo, according to one international watchdog. Historically, Russia has done worse than smear journalists like Aro. It's snuffed them out.

As I check into Moscow's Golden Ring Hotel, I know that any of my electronic devices can easily be compromised. If I take the chance of hooking my computer or phone up to the hotel Wi-Fi, I'm practically begging for the Russian government to peek inside. It wouldn't be the first time a government has gotten into my private files. In 2014, sources first approached me with the news that my own U.S. government was monitoring my computer traffic and, likely, my phones. Three forensics experts confirmed unauthorized remote intrusions of my work and personal computers. I wasn't the only one. Within a few months, the Edward Snowden scandal broke and America learned the U.S. government had been spying on ordinary citizens as well as journalists. As recently as January of 2017, my forensics expert and sources indicated I was still under surveillance. Soviet-style tactics at work in the good ole U.S. of A.

Oddly enough, the Russia journalism conference is what really opens my eyes to the global nature of the smear. As I speak with other attendees, I'm faced with further evidence that the United States isn't the only place where character assassins are intimidating reporters who are out of step with the prescribed narrative. Propagandists around the world are exploiting the same methods. The conference refers to this phenomenon as the "post-Mainstream media"—a world where reporters who go off script are censored, bullied, smeared, and silenced.

From what I can tell, out of several hundred journalists at the Moscow event, I'm the only one who's currently working in national news inside the United States. I meet colleagues from the United Kingdom, Lebanon, China, Syria, Japan, South Africa, India, and Sri Lanka. They may not fully agree on much—they hold philosophical beliefs that range from left to right—but they each relay stories of growing censorship and smear campaigns at the hands of powerful state and corporate interests.

At our first session, one speaker notes that "Journalists are the object of manipulation attempts by state authorities and those in business who try to disseminate false information." Oddly enough, this observation comes from Russia's own foreign ministry commissioner for Human Rights, Democracy and the Rule of Law: Alexi Volin. Volin goes on to say that some "journalists are ostracized, criticized for their opinions and [placed on] sanctions list, where they are banned from some countries for doing their jobs. It's the post mainstream era. It's new censorship."

Russia's director general of the state-run Rossiya Segodnya International Media Group, Dmitry Kieselev, describes use of Goebbels-type propaganda tactics around the globe. "Information noise [is intentionally] created so that we have too much information and we get lost in it." Some of the information is intentionally false, he says, to confuse the truth.

Beyond the smear, some journalists around the world find themselves physically attacked when they go up against the politically powerful. Ahmed Dawa, director general and editor-in-chief of the Syrian Arab News Agency, tells the conference that forces sometimes target the homes of uncooperative journalists with mortar shells in that country's brutal civil war. Other interests, says Dawa, are responsible for reporting prefabricated, false news. "We didn't know where the truth was and who was in charge," says Dawa, "but it was a preplanned campaign. An information war." In retrospect, I see that we're discussing "fake news" several months before it came to be called that.

WikiLeaks founder Julian Assange addresses us via teleconference from the Ecuadorian embassy in the United Kingdom. He's been holed up there under asylum for more than three years after exposing uncomfortable U.S. government secrets on his website. As American officials reportedly investigated WikiLeaks and Assange for possible criminal charges, sexual assault allegations were lodged against him in Sweden. He sought asylum at the Ecuadorian embassy in London fearing that the Swedes would extradite him to the United States to face unannounced criminal charges under the Espionage Act related to his WikiLeaks website. I don't know the truth of all the claims against Assange. I only know that it's within the realm of the possible that he's being smeared because of his work. He's upset some of the most powerful people in the world. Appearing live on big screens in the Rossiya Segodnya auditorium, Assange tells us how the Internet is being used to manipulate opinion. He warns us that Google isn't what it seems. He says that Google's Eric Schmidt is on board with the Hillary campaign. He describes how Google, Twitter, and Facebook have all been used to promote political causes.

I'm most intrigued, perhaps, when I hear a question during one session from an audience member who identifies himself as British journalist Neil Clark. He stands up and recounts his experience trying to present economic and foreign policy viewpoints that differ with the established narratives. He says for that, he was subjected to an artful and persistent smear campaign that marginalized him, succeeded in removing him from the ranks of mainstream journalism, and turned him a controversialized target. After the session, I catch up with Clark in the lobby of the Rossiya Segodnya building outside the great hall and ask to hear more of his story.

"I see a big change really in the British media . . . particularly in the last five years," Clark tells me. "The parameters of the things that we can sort of say and write are much narrower now than they used to be."

His timeline coincides with my own observations. In the past five years I, too, have seen an incredible crackdown on journalists reporting viewpoints and facts contrary to powerful interests. One way we're stopped is through nasty, organized smears.

I ask Clark to elaborate. He seems hesitant. It's a long story. He doesn't know me. *Could I be part of the effort to discredit him?* he wonders. I chat him up and ask a few more questions. He decides to open up. He describes how he became victim of a diabolical smear operation that's gone on for the better part of a decade. It's used every classic tool: disparaging his work to employers, relentlessly pursuing him on social media, manipulating and controlling Wikipedia pages, deploying astroturf, making counteraccusations, and posting negative comments about his book online.

"I call it the new McCarthyism," Clark continues. "And I don't think that's overstating it. This very pernicious gatekeeping [is] going on. The targeting of any journalist who really puts his head above the curb on certain issues, and foreign policy is the number one sort of no-go area . . . if you want to write about this stuff, you may find it hard to get published in the mainstream, but if you do get something in, then you're likely to be targeted and smeared. Portrayed as sort of working for the enemy."

I ask what originally triggered the harassment. Clark says it began back on December 31, 2005, when he published in the *Daily Telegraph* a critical review of a pro-Iraq war neocon book. The next day, he says, a relentless campaign began to controversialize and discredit him in the eyes of newspapers that commissioned his work.

"I don't think of myself as putting anything extraordinary out, I'm pretty mainstream," Clark says. "My views are what I would call to the mainstream left of the '60s and '70s. However, the sort of shift has been so far in the other direction that when you're putting forward views that were in the mainstream in those days, it's now sort of smeared or portrayed as some sort of fanatical extremist by neocons. And these are people who are the real extremists, this is the Orwellian factor—people who are doing this smearing . . . are the real extremists."

He visibly winces as he describes the attacks.

"And this is a kind of bullying intimidation that's meant to silence a journalist and also push you out of the mainstream. They don't want you in the mainstream. They're terrified of you being in the mainstream outlets. And looking at my journalism and journalists like me, we find it harder to write on some of our foreign policy in the mainstream than we did ten, fifteen years ago."

After we finish talking, Clark strides over to a pretty, blond woman who's waiting for him. He introduces her as his wife. He says she's been damaged in the fallout of the smear campaign against him. She's also a writer. As part of the harassment campaign, they went after *her* work, too.

Several months after the conference, Clark details the sordid account of his harassment in an online blog. Here, he reports how his attackers used Twitter to falsely paint him as anti-immigration and an "obscure far-right blogger," in order to smear him in the eyes of left-leaning Twitter users. Conversely, they smeared him in the eyes of right-leaning Twitter users by falsely portraying him as a hardline communist. One stalker plastered Twitter with tweets calling him a "plagiarist" and a "fraud."

Clark says his attackers also used Wikipedia. One obsessive volunteer Wikipedia editor made repetitive, derogatory changes to his biography— "an astonishing 107 changes over the course of . . . three days," by Clark's count. One edit was made to refer to Clark as a "Srebrenica denier/ genocide denier." Mysterious trolls also popped up to criticize Clark in the comment sections of online articles. They posted negative reviews about his book. They wrote to Clark's employers falsely accusing him of plagiarism and bad acts of journalism.

Clark is fighting back the only way he knows how. Like Jessikka Aro, he launched an online crowd-sourcing campaign to raise legal funds to challenge his attackers. The long campaign against him has taken its toll. It's hit his family, his reputation, and his livelihood. It's consumed him. How can it not? But he insists it won't defeat him.

Back in the U.S.A.

On the home front, the left and right become more entrenched in their respective positions, and jockey to corner the market in labeling "fake news." The media hasn't responded to its campaign missteps with self-correction or self-reflection; they've dug in. Following a year-and-a-half-long self-declared war against President Donald J. Trump, they audaciously declare that it's *he* who first picked the fight. *Washington Post* headlines include "Donald Trump's War on the News Media Is Serious," and "President Trump Is Losing His War with the Media." *Politico* joins in with "Trump's Dead-End War with the Media."

Moving into 2017, the *New York Times* solidifies its intention to use its news platform take down President Trump. It assigns a large, powerhouse team to cover the White House. Two of the six reporters are Glenn Thrush and Maggie Haberman, both formerly of *Politico*. Thrush is the one who referred to himself as a "hack" in emails revealed by WikiLeaks, as he sought advance clearance of his political stories from Clinton campaign chair Podesta. Haberman is the one whom Clinton campaign emails called a "friendly" that they used to "tee up stories for us," and remarked that they were "never . . . disappointed . . . [W]e can . . . do the most shaping by going to Maggie." The *Washington Post*'s Erik Wemple, *Politico*'s Hadas Gold, and *Huffington Post*'s Michael Calderone write stories about the promotions of Thrush and Haberman, omitting any mention of the recent controversies surrounding them.

In March 2017, former Democratic National Committee Chair Donna Brazile finally admits that, as a CNN contributor, she'd "share[d] potential town hall topics with the Clinton campaign . . . My job was to make all our Democratic candidates look good, and I worked closely with both campaigns to make that happen. But sending those emails was a mistake I will forever regret."

A *Guardian* article connects WikiLeaks' Julian Assange to Russia and then to Trump, as if to imply a Trump connection to Russia—and goes viral. After the fact, it's revealed that in making its assertions, the *Guardian* had falsely attributed comments to Assange that he never actually made. The *Guardian* later "amended" its article to remove a sentence that had stated Assange "has long had a close relationship with the Putin regime." *The Intercept*'s Glenn Greenwald notes that the *Guardian* article was "spread all over the internet by journalists, causing hundreds of thousands of people (if not millions) to consume false news," underscoring "that those who most flamboyantly denounce Fake News, and want

Facebook and other tech giants to suppress content in the name of combatting it, are often the most aggressive and self-serving perpetrators of it." To the chagrin of the press, Trump—a master of branding—has so thoroughly co-opted the notion of "fake news" and turned it on the mainstream media that people now commonly refer to it as his invention.

Meantime, a rash of anti-Semitic bomb threats is accompanied by media demands for President Trump to condemn them (which he does), as if he's somehow responsible for them. One article accuses Trump of refusing to "accept that his allies are targeting Jews." An anti-Trump reporter, Juan Thompson, takes to Twitter to criticize the racism and anti-Semitism, writing: "Another week, another round of threats against Jewish [people]. In the middle of the day, you know who's at a [Jewish community center]? Kids. KIDS." A few days later, the FBI arrests that very reporter, Thompson, for allegedly making eight bomb threats against Jewish community centers. An African American and a Bernie Sanders supporter, Thompson was decrying the racist threats while making them himself, with intent to "injure, kill, harass and intimidate," according to the FBI. *Huffington Post* reports the arrest but makes no mention of the reporter's political affiliations, or the twist that he'd criticized Trump and blamed others while making the anti-Semitic threats himself.

As for David Brock, on March 22, 2017, it's announced he has suffered a heart attack at his Washington D.C. offices and is recovering. At the time, he's in the middle of devising a four-year plan to reorganize Media Matters. He's desperately seeking a new place of relevance in a landscape that he helped create, but one that's seemed to have evolved beyond his mastery. In a confidential presentation to donors, Brock claims that the "next generation of conservative misinformation" is "the proliferation of fake news and propaganda now threatening the country's ecosystem." He also takes credit for convincing CBS and ABC to stop allowing Trump to do telephone interviews during the campaign (which had made Trump a constant presence on the news). Brock promises new strategies to use reporters to "move the needle and [shape] coverage." He announces five new "issue teams" focused on "gun violence and public safety, LGBT equality, reproductive health and gender equality, climate and energy, and economic policy." He promises to "amplify" the progressive message and "change the narrative on how these issues are covered in the media." After Hillary's devastating presidential loss, Media Matters returns to a successful smear campaign of the past, restarting its War on Fox. Beginning in mid-February of 2017, the group publishes one blog after another attacking Fox's most famous and notorious personality: Bill O'Reilly. The campaign hits O'Reilly for a dozen perceived offenses. In one example, Media Matters accuses O'Reilly of racism and demands he be fired for comparing the hairdo of African-American Congresswoman Maxine Waters to a James Brown wig. (Media Matters apparently sees no parallel to the many media figures who lampooned Donald Trump's "wig.") By late February, Media Matters finds a golden nugget—its grain of truth—when the *New York Times* reports that O'Reilly and Fox News "have paid $13 million in settlements for sexual harassment, sparking an advertiser boycott of his show and leading to his ouster from the channel." Media Matters shifts focus from demanding O'Reilly be fired for the wig comment to demanding he be fired because he is, says Media Matters, a sexual predator. Media Matters prints a list of O'Reilly Factor advertisers and pressures them to cancel their sponsorships. It reprints critical quotes about O'Reilly from CNN's Brian Stelter and the Washington Post's Erik Wemple. It publishes the names, email addresses, phone numbers, and Twitter handles for 21st Century Fox's board of directors prior to their meeting to take up the status of the embattled O'Reilly.

On April 19, just a few weeks after the campaign to fire O'Reilly begins, it's announced he's out at Fox. Media Matters has issued 40 blogs addressing O'Reilly in two months and takes a victory lap when the ouster becomes official. And the group can't help but bring up one of its earlier Fox News targets: Glenn Beck.

"Almost six years after former Fox News host Glenn Beck insisted that Media Matters had nothing to do with the decline in his show's advertising and its eventual termination, he went on his radio program to blame Media Matters for Fox dropping host Bill O'Reilly," writes Media Matters.

After his Fox departure is made public, O'Reilly issues a statement saying, "It is tremendously disheartening that we part ways due to completely unfounded claims. But that is the unfortunate reality many of us in the public eye must live with today."

Indeed, Media Matters and Brock have proven they can shape the news and influence the media landscape. But as the election of Donald Trump proved, their influence isn't boundless. Part of that is because many people are growing wise. The work of propagandists, left and right, isn't as invisible as it once was. And Brock faces cynicism from his own side.

A campaign postmortem published in *The Daily Beast* is entitled "Dems to David Brock: Stop Helping, You Are Killing Us." In the article, a senior ex-Clinton staffer calls Brock and his organizations: "useless— you might as well have thrown those [tens of] millions of dollars down a well, and then set the well on fire." A former Obama administration official remarks, "I don't know what the fuck [Brock's network] did besides raise a ton of money, and I don't think the after-action report on 2016 says we need more David Brock. Probably the opposite is true."

I run into a longtime, national investigative journalist in Washington, D.C. He quickly turns the conversation to the sorry state of news.

"But I think the pendulum will swing back the other way," he remarks.

"Really?" I ask.

"Sure," he says. "It has to. It can't sustain itself like this. It'll come and go."

For now, one thing you can count on is that most every image that crosses your path has been put there for a reason. Nothing happens by accident. What you need to ask yourself isn't so much *Is it true*, but *Who wants me to believe it—and why?*

Index

||||||||||||

Abedin, Huma, 150, 171, 244
Acosta, Jim, 273
Adams, Scott, 126–27
Adelson, Sheldon, 87, 170, 182
Aguilar, David, 156–57
Ailes, Roger, 25, 110
Akin, Todd, 97–98
Alinsky, Saul, 17–18, 222
Allen, Mike, 147–48, 151–53, 162–63, 172
Ambinder, Marc, 146–48
Ardoin, John, 97
Aro, Jessikka, 275–77, 281
Asher, James, 77
Assange, Julian, 259–60, 279, 282
Auerbach, David, 128
Ayers, Bill, 200
Aziz, Jalil Ibn Ameer, 131–32

Bachmann, Michele, 99
Baier, Bret, 207–8
Baker, Peter, 213
Baquet, Dean, 235
Barbaro, Michael, 219
Bay, Michael, 124
Beck, Glenn, 54, 59–66, 268, 284
Berger, Daniel, 103–4

Berman, Rick, 84–85
Bernstein, Carl, 18, 148
Biden, Joe, 52–53, 182
Bin Laden, Osama, 181
Blitzer, Wolf, 211–12
Blumenthal, Max, 78–79
Blumenthal, Richard, 90
Blumenthal, Sidney, 28–32, 76–80, 98
Boehlert, Eric, 55–56
Boehner, John, 134
Bolton, John, 99
Bonner, Mary Pat
    2016 campaign, 171, 196
    financial take of, 103, 108, 114, 117–18
    fundraising of, 45–46, 100, 103
Bookbinder, Noah, 108
Boortz, Neal, 54
Bork, Robert, 15
Bossie, David N., 133
Brazile, Donna, 210–11, 282
Brewer Lane, Rowanne, 218–20
Broaddrick, Juanita, 27
Brock, David, 35–66
    American Bridge and, 95–104, 154–55, 208
    American Democracy and, 109–11

Brock, David (*cont.*)
  American Independent Institute and,
      111–13
  anti-fake news movement and, 266–67,
      269, 283
  Citizens United decision, 95
  CREW and, 107–13, 229
  empire of, 36–40, *38–39*
  financial take of, 36, 116–18
  Franklin groups, 113–14
  Hillary Clinton and 2008 campaign,
      55–57
  Hillary Clinton and 2016 campaign,
      98–99, 144, 229, 241
    anti-Sanders efforts, 181–83, 195–99
    Correct the Record, 101–4
    Pizzagate, 243–44
    postmortem, 247–48, 285
    shaping the narrative, 154–55,
        170–74, 208
    True Blue, 114–15
    Trump and racist smears, 101–2, 226
  Hillary Clinton and liberal birth,
      41–43, 44
  Hillary Clinton and Troopergate, 24
  liberal birth of, 42–44
  Media Matters and, 36, 42–57
    Beck and, 59–66
    double standards, 52–54
    early smears, 46–49
    founding, 42–43
    Gerth and, 54–56
    Imus smear, 49–52
    money magnet, 44–46
    Obama and, 57–59
    post–2016 campaign reorganization,
        111, 266, 283–84
  Message Matters and, 104–7
  Thomas and Hill hearing, 16, 40–41
Brown, Michael, 245–46, 256–57
Brown, Ron, 25
Brown, Scott, 96–98
Brown, Susan, 245–46
Browning, Dolly Kyle, 27

Bruning, Jon, 96
Buchanan, Pat, 197
Budowsky, Brent, 179
Bump, Philip, 240–41
Burke, Dennis, 159–60
Bush, Billy, 239
Bush, George H. W., 28, 87
Bush, George W., 146
  2004 campaign and swiftboating,
      74–75
  military service and Dan Rather,
      255
  think tanks and, 89–91
  use of PR firms, 82–83
Bush, John Ellis "Jeb," 2016 campaign,
      99–100, 110, 155
  debates, 193
  media collusion, 183
  super PACs, 86, 202
Byrd, Robert, 53

Calabresi, Massimo, 150
Calderone, Michael, 282
Cameron, David, 189
Cardona, Maria, 216–17
Carlson, Gretchen, 56
Carlson, Tucker, 4
Carrey, Jim, 121
Carson, Ben, 110
Carter, Jimmy, 191
Carville, James, 19–20, 23
Cauterucci, Christina, 191–92
Chafee, Lincoln, 190
Chaffetz, Jason, 98, 173
Chait, Jonathan, 225
Chavez, Hugo, 181
Chiachiere, Ryan, 49
Christie, Chris, 99, 111, 204
Chung, Johnny, 260
Cillizza, Chris, 224
Clapper, James, 264
Clark, Neil, 279–81
Clift, Eleanor, 178
Clifton, Eli, 112

Clinton, Bill
1992 campaign, 18–23
1996 campaign, 25–27, 260
2016 campaign, 189–90, 232, 240, 241–42
email proof of transactional journalism, 153–54
Lewinsky affair and, 28–32, 34
presidential scandals, 23–25
Wen Ho Lee case, 254–55
Whitewater controversy and, 20–23, 54–55, 176
womanizing of, 18–20, 24, 25–34, 134, 189–90, 240
Clinton, Chelsea, 151–53, 233, 241
Clinton, Hillary
1992 campaign, 18–23
2008 campaign, 55–57, 76–77, 256
2016 campaign, 167–84, 189–200, 209–48, 265
Adams and shadowbanning, 126–27
anti-Sanders efforts, 181–83, 195–99
audience-stacking, 190–94
"basket of deplorables" comments, 229–30
Brazile and CNN debate questions, 210–11, 282
Brock and super PACs, 98–104, 114–15, 144, 154–55, 170–74, 179, 198–99, 208, 209–10
the cash, 168–70
the collusion, 177–84
Comey and, 244–45, 246
DNC leaked emails, 170–74, 182–83, 210–13, 216–18, 220, 241–43, 259–60, 261
electoral map, 240–41, 247
email controversy, 172–74, 177–78, 181, 235–36
general election, 214–48
Gerth smears, 174–77
health issues, 230–33
Iowa caucuses, 195, 201
outside group spending, 168–70

Pizzagate, 1–2, 243–44, 268
public polls, 237–38, 239, 246
shaping the narrative, 144–45, 170–74
Wall Street speeches, 154, 196
Alinsky and, 17–18
anti–fake news movement and, 267–68
Benghazi attack, 44, 78–80, 98, 123–25, 138, 149–50, 174
Blumenthal and, 28–32, 76–80, 98
email proof of transactional journalism, 146–53, 154, 163, 216–18, 220
Lewinsky affair, 28–29, 31–32
Whitewater controversy and, 20–23, 54–55, 176
Cohen, Michael, 262–63
Comey, James, 244–45, 246
Conway, Kellyanne, 240–41, 271–72
Cooney, Phil, 89–90
Cooper, Anderson, 190, 211
Cooper, Rebecca, 150
Costolo, Dick, 122–23
Cruz, Ted, 110, 201, 203, 205, 208, 209, 211

D'Alessandro, Anthony, 124
Daou, Peter, 114
Davis, Lanny, 196
Dawa, Ahmed, 278–79
Dean, Howard, 60, 233
Denvir, Daniel, 183
Devine, Tad, 197–98
Dietl, Bo, 52
Dietrich, Marlene, 10–11
Dilanian, Ken, 148–49
Dobbs, Lou, 66
Dodson, John, 158–61
Dole, Bob, 25, 260
Dole, Elizabeth, 96
Drogin, Bob, 255
Drum, Kevin, 183
Dukakis, Michael, 87
Dyson, Robert, 95

Earnest, Josh, 154
Eban, Katherine, 160–61
Ebell, Myron, 89–90
Edwards, Haley Sweetland, 112
Emanuel, Rahm, 31
Erdely, Sabrina Rubin, 257
Estrich, Susan, 19

Fabiani, Mark, 54–55
Fallon, Brian, 184
Feldstein, Mark, 4–5, 9
Fiorina, Carly, 93, 205, 212
Fisher, Max, 124
Fitzgerald, Gerald, 97
Flowers, Gennifer, 18–20
Flynn, Michael, 263–64
Flynt, Larry, 32–34
Foster, Vincent, 25
Fouhy, Beth, 150
Friedman, Dan, 192
Frisch, Karl, 60–62, 65, 111

Gandhi, Mahatma, 52
Gerth, Jeff, 54–56, 154
    2008 campaign, 55–56
    2016 campaign and smears against,
        174–77
    Whitewater and, 20–23, 54–55
Gibson, John, 54
Giuliani, Rudy, 230
Glasser, Susan, 152, 213, 234–35
Glastris, Paul, 112
Glaze, Mark, 108
Goebbels, Joseph, 11–12, 136, 222
Goldwater, Barry, 23
Gore, Al, 81, 260
Gowdy, Trey, 111, 173–74
Grace, Nancy, 59
Gracen, Elizabeth Ward, 27
Graham, David, 225
Graham, Lindsey, 173
Grassley, Charles, 158, 160, 184
Greenwald, Glenn, 106, 271, 282–83
Gregory, David, 221

Griffin, Ken, 196
Grim, Ryan, 246
Grove, Lloyd, 197
Gruber, Jonathan, 133–34

Haberman, Maggie, 171–72, 184, 213, 282
Hagel, Chuck, 53
Haley, Nikki, 99
Halperin, Mark, 76–77
Hamilton, Alexander, 9
Hannity, Sean, 56–57
Hart, Gary, 28, 253
Harwood, John, 183
Hasson, Peter, 138
Hástings, Michael, 149–50
Hatch, Orrin, 16
Hearst, William Randolph, 253
Hebert, Josef, 255
Heilemann, John, 76–77
Hemings, Sally, 9
Hill, Anita, 16, 23, 31, 40–41
Hitchens, Christopher, 31–32
Hitler, Adolf, 11, 235
Hoffenberg, Steven, 169–70
Holbrooke, Richard, 147
Holder, Eric, 256
Horton, Willie, 87
Huang, John, 260
Hubbell, Webb, 22
Huckabee, Mike, 110
Hughes, Dana, 148
Hunter, Laura, 271
Hussein, Saddam, 190

Imus, Don, 49–52
Ingraham, Laura, 162
Isikoff, Michael, 30
Issa, Darrell, 173

Jarrett, Gregg, 56
Jefferson, Thomas, 9
Jeffery, Clara, 183
Jewell, Richard, 254
Johnson, John H., 252–53, 272–73

Johnson, Lyndon, 13
Johnson, Ron, 99
Johnson, Simon, 81–82
Jones, Alex, 134
Jones, Anthony "Van," 66
Jones, Paula, 25–26, 27
Josi, Christian, 133–35
Juntos, Creciendo, 81

Kaine, Tim, 135
Kasich, John, 110
Katzenberg, Jeffrey, 171
Kennedy, Anthony, 15
Kennedy, Edward "Ted," 15
Kennedy, John F., 13, 191, 209
Kerry, John, 74–75, 178, 263
Ketcham, Christopher, 112
Kieselev, Dmitry, 278
King, Martin Luther, 252
King, Steve, 97
Kinnock, Neil, 97
Kislyak, Sergey, 263–64
Klein, Ezra, 124
Koch brothers, 87–88, 155, 166, 182
Kornblut, Anne, 150
Kucinich, Jackie, 178
Kurtz, Howard, 223, 229

LaCapria, Kim, 138
Lavrov, Sergey, 263
Leahy, Patrick, 71–72, 108
Lee, Spike, 115
Lee, Wen Ho, 254–55
Legum, Judd, 128–29
Leidner, Gordon, 191
Lerner, Lois, 123
Lewandowski, Corey, 215–16
Lewinsky, Monica, 28–32, 34
Liasson, Mara, 56
Libowitz, Jordan, 109
Lichter, S. Robert, 137
Limbaugh, Rush, 54, 112
Lincoln, Abraham, 191
Livingston, Bob, 33

Lowell, Abbe, 173–74
Lucas, Fred, 216
Lynch, Loretta, 22
Lyons, Gene, 22

McCain, John, 60
    2008 campaign, 56, 57, 93, 218
    2016 campaign and Trump, 185–86
McCarthy, Joseph, 229
McCarthy, Kevin, 134
McCaskill, Claire, 98, 197
McCloskey, Pete, 215
MacDonell, Allan, 33–34
McFadden, Cynthia, 180
McGuirk, Bernard, 49–50
McKay, Rob, 95
McKenna, Matt, 153–54
McKinley, William, 253
Mair, Liz, 92–93, 188, 204, 205–6
Manafort, Paul, 215–16, 227
Manjoo, Farhad, 231
Margolis, Jim, 179
Marshall, Brad, 199
Martinez, Alberto, 187–88
Martinez, Susana, 99
Matthews, Chris, 46–47, 206–7
Matzzie, Tom, 57
Mayberg, Louis, 109
Medvedev, Dmitri, 263
Melson, Kenneth, 159
Merica, Dan, 210
Merrill, Nick, 210
Messina, Jim, 189, 201–3
Milbank, Dana, 212, 226
Miller, Mark Crispin, 12–13, 14
Miller, Myra Belle "Sally," 18
Miller, Zeke, 251–52
Mills, Cheryl, 177, 181
Miranda, Luis, 216
Mitchell, Andrea, 181
Mitchell, George, 147
Mook, Robby, 102
Moore, Michael, 61
Morell, Mike, 243

Morris, Dick, 19
Mosseri, Adam, 270
Murdoch, Rupert, 25
Murray, Craig, 260
Murrow, Edward R., 229

Nakoula, Nakoula, 79–80
Netanyahu, Benjamin, 258
Nicholas, Peter, 153–54
Nixon, Richard, 191, 215
Norquist, Grover, 90–91

Obama, Barack
    2008 campaign, 53, 56–57, 76–77, 256
    2012 campaign, 86–88, 95–96, 202
    2016 campaign, 225, 259
    Affordable Care Act (Obamacare), 58,
        105–6, 133–34, 153–54
    #AskPOTUS town hall, 122–23
    astroturf and climate change, 135–36
    Benghazi attack, 98, 137, 267
    "birther" smear, 77
    email proof of transactional
        journalism, 145–46
    fake news and, 8, 265–66
    Fast and Furious case, 159–61
    Media Matters and Brock, 57–59
O'Donnell, Rosie, 59
O'Malley, Martin, 182, 198
O'Reilly, Bill, 54, 284
Oswald, Lee Harvey, 13, 209

Packer, Katie, 203–4
Page, Clarence, 224
Palermo, Rachel, 216
Palin, Sarah, 93
Palma, Bethania, 172
Palmieri, Jennifer, 178, 179–81, 183, 213
Patrick, Deval, 97
Paul, Rand, 93, 110
Paul, Ron, 197
Paustenbach, Mark, 212, 216–17
Pelosi, Nancy, 264
Pence, Mike, 99, 225, 263

Perot, Ross, 25, 28
Perry, Rick, 93, 99–100
Peters, Jeremy, 150
Pielke, Roger, Jr., 128–29
Pike, Drummond, 45, 63
Pincus, Walter, 255
Podesta, John, 129
    2008 campaign, 57
    2016 campaign, 195–96, 213
        leaked emails, 99, 102, 170–71, 178,
            243–44
Portman, Rob, 99
Priebus, Reince, 193
Psaki, Jen, 178
Pulitzer, Joseph, 253
Putin, Vladimir, 2, 227, 250, 258–64,
    277

Qaddafi, Muammar, 78–79

Ramos, Jorge, 168, 184–85, 185
Rangel, Charles, 108
Rather, Dan, 228, 255
Reagan, Ronald, 15, 191, 214
Real Anita Hill, The (Brock), 16, 41
Redstone, Sumner, 52
Reid, Harry, 53, 259
Reines, Philippe, 146–53, 163–64, 173
Reynolds, Maria, 9
Rhodes, Ben, 268–69
Rice, Donna, 253
Ricketts, Joe, 196
Ricketts, Marlene, 204
Robinson, Eugene, 224
Roff, Peter, 137
Rollins, Ed, 214–16
Romney, Mitt
    2012 campaign, 79, 86–88, 95–96, 98
    2016 campaign and Trump, 167
Rosenberg, Alyssa, 124
Ross, Dennis, 147
Rothenberg, Stu, 240
Rove, Karl, 90, 95, 108, 202–3
Rubio, Marco, 99, 204–5

Rucker, Philip, 185–86
Ryan, Paul, 99

Saban, Haim, 184–90
Safer, Morley, 84
Salazar, Ken, 197
Sanders, Bernie, 2016 primary campaign,
     181–83, 195–200
   Brock and anti-Sanders efforts, 115,
     181–82, 195–99
   Iowa caucuses, 195, 201
   Wasserman-Schultz and, 6, 182,
     193–94
Sargent, Greg, 217–18
Sargent, Jenni, 273
Savage, Kaye, 41
Savage, Michael, 54
Scaife, Richard Mellon, 23–24, 32
Scarborough, Joe, 221
Schieffer, Bob, 71–72
Schmaler, Tracy, 71–72, 162–63
Schmidt, Eric, 265, 279
Schneiderman, Eric, 242
Schumer, Charles, 264
Schweizer, Peter, 178–79
Sessions, Jeff, 15, 263–64
Silberstein, Stephen M., 45, 114
Silver, Nate, 128, 246
Simons, James, 168
Singer, Paul, 196
Sirota, David, 115
Slaughter, Louise, 60
Sloan, Melanie, 108
Smerconish, Michael, 54
Smith, Ben, 65
Snowden, Edward, 106, 277–78
Soghoian, Christopher, 83
Soros, George, 35, 45, 59, 61–63, 100, 168,
     201, 208, 268
Spahn, Andy, 171
Starr, Ken, 29
Steele, Michael, 221
Stein, Ben, 56
Stelter, Brian, 231, 284

Stephanopoulos, George, 269–70
Stevens, Christopher, 123–24, 149
Stewart, Jim, 255
Steyer, Tom, 128
Stone, Roger, 134–36, 214–15, 233,
     242–43
Streisand, Barbra, 229–30
Sullivan, Jake, 150
Susman, Gary, 124
Sussman, Donald, 168

Tanden, Neera, 102, 171, 195–96
Taylor, Goldie, 224
Terry, Brian, 158–59
Thomas, Clarence, 16, 19, 40–41
Thomas, Pierre, 255
Thompson, Juan, 283
Thrush, Glenn, 213, 282
Timberg, Craig, 261
Todd, Chuck, 180, 264
Tomasky, Michael, 174–75
Tomsheck, James, 156–57
Trie, Charlie, 260
Trump, Donald
   2016 campaign, 2–3, 184–90, 214–48
     abortion question, 206–8
     Access Hollywood tape, 238–40
     Adams and shadowbanning, 126–27
     alleged Russia connection, 2, 227,
       243, 250, 258–64
     anti-smear candidate, 166–70,
       184–90, 192–93
     Chicago protests, 200–201
     debate performances, 192–93
     electoral map, 240–41, 247
     fact-checking, 139, 234–35
     first big hit piece, 218–20
     Florida primary, 204–5
     general election, 214–48
     illegal immigration, 184–85, 187–88,
       258
     Indiana primary, 209
     Iowa caucuses, 201–2
     McCain skirmish, 185–86

Trump, Donald (*cont.*)
    Mair and super PAC, 93, 188, 204,
      205–6
    Melania smears, 205, 209, 222–24
    outside group spending, 168–70,
      188–89
    public polls, 237–38, 239, 246
    RNC speech, 221–22
    Sarasota town hall, 201–3
    South Carolina primary, 203–4
    summer media story line of, 222–30
    super PAC rivalry, 214–16
    Super Tuesday, 208–9
    tax returns, 209, 235–36
    Utah primary, 205
    the wildcard, 184–88
    Wisconsin town hall, 206–7
  fake news and, 258, 271–72, 273,
    282–83
  Full Measure interviews, 207, 234
  hate crimes and, 250–52, 283
  inauguration of, 115
Trump, Melania, 205, 209, 222–24
Tucker, Will, 84, 92, 189
Twohey, Megan, 219
Tyson, Mike, 206

Van Natta, Don, Jr., 55
Vogel, Ken, 212
Volin, Alexi, 278

Walker, Scott, 93, 110, 155
Warren, Elizabeth, 96, 97
Wasserman-Schultz, Debbie, 6, 182–83,
    193–94
Waters, Maxine, 284
Watson, Paul Joseph, 172
Weiner, Anthony, 107, 244–45, 246
Wemple, Erik, 124, 163–64, 282,
    284
West, James, 223
Whitman, Christine Todd, 90
Willey, Kathleen, 25–27, 31
Williams, Armstrong, 83
Williams, Brian, 257–58
Wolking, Matt, 162
Wong, James, 156–57
Woodhouse, Brad, 101, 110, 198
Woodruff, Judy, 183
Woodward, Bob, 148
Wright, Betsey, 19
Wright, Jeremiah, 77
Wynette, Tammy, 19

About the Author

||||||||||||||||||||||||||||||||||||||||||

SHARYL ATTKISSON is the *New York Times* bestselling author of *Stonewalled*, a five-time Emmy Award winner, and the host of Sinclair's national investigative television program *Full Measure with Sharyl Attkisson*. As a working journalist for more than thirty years, she has covered controversies under the administrations of Bill Clinton, George W. Bush, and Barack Obama, emerging with a reputation, as the *Washington Post* put it, as a "persistent voice of news-media skepticism about the government's story." She is a recipient of the Edward R. Murrow Award for investigative reporting and has reported nationally for CBS News, PBS, and CNN.

ALSO BY
SHARYL ATTKISSON

STONEWALLED
My Fight for Truth Against the Forces of Obstruction, Intimidation, and Harassment in Obama's Washington

Available in Paperback and eBook

"Attkisson offers a harrowing and gripping account of journalism as practiced these days in Washington."
—Jeff Gerth, Pulitzer Prize winning former investigative reporter for the *New York Times*

Seasoned CBS reporter and author of *The Smear*, Sharyl Attkisson reveals how she was electronically surveilled while digging deep into the Obama Administration and its scandals, and offers an incisive critique of her industry and the shrinking role of investigative journalism in today's media.

Discover great authors, exclusive offers, and more at hc.com.